State of the Parties 2022

State of the Parties 2022

The Changing Role of American Political Parties

Edited by
John C. Green, David B. Cohen,
and Kenneth M. Miller

ROWMAN & LITTLEFIELD
Lanham • Boulder • New York • London

Published by Rowman & Littlefield
An imprint of The Rowman & Littlefield Publishing Group, Inc.
4501 Forbes Boulevard, Suite 200, Lanham, Maryland 20706
www.rowman.com

86-90 Paul Street, London EC2A 4NE

British Library Cataloguing in Publication Information Available

Library of Congress Cataloging-in-Publication Data

Names: Cohen, David B., 1967– editor. | Green, John Clifford, 1953– editor. | Miller, Kenneth P. (Political scientist), editor.
Title: State of the parties 2022 : the changing role of American political parties / edited by David B. Cohen, John C. Green, and Kenneth M. Miller.
Description: Lanham, Maryland : Rowman & Littlefield, 2022. | Includes bibliographical references and index.
Identifiers: LCCN 2022019264 (print) | LCCN 2022019265 (ebook) | ISBN 9781538164846 (cloth) | ISBN 9781538164853 (paperback) | ISBN 9781538164860 (epub)
Subjects: LCSH: Political parties—United States. | Presidents—United States—Election—2020. | United States. Congress—Elections, 2020. | Party affiliation—United States. | Political culture—United States.
Classification: LCC JK2261 .S825 2022 (print) | LCC JK2261 (ebook) | DDC 324.273—dc23/eng/20220729
LC record available at https://lccn.loc.gov/2022019264
LC ebook record available at https://lccn.loc.gov/2022019265

Contents

Tables

Figures

Acknowledgments

This volume is the product of three decades of scholarship. In 1993, the first edition of *State of the Parties* originated from research coordinated at the Ray C. Bliss Institute of Applied Politics on the changing role of political parties in American politics. The impact of the 1994 midterm elections was assessed soon thereafter in the second edition, while the third through eighth editions examined further changes following the 1996, 2000, 2004, 2008, 2012, and 2016 presidential elections, respectively. The ninth edition examines changes following the historic 2020 election and subsequent unprecedented events.

Our goal, as it has been from the very beginning, has been to bring together academics from around the country to explore the state of party politics in the United States and to highlight new avenues of research. As a collection, the scholarship in this volume observes the "state of the parties" in the nation at the outset of the second decade of the twenty-first century. Over the span of thirty years, we have been continually privileged to illuminate the "best and brightest" party scholars. This edition was no exception and includes a strong mix of veteran and emerging scholars in the field of party politics. We are grateful for their participation.

The development of this volume was greatly aided by Kim Haverkamp, Manager of Marketing and Events at the Bliss Institute. Kim was not only instrumental in organizing the virtual State of the Parties Conference in November 2021 where these chapters were first presented (the first time it was conducted remotely due to the COVID-19 pandemic), she was also responsible for compiling the chapters, managing the layout, and helping meet the demands of her pesky editors. We would also like to thank our other colleagues at The University of Akron and our student assistants at the Bliss Institute who participated in the virtual conference. We also owe a debt of thanks to Jon Sisk, Sarah Sichina, and their associates at Rowman & Littlefield for once again publishing this volume. Finally, we would like to recognize our spouses, Lynn Green, Dawn Cohen, and Erin Grady, because without their unwavering support, encouragement, and love, *State of the Parties* would not have been possible.

Chapter One

The State of the Parties

Continuity and Change in 2020

John C. Green, Kenneth M. Miller,
and David B. Cohen

In the "election that (almost) broke America" (Sabato, Kondik, and Coleman 2021), former Vice President Joseph Biden defeated the incumbent president, Donald Trump. The results of the 2020 Electoral College overturned the results of the 2016 election, when Trump unexpectedly won an Electoral College majority despite losing the national popular vote. An unusually contentious and controversial president, Trump repeatedly broke long-established norms of American politics during his two campaigns and single term. This pattern culminated in his unwillingness to concede the election in a timely fashion, leading to a less than peaceful transition of power.

Waged under difficult conditions, the 2020 campaign resulted in "an election like no other" (Smith 2020) and ended in an "imperfect tie" (Busch and Pitney 2021). Despite the Democratic Party success at the presidential level, Republicans did unexpectedly well in down-ticket races, including a net gain of fourteen seats in the US House of Representatives, two state legislative chambers, and one gubernatorial office. When President Biden was inaugurated on January 20, 2021, the Democrats had unified control of the federal government by the slimmest of margins: five seats in the House, and 51 votes in the Senate, based on the tie-breaking vote of newly elected Vice President Kamala Harris—the first woman, African American, and Indian American to serve in the post.

This collection of chapters is the ninth in the series of assessments of the "state of the parties" in the United States (Shea and Green 1994; Green and Shea 1996, 1999; Green and Farmer 2003; Green and Coffey 2006, 2010; Green, Coffey, and Cohen 2014 and 2018). These volumes were based on papers delivered at the quadrennial "State of the Parties Conference" sponsored by the Ray C. Bliss Institute of Applied Politics at The University of Akron, following the 1992 election and continuing through 2020. Due to the generosity and with the permission of Rowman & Littlefield, the publisher of these books, the previous editions of the *State of the Parties* are posted on the Bliss Institute website at https://uakron.edu/bliss/research/. We invite all students of American political parties to visit the free and open archive to access this extraordinary body of research.

As with past editions, this book is a collection of chapters by prominent and emerging scholars examining the "state of the parties" from a variety of perspectives. These chapters reveal American political parties to be vibrant and dynamic institutions, central to democratic politics, and worthy of special study. Indeed, such inquiry is especially important given the deep divisions in the American body politic, and innovations—for good or ill—in the organization and operation of party politics in the United States. But before turning to these chapters, a brief review of the events leading up to and during the 2020 election will help put this scholarship in context.

THE TRUMP PRESIDENCY AND 2020 ELECTION

An Atypical and Impactful Presidency

The 2020 federal election was held in some of the most remarkable circumstances in a century. It was the first presidential election ever held during a global public health pandemic in the United States (the closest parallel would be the midterm elections held during the influenza pandemic of 1918). Efforts to slow the spread of the SARS-CoV-2 virus resulted in the most severe economic slowdown since the Great Depression (Wheelock 2020). Demonstrations for racial justice reached a crescendo in 2020 after the murder of George Floyd by a Minneapolis police officer. The incumbent president had spent most of his term breaking the norms long associated with his office and had been impeached by the House of Representatives (later acquitted by the Senate), making him the first impeached president in American history to run for reelection. Any one of these conditions would have invested the election with a sense of consequence—but occurring simultaneously, they raised both its controversy and stakes.

President Trump's job approval had been low but remarkably stable throughout his term. The first president to never reach 50 percent approval during their tenure since Gallup began measuring job approval in 1938, Trump enjoyed no initial honeymoon period, and few events of his presidency affected his approval rating either way (Jones 2021b). But strong economic conditions that favored the incumbent through 2019 cratered with COVID-19: quarterly GDP contracted by more than 30 percent in the second quarter of 2020 and unemployment spiked over 15 percent in April, receding to a still high 8 percent in September.

Conditions in the country had taken a serious downward turn, but would structural forces have their usual effects, and would voters blame the party occupying the White House? Most major election forecasts projected a loss for the incumbent president (though not all, see, e.g., Norpoth 2021). Whether modeling the outcome on presidential job approval alone (Abramowitz 2021), or using trail heat polls, index of economic indicators, and quarterly growth (Erikson and Wlezien 2021), Trump was projected as the underdog. Predictions from media outlets *FiveThirtyEight*, the *Economist*, and *RealClearPolitics* based on combinations of matchup polls and prior election results reached the same conclusions as the projections from academics. But these predictions were cautious ones. Trump's job approval rating was consistently in the low 40s, slightly lower than at the same point of the Barack Obama and George W. Bush presidencies (who went on to win) and slightly higher than at the same point of the George H. W. Bush and Jimmy Carter presidencies (who went on to lose). After all, Donald Trump had surprised most observers by winning the Electoral College by a comfortable margin in 2016 despite losing the popular vote.

Like George H. W. Bush, Bill Clinton, and George W. Bush before him, Trump was initially elected without coattails, with the Republicans losing six House seats and two Senate seats. Despite these congressional losses, the Republicans had unified control of the federal government for the first two years of the Trump administration: a majority in the House and control of the Senate with a 50-50 split and Vice President Mike Pence as the tie-breaking vote for the first two years of Trump's term. This situation gave the Republicans a brief window to pass the Tax Cuts and Jobs Act of 2017, a sweeping tax cut for higher incomes and elimination of the individual health insurance tax penalty, which was signed by President Trump three days before Christmas, the principal legislative policy achievement of his presidency. And though Republicans gained two Senate seats in the 2018 midterm, the Democrats won forty-one seats and control of the House of Representatives for the first time since 2010.

Trump's two main policy objectives, restriction of immigration and trade protectionism, were not pursued through Congress. On immigration, Trump was repeatedly frustrated in his attempts to fully fund the construction of more physical barriers on the US border with Mexico but used executive authority to increase enforcement and reduce the number of approved applications for immigration and asylum. On trade, the Trump White House quickly pulled the US out of the Trans-Pacific Partnership (TPP) negotiations and replaced the North American Free Trade Agreement (NAFTA) with the United States-Mexico-Canada Agreement (USMCA) in early 2020.

Trump's policy efforts on these two fronts reoriented long-standing Republican Party positions on these issues. The Republican Party still stood for lower taxes and less regulation on business but was rebranded as a party of trade protectionism and opposition to immigration. This was a shift for the brand was a rejection of the 2013 "autopsy" report by the Republican National committee that recommended outreach to minority communities and more inclusive rhetoric (Walshe 2013). Instead, Trump brought the Republican Party along to ride the nationalist populist tidal wave that was sweeping over the United States and elsewhere around the world.

But the Trump presidency's most substantial impact, and the one that will last far longer than his one short term, was on the Supreme Court. Trump appointed, and a Republican-led Senate confirmed, three new justices: Neil Gorsuch in the opening months of 2017 after Senate Majority Leader Mitch McConnell successfully blocked President Obama's effort to fill the late Antonin Scalia's seat in 2016; Brett Kavanaugh to replace the retiring Anthony Kennedy; and Amy Coney Barrett to replace Ruth Bader Ginsburg, who passed away just forty-five days before the 2020 election. The net effect of these appointments is that conservative justices will likely hold the majority on the Supreme Court into the 2050s (Cameron and Kastellec 2021).

The 2020 Presidential Primary Season

By the time the calendar turned to 2020, Donald Trump already spent three years campaigning for reelection, having announced his intention to seek another term at his 2017 inauguration. As is usually the case with a sitting president, no Republican mounted a serious challenge to Trump in the GOP primaries. But in the early days of his presidency a 2020 primary challenge seemed plausible, if not likely. Some Republican elite "never-Trumpers" remained vocal after 2016 (Saldin and Teles 2020), and a handful of sitting Republican legislators such as Senators Mitt Romney (R-UT) and Lisa Murkowski (R-AK) and Representative Justin Amash (R-MI) would not endorse Trump in 2020. However, these small hints of party fracture amounted to little, as the party was firmly unified behind Trump in the 2020 primary season.

Donald Trump had great success in taking over the Republican Party machinery at the national, state, and local levels. Ronna Romney McDaniel, the niece of his nemesis Mitt Romney, was Trump's handpicked choice to lead the Republican National Committee (RNC). McDaniel brought the RNC firmly in line behind the president, giving Trump an usual level of control over the organization (Heersink 2018). In contrast, the Democratic Party was in disarray and searching for a path forward after the party's clear establishment choice, Hillary Clinton, had fallen short (Brazile 2017). In the months and years after the 2016 election, the Democratic Party continued to grapple with a schism between the establishment and progressive wings that spilled into the 2017 and 2018 nominating contests (Masket 2020). Strategic politicians might typically balk at challenging a sitting president, but Democrats were energized and perceived that Trump was vulnerable even before the COVID-19 pandemic struck. However, they were not unified behind a single vision of what sort of candidate was best to take on Trump.

It was no surprise, then, that the record Democratic field of challengers (29 candidates in total) was wide and deep, including senators, governors, members of Congress, and one former vice president. Establishment Democrats, having seen what had occurred in the Republican primaries four years earlier, were concerned that the large field of candidates would split the vote and allow an outsider to capture the nomination. Due to his long service and subsequent name recognition, Joe Biden emerged as an early front-runner. However, after his strong showing against Hillary Clinton in the 2016 nomination contests, Senator Bernie Sanders (I-VT) posed a formidable challenge, with many progressives eager to renew the struggle over the direction of the party.

The crowded nomination field winnowed slowly. Several potentially viable establishment candidates, including Senators Cory Booker (D-NJ), Kamala Harris (D-CA) and Kirsten Gillibrand (D-NY), Governors Steve Bullock (D-MT) Jay Inslee (D-WA) and John Hickenlooper (D-CO), failed to achieve much momentum and dropped out before the Iowa Caucuses. By the end of 2019, the major candidates remaining in the race were Biden, Sanders, and Senators Elizabeth Warren (D-MA) and Amy Klobuchar (D-MN), and Mayor Pete Buttigieg (D-IN). Biden's anemic fundraising raised serious doubts about his campaign. Believing that no establishment candidate had emerged as a strong enough alternative to Sanders, billionaires Tom Steyer and Michael Bloomberg eventually joined the race, self-financing lavish campaigns.

The Iowa caucuses offered little clarity. Pete Buttigieg appeared to narrowly beat Bernie Sanders, but technical glitches meant that full results were not known for six days—just before the New Hampshire primary. Sanders narrowly edged out Buttigieg in New Hampshire on February 11. Then on February 22, Sanders convincingly won the Nevada caucuses. For the moment, it looked like Sanders had momentum and could win the nomination.

The party establishment suddenly rallied around Biden as an alternative to Sanders. A critical movement came when Majority Whip Jim Clyburn (D-SC), the highest-ranking Black leader in the House of Representatives, endorsed Biden. Biden then easily won the South Carolina primary on February 29 with almost one-half of the vote in a crowded field. On the eve of Super Tuesday, Buttigieg and Klobuchar dropped out and endorsed Biden. Biden rode this momentum to victory in several key states, triggering Warren and Bloomberg to drop out the following day, also endorsing Biden. The stage was set for a Biden-Sanders contest, but one week later, restrictions on public gatherings began to roll out and the public began to confront the reality of a pandemic. Unable to campaign effectively, Sanders lingered in the race until early April, and eventually endorsed Biden as well.

The 2020 General Election Season

As the presumptive nominee, Joe Biden faced a serious challenge: a disorganized and divided party and a well-organized and well-funded opponent. However, the Democrats quickly came together around the goal of regaining the White House. With the help of the party organization and many prominent leaders, Biden's finances improved steady and dramatically. Opting for a "basement strategy" for campaigning in the spring and summer, Biden stayed out of the limelight while President Trump confronted the pandemic publicly—and problematically. Adding to the president's challenges was a wave of racial unrest unleashed by the murder of George Floyd by a white police officer during an arrest.

The parties' national conventions normally serve to promote the nominees and kick off the general election campaign. But because of the coronavirus pandemic both parties had to reduce the scale of their events. The Democratic Party opted for a muted online/television event based in Milwaukee but with little in-person activity. Meanwhile, the Republicans labored furiously to keep the in-person convention, attempting to relocate from Charlotte, North Carolina, to Jacksonville, Florida, before finally settling on multiple venues, which included a live outdoor event on the South Lawn of the White House—a decision that brought a wave of criticism as it likely violated the Hatch Act. Neither candidate received a detectable "convention bounce" in the polls.

The pandemic constrained the campaigns' ability to host rallies that media outlets like to cover, that campaigns like for steering coverage and narrative, and that help drive volunteers and organizing. The Trump campaign remained committed to large in-person events as much as possible because rallies were the president's favorite form of campaign event. Rallies also allowed Trump to try to downplay the pandemic as much as possible.

The Democratic campaign centered on the message that Joe Biden would return stability to the Oval Office and would more effectively combat the coronavirus pandemic. Republicans primarily cast Trump as someone to restore order, leaning on images of unrest surrounding Black Lives Matter protests and returning to the primary 2016 theme of the danger of immigration. Republican messaging tried to remind voters that before the virus emerged from China, the United States had experienced economic growth. However, this message was a complicated one for an incumbent facing so many different challenges.

With in-person events reduced and more Americans staying home, social and mass media were even more important for carrying campaign messages. Both campaigns raised extraordinary amounts of money. Trump's close partnership with the RNC raised over $1 billion, and the Biden campaign also raised more than $1 billion, benefiting from a surge in large donations and Super PAC spending. In fact, Team Biden outspent Team Trump in the last two months of the campaign. The total cost of the presidential campaigns reached a record shattering $5.7 billion (OpenSecrets 2022a). Just like in 2016, Trump received a greater share of his donations from small donors compared to his Democratic opponent, but small donors surged across the political spectrum—alongside an expansion of large donations and "outside" spending (OpenSecrets 2022b 2022c, 2022d).

Public polls of the presidential matchup painted a picture of a frozen race. Surveys from most reputable organizations estimated the incumbent president to be behind from six to eight points nationally, with a smaller-than-typical share of the electorate undecided. Biden was polling ahead in most key battleground states as well, usually by smaller margins. These poll results prompted some progressive activists and analysts to predict a "blue wave" that would sweep many down-ticket Democrats into office along with Biden. Others were cautious—and on the conservative side hopeful. Although President Trump appeared to be well behind Biden, he had won the presidency with just 46 percent of the popular vote in 2016.

COVID-19 hung over nearly all aspects of the campaign. President Trump's affinity for rallies was challenged by pandemic restrictions on large, especially indoor gatherings. But the Trump campaign was eager to project images of normalcy and turned to more outdoor events, especially at airports with the added benefits of rapid travel to and from venues and the presidential backdrop of Air Force One. The Biden campaign recognized the necessity of events for organizing and for press coverage but wanted to provide a contrasting signal about Biden's approach to the pandemic. The Biden campaign held fewer, smaller events, emphasizing social distancing, and having the additional benefit of reducing the opportunities for a gaffe-prone candidate to speak unscripted.

The first presidential debate on September 29 was the unruly affair that many expected, as Trump adopted the same strategy as in 2016 of repeatedly interrupting his opponent. Two days later in an early-morning tweet, President Trump announced he and First Lady Melania Trump had tested positive for the coronavirus. Later that afternoon, Trump was flown by Marine One in a dramatic televised event to Walter Reed National Military Medical Center in

Bethesda, Maryland, where he was treated and released a couple days later. Due to Trump's COVID-19, the second debate for October 8 was changed to a virtual format, but Trump pulled out of the debate. The candidates had a second and final debate on October 22. Tracking polls suggested that these debates had little effect on the race.

As Election Day approached, Biden still seemed likely to win, but polls in key battleground states such as Michigan, Pennsylvania, and Wisconsin showed a close and hotly contested race. Election night was tense as local officials struggled to process an unusual combination of in-person, absentee, and mail-in ballots. Indeed, the outcome remained uncertain several days later until Saturday, November 7, when all the major television networks' news desks "called" the election for Biden. The results of the presidential election were consistent with overall projections, but contained some big surprises, including another embarrassing outing for many of the major polling operations (Kennedy et al. 2021).

Overall, Biden won 51.9 percent of the national popular vote and 306 Electoral College votes. He flipped Pennsylvania, Michigan, and Wisconsin back into the Democratic column from 2016, but by margins smaller than anticipated. More surprisingly, Arizona and Georgia both went to the Democratic candidate by very narrow margins. Indeed, Biden carried the three closest states by a total of about 43,000 votes (Georgia, Arizona, and Wisconsin). More broadly, 2020 was yet another recent example of a president without coattails: Democrats picked up just three Senate seats (two of them in special elections weeks later in Georgia) but lost fourteen House seats.

With absentee and mail-in voting expanded, unparalleled campaign spending, and with the combined conditions of economic distress and a global pandemic making politics more salient for more Americans, turnout soared by about seven percentage points higher compared to 2016: 66 percent of eligible voters, 62 percent of voting age population. This increase in turnout occurred in all 50 states but was especially higher where voting by mail was adopted or expanded (Desilver 2021).

Breaching yet another norm, Trump did not concede the race—until shortly before Biden was inaugurated in January 2021.

Post-Election and January 6

One cannot discuss the 2020 presidential election without reviewing the unprecedented events that occurred after Election Day, culminating in the occupation of the United States Capitol by supporters of Donald Trump on January 6, 2021. The groundwork for the events that day were laid by Trump dating back to before the 2016 election. But at rallies, in tweets, in press conferences, and presidential debates during the 2020 campaign, Trump sowed the seeds of doubt about the upcoming election. The COVID-19 pandemic exacerbated these allegations as primary elections were delayed, election laws were adapted to the novel circumstances, and absentee voting—especially mail-in ballots—was actively encouraged. Trump assailed these developments and claimed that the election would be rife with voter fraud. For instance, during the first presidential debate with Democratic Party nominee Joe Biden, Trump declared presumptively to a worldwide audience that "it's a rigged election" (Peters and Woolley 2020a).

After the election was over, and it became apparent that Donald Trump would likely lose key battleground states, Trump declared victory. In the early morning hours of November 4 in the East Room of the White House, Trump angrily announced: "This is a fraud on the American public. This is an embarrassment to our country. We were getting ready to win this election. Frankly, we did win this election" (Rev.com 2020). Trump would continue to push the narrative that he won in various tweets after the election: "We are up BIG, but they are trying to STEAL the Election. We will never let them do it. Votes cannot be cast after the Poles [*sic*] are closed!" (Peters and Woolley 2020b).

For the next 63 days leading up to the certification of the electoral vote count on January 6, Trump and his lawyers, aided and abetted by many Republican officeholders and officials, continued to assert that he won the election. Trump disputed the election results in court, in public rhetoric, and behind the scenes in a pressure campaign of state election officials. None of these efforts were successful. As election certification date rapidly approached, Trump ramped up pressure on Vice President Mike Pence to refuse certification of the electoral votes of disputed battleground states, while simultaneously encouraging loyal members of Congress to object to the votes in those states during the roll call. He also encouraged supporters to travel to Washington, DC, to protest the election results (Shaw 2020).

President Trump was the headliner at the late-morning "Save America" rally on January 6 at the Ellipse at which he stirred up the crowd for over 70 minutes:

> Now it is up to Congress to confront this egregious assault on our democracy. . . . We're going to walk down to the Capitol. . . . [Y]ou'll never take back our country with weakness. You have to show strength and you have to be strong. We have come to demand that Congress do the right thing and only count the electors who have been lawfully slated. (Peters and Woolley 2021b)

The rally attendees heeded Trump's call to march to the US Capitol, where a very large crowd had already gathered. What transpired over the next few hours was a scene never before witnessed in US history: an angry mob of American citizens breaking into and vandalizing the US Capitol, occupying the seat of their own government, and interrupting its lawful proceedings.

During the occupation, Trump's Twitter feed seemed to encourage the mob and continued to list his grievances about the election, even when he eventually asked his supporters to leave the Capitol grounds:

> I know your pain, I know you're hurt. We had an election that was stolen from us. It was a landslide election and everyone knows it, especially the other side. But you have to go home now. We have to have peace. We have to have law and order. We have to respect our great people in law and order. We don't want anybody hurt. It's a very tough period of time. There's never been a time like this where such a thing happened where they could take it away from all of us—from me, from you, from our country. This was a fraudulent election, but we can't play into the hands of these people. We have to have peace. So go home. We love you. You're very special. You've seen what happens. You see the way others are treated that are so bad and so evil. I know how you feel, but go home, and go home in peace. (Peters and Woolley 2021a)

After several hours, the occupation ended, resulting in five deaths, numerous injuries, and millions of dollars in damage. Later that evening, members of Congress resumed the interrupted proceedings, and the 2020 election was certified shortly before 4 a.m. on January 7.

A second impeachment of Donald Trump—the only time an American president has been impeached more than once—would follow swiftly. On January 13, 2021, exactly one week after the Capitol siege, Trump was impeached on a single charge of "incitement of insurrection" by a vote of 232–197 with 10 Republicans voting in favor. The Senate trial would occur a month later after Trump had left office, and although Trump was acquitted, the 57–43 vote comprised a clear majority of the US Senate voting to convict including seven Republicans.

THE STATE OF THE PARTIES

The rest of this book examines the impact of the 2018 and 2020 elections on the "state of the parties," noting both change and continuity. This examination proceeds in four parts: a review of the state of the two-party system, partisan voters (with a special look at the role of region), partisan activities, and women in party politics.

The State of the Parties

In chapter 2, Morris Fiorina discusses the "unstable majorities" in presidential and congressional elections over the last twenty years. He argues that "catch-all" political parties of the mid-twentieth century have been replaced with ideological parties, whose core constituencies represent only a minority of the electorate. The result is the "most electorally competitive period in American history," characterized by polarized politics and policy overreach once in office. He explores the possibility of broader and more stable coalitions among Democrats and Republicans.

In chapter 3, Byron Shaffer and Regina Wagner examine how the long-standing conflict over the internal structure of American political parties contributes to unstable majorities. A key distinction is between "organizational" parties, once prominent and focused on electoral success, and "volunteer" parties, now dominant and focused on ideological goals. They show that the growth of volunteer parties has contributed to polarization, unstable government, and attenuated representation, creating a conflict between party activists and voters. They conclude that lamentations about the state of American politics are in large measure lamentations about the state of the parties.

In chapter 4, Robert Boatright examines an element of the unstable majorities—primary challenges to sitting members of Congress. He describes the last five decades of such challenges and then explores three theories that help account for the patterns over time: partisan electoral swings, activities by ideological interest groups, and presidential politics. Boatright finds that all three theories are helpful, but their relative importance varies over time and by party. Each of these factors reflects weaknesses in party politics.

Partisan Voters

In chapter 5, Alan Abramowitz documents political polarization in public opinion. He finds that the ideological divide between self-identified Democrats and Republicans widened in 2020. It now includes a wider variety of issues, the size and scope of the welfare state, abortion, LGBTQ rights, race relations, immigration, gun control, and climate change. This new partisan-ideological consistency has profound political consequences, including hostility toward the opposing party, high levels of party loyalty, and increased straight-ticket voting.

In chapter 6, Anita Manion, David Kimball, and Adriano Udani explore the sources of public beliefs that the 2020 election was "stolen," views that contributed to the occupation of the US Capitol on January 6, 2021. They find that the growth of affective polarization provided the fuel for these views, while President Trump provided the spark with his allegations of voter fraud, and other Republicans provided an accelerant by amplifying those claims. Consequently, the American public remains bitterly divided over the legitimacy of the 2020 election.

In chapter 7, Stephen Medvic and Berwood Yost report on voter self-identification with major party factors in the swing state of Pennsylvania. They find that both major parties have two major factions: the "Trump" versus "Traditional" Republicans and the "Progressive" versus "Centrist" Democrats. These factions are based primarily in ideology but tap into the major social characteristics of each party's coalition: for the Republicans, race and religion, and for the Democrats, race and age.

In chapter 8, David Damore, Karen Danielsen, and Robert Lang report on voting behavior by the country's largest metropolitan areas, providing an insightful look at new trends in substate regionalism. These large and growing metropolitan areas are an important way to win key states. In 2020, the Biden campaign was able to capitalize on this opportunity to win Georgia, Arizona, Wisconsin, Michigan, and Pennsylvania.

In chapter 9, John Davis reports on Republican ascendency in Arkansas, an example of Republican gains in a once solidly Democratic state. The GOP grew slowly in Arkansas in three stages, with the shift gaining momentum after 2010. The underlying process was movement of white conservative voters away from generations-old support for the Democratic Party to a consistent support for the Republicans.

Party Activities

In chapter 10, Kenneth Miller reports on congressional campaign spending in 2018 and 2020. He finds that the congressional finance system has been fully nationalized, with the candidates in the most competitive races providing less than half of the funds spent. The bulk of the funds in these competitive races are provided by formal and informal party organizations who are ruthlessly focused on winning elections, and allied interest groups, who are more motivated by policy goals. At the same time, national sources of funds from individual donors are large, diverse, and largely uncoordinated.

In chapter 11, Paul Beck highlights the "ground game" in 2020, finding that both major parties were quite active in 2020 with two-fifths of voters reporting a party contact, up slightly from 2016. Interestingly, the parties did not concentrate their contacts disproportionately on the small number of battleground states in 2020 compared to recent elections. This pattern could reflect the relative ease of contacting voters via telephone, social media, and the Internet, but some of these contacts may have been for fundraising rather than voter mobilization purposes.

In chapter 12, Ronald Rapoport and W. Henry Crossman report on the shift of Tea Party activists from opposition to Donald Trump during the 2016 presidential campaign to strong supporters of Trump over the course of his administration. In addition, their issue priorities changed to match Trump's, their issue positions shifted, and their views of the Tea Party improved as well. The move from Tea Party to Trump Party helped solidify the president's support in advance of the 2020 election.

Women and Party Politics

In chapter 13, Laurel Elder describes the partisan differences of women candidates and officeholders. Although Republican women made gains in the 2020 election, the Democratic Party is still more favorable to the recruitment and election of women candidates—as exemplified by the election of Vice President Kamala Harris. Elder argues that this pattern reflects differences in party culture, as well as the effects of the regional and racial realignments of the last several decades. The GOP has a great opportunity to improve in this regard.

In chapter 14, Shannon McQueen reports on the impact of Trump's 2016 election on the perceptions and activities of women's organizations. Democratic and nonpartisan groups were able to recruit a larger number of women candidates as well as activists and donors because of the negative reaction of many women to the Trump campaign and administration. This surge in activism benefited from the overlap of activated women with younger, minority, LGBTQ, and progressive candidates. In contrast, Republican women's groups reported no major change due to Trump's election.

In chapter 15, Paul Herrnson and Jennifer Heerwig consider the impact of a recent innovation in federal campaign finance—Super PACs—on the prospects for women's role in politics. They conclude that Super PACs, as they presently operate, represent a new form of inequality for women. These new organizations exhibit a large gender gap among their donors than other organizational aspects of campaign finance. One reason for this pattern is the tendency of women donors to focus on Super PACs that seek to elect women candidates.

UNANSWERED QUESTIONS

These chapters provide a detailed review of the "state of the parties" after 2020. But they also raise unanswered questions about the "state of the parties" in the future. Among the most important are:

- What will be the legacy of the Trump loss in the Republican Party? Parties typically turn away from losing candidates, but will Trump maintain a grip on the party after he is out of office?
- Has the Democratic Party returned to the center with the election of Joe Biden? Or was the Democrats' election campaign simply "not Trump." With Trump gone, is there sufficient glue to hold the coalition together?
- How will both parties adapt to social media's elevated importance in politics and campaigns?
- Can the trend of growing campaign spending continue? Will the parties' vast pools of individual donors stay engaged?
- Will the high level of partisan polarization persist in the Presidency and the Congress? Or will polarization decline, reducing political tensions but also limiting the responsiveness of American government?

Part I

STATE OF THE PARTIES

Chapter Two

An Era of Unstable
Majorities Continues

Morris P. Fiorina

In *Unstable Majorities* (Fiorina 2017), published shortly after the 2016 elections, I addressed the enormous changes in American electoral politics that have occurred during my lifetime. From a "Tweedledum and Tweedledee" era of centrist party competition that prevailed in the mid-twentieth century, our country transitioned to the polarized partisan warfare that prevails today. The result is a politics of gridlock that many observers believe threatens the very future of American democracy.

Unfortunately, the elections of 2018 and 2020 generally are consistent with the arguments I offered in the 2017 book, suggesting that the forces underlying today's polarized politics have not abated and may even have grown stronger. I begin by summarizing the earlier argument then move to a brief discussion of the more recent elections, concluding with some critical thoughts about what some people in the political order see as possible future paths for the parties.

RECAPITULATION

Unstable Majorities was the culmination of an argument I have been developing for at least two decades (Fiorina 2002), in recognition that the literature on political parties from the 1960s and 1970s no longer explained party behavior evident since the turn of the century. As Drutman (2020) recounts in his recent book, for the first two centuries of political life under the Constitution the Madisonian system of federalism and separation of powers averted the fears of the Framers that "two great parties" would arise and lead to the demise of the Republic. For more than 150 years after the arrival of mass parties in the Jacksonian era, the parties were loose coalitions of factions that spanned geographic divides—"big tents" in common parlance. Significant third parties were common in the nineteenth century, and for much of the twentieth century, Drutman argues that the United States had a de facto four-party system, wherein each party had "conservative" and "liberal" wings (similar to, but slightly different from James McGregor Burns's (1964) argument in *The Deadlock of Democracy* that both parties had presidential and congressional wings).[1] Beginning in the 1990s however, the not-well-understood process of party sorting created two ideologically distinct, cohesive parties reminiscent of the government and the loyal opposition in mid-nineteenth century Britain, and the Christian Democrats and Social Democrats of some continental democracies. Ironically, as the dominant parties in Europe became more like the convergent parties of the mid-twentieth century United States, American parties became more like the polarized parliamentary parties of mid-nineteenth-century Europe—yet another example of American exceptionalism (Fiorina 2017, chapter 8).

Possibly as a consequence of the parties' abandonment of the "big tent" notion, a smaller proportion of the American public now claims adherence to the two parties than previously. From three-quarters of the electorate declaring Republican or Democratic affiliation in the Eisenhower era, the proportion has fallen to about 60 percent willing to claim adherence today.[2] The decline in adherents has occurred primarily among Democrats, who have lost significant ground to Independents; Republican have about the same proportion of identifiers today as in the Eisenhower era. (Some commentators thought—briefly—that Obama's victory in the 2008 elections heralded a new Democratic alignment, but the 2010 midterm elections put a quick end to that notion.) The consequence of these trends is that the United States now has two minority parties. Neither party can win on their own as the Democrats— theoretically—could in the New Deal Era. To win, today's parties must hold their base and gain the support of a majority of independents and perhaps a few defectors from the other side. The result is the arrival of the most electorally competitive period in American history (Fiorina 2013). Beginning with the Clinton victory in the three-way 1992 election, and accelerating in the 2000s, control of the presidency and both houses of Congress are in question in nearly every election.

The traditional literature holds that majoritarian electoral systems with single-member districts produce centrist politics: two "catch-all" parties compete for the middle of the electorate. In the second half of the twentieth century the notion that the parties would make overlapping appeals in an attempt to capture the center became a kind of master theory of American politics, an idea formalized in the attention bestowed on the median voter (Downs 1957; Black 1958). But by the 1990s it was clear that theory and reality no longer meshed. On the contrary, Democratic and Republican candidates adopted positions far from the center even in the most competitive districts, and although candidates might make some tentative attempts to move toward the center in the general election, various considerations, including the danger of being labeled a flip-flopper, kept them close to the distinct positions that they advocated in their party primaries (Bafumi and Herron 2010). The link between close elections and policy moderation that once seemed axiomatic now seems weak, if not nonexistent.

Why has this happened? I believe the answer is twofold. The first part of the answer is that the parties sorted. Students today find it difficult to believe that two generations ago, there were Republican representatives and senators who were more liberal than many Democratic representatives and senators. There were Democrats in Congress who opposed environmental legislation and Republicans who favored it, Democrats who strongly opposed gun control, and Republicans who favored it, Democrats who were pro-life and Republicans who were unabashedly pro-choice. The most racially liberal *and* the most racially conservative representatives and senators were both in the Democratic Party. No more. Today, party labels immediately tell us with a high degree of confidence where those bearing them stand on a wide array of issues. The conditional probability that a voter takes a liberal (conservative) position on abortion given that they have a liberal (conservative) position on taxation is much higher than it was just a few decades ago.[3] More colloquially, the average Democrat disagrees with the average Republican on more issues today than previously (Abramowitz, chapter 5 in this volume).

This process of sorting began in mid-nineteenth century at the elite level as shown by Carmines and Stimson (1989), becomes evident at the mass level in the 1980s as shown by Abramowitz and Saunders (1998), and shows up with a vengeance in elections in the new century.[4] The underlying causes of the sorting process are not well understood (Fiorina and Abrams 2011, chapter 5), although some parts of the explanation seem clear enough. Social changes had an impact. As African Americans migrated north after World War II, they became a more important political force in northern cities, pushing the northern wing of the Democratic Party in a more racially liberal direction, which heightened tensions with its southern wing. Meanwhile, the growth of the Sun Belt increased the political importance of the region and stimulated the Republicans to move in a more conservative direction, not only to capture disaffected Democrats but to attract support in the new areas experiencing rapid economic development.[5]

Other parts of the sorting process are more difficult to understand. In 1960, if someone had foreseen that abortion would become a major issue in the decades ahead, which party would observers have predicted would become the pro-life party? More likely the Democrats, given the heavy presence of northern Catholics and southern Baptists in the party. Similarly, which party would become the environmental party? More likely the Republican Party, given its association with Theodore Roosevelt and conservation, whereas the Democratic Party included workers in heavy manufacturing and extractive industries whose jobs might be threatened by environmental regulations. Political alignments didn't work out that way, however, and it is clear that the sorting process was strongly affected by politics, specifically political entrepreneurs who engaged in coalition building (e.g., Baylor 2018).

Catch-all parties must engage in internal compromising to arrive at policy platforms and candidate nominations acceptable to all parts of their heterogeneous membership. In the ideological parties that operate today, that process is severely truncated. At one time Republicans were competitive in highly urbanized states such as New York and Illinois, and Democrats were competitive in rural states in the Great Plains and the Mountain West.[6] Today, the urban-rural divide is one of the defining cleavages in the party system. Another defining cleavage is race. Until 1964 Republicans got a fair percentage of the Black vote; today it is overwhelmingly Democratic. Before the 1990s both parties contained majorities of churchgoing worshippers; today the Democrats are the party of "nones" and Republicans the party of weekly churchgoers. College degrees once were too rare to provide the basis of an electoral cleavage; in the past two elections they have become a significant cleavage. Each party now compromises over a much narrower range of the various policy dimensions than they did in earlier decades. The resulting compromises in the Republican Party are likely to be much farther from those in the Democratic Party than was the case in earlier decades.

The second part of the explanation for the changing nature of party competition is a change in the nature of the two parties. What is a party? According to Edmund Burke, a political party is "a body of men united for promoting the national interest upon some particular principle upon which they are agreed" (Commager 1949). Most observers take a somewhat earthier view, such as a political party "is a group of persons organized to acquire and exercise political power" (Duverger 2021). In short, the principle on which party members agree is winning elections. I suggest that in the past generation we have seen a transition in American parties from something like those in the second definition to something more closely resembling the parties in the first definition.

From the Jacksonian Era to the mid-twentieth century, electoral victory for a party brought control of public sector jobs, government contracts, insider information—all the components of what Plunkett considered to be "honest graft" (Riordan 1963). Civil Service reforms were the first attack on this system and beginning in the 1960s public sector unionization shifted power from the parties to increasingly powerful interest groups that have become a dominant force in today's Democratic Party. Meanwhile the adoption of universalistic policies and entitlements weakened the role of the parties as providers of particularized benefits. Further constraining old time party activities were the adoption of conflict-of-interest laws and changing media practices—journalists transformed from "lapdogs to junkyard dogs" in Sabato's (1991) phraseology. Together, and in combination, these reforms and societal changes greatly diminished the material rewards of participating in party politics (Fiorina 2002).

Clark and Wilson (1961) argued that incentives fall into three categories: material, purposive, and solidary. With material rewards diminishing space opened up for party participation motivated by purposive and solidary motives. Rather than attend party functions, donate, or work for a party because it was a job requirement or in the hope of making a valuable contact, people became party activists because they wished to help end, or as Hersh (2020) suggests, *feel like* they were helping to end abortion, helping to end gun violence, stopping global warming, achieving justice for marginalized groups, and a host of other issues. The result is that today's parties look more like those envisioned by Burke than anyone would have imagined a generation or so ago.

In sum, the American parties today are much different from the political organizations that operated until the late nineteenth century. The parties are more homogenous, and they are operated by ideologically and policy-motivated members. When Republican candidate Barry Goldwater declared in 1964 that he would rather be "right than president," worldly-wise political observers smirked. Today's parties are full of people who would rather be right than winners—or at a minimum, have convinced themselves that losing today will result in victory in the future. Rather than close electoral competition driving parties to the center, close competition today drives the parties to *overreach*. When they do win control of an elective institution, especially when they win control of all three at the same time, they attempt to impose the position of the party on the larger electorate. This occurs even if they realize that their positions are not majority supported because they likely will soon lose power anyway. "Strike while the iron is hot" rather than seek victory in the center is the mantra of today's parties. We see Bill Clinton in 1994, George W. Bush in 2004, and Barack Obama in 2008 behave similarly to Franklin Roosevelt in 1936 and Lyndon Johnson in 1964, despite winning elections nowhere near as impressively as their mid-century predecessors.

Overreach, of course, is a self-fulfilling strategy. Fearing they will lose the next election, parties overreach which raises the likelihood that in fact they will lose the next election, as voters not committed to the party's platform experience a version of political "buyer's remorse." For example, according to Gallup, when Obama was elected in 2008, Americans were evenly split on whether they had elected a liberal (43%) or a moderate (45%). But a year later after which the Democrats advocated cap-and-trade environmental legislation and Obamacare, a significant chunk of voters decided that Obama in fact was a liberal (54%) rather than a moderate (34%) (Saad 2009). The 2010 electoral bloodbath followed the next year.

THE 2018 AND 2020 ELECTIONS

Table 2.1 is an update of party control of the three national elective institutions. The two most recent elections have put an exclamation point on the fact that we are living in the most unstable electoral period in American history. There are eight possible patterns of control of the three elective institutions. The elections between 2000 and 2016 inclusive saw six of these patterns realized. The 2018 elections gave us a seventh, and had Donald Trump not inexplicably helped the Democrats win both Georgia runoffs, the 2020 elections would have given us all eight logically possible patterns in twenty years of elections.

The 2018 elections somewhat fit the overreach account. Originally, I thought that Trump might evade the overreach fate that recent presidents have suffered. In a number of noteworthy respects, the positions he took in the campaign (e.g., trade, immigration, Russia) were not those held by the traditional Republican base, but once in office, he largely ceded the policy agenda to congressional Republicans. Their attempt to repeal the Affordable Care Act proved futile—success in this regard probably would have made the 2018 election outcome even worse for them. Many observers thought that a large infrastructure proposal would be a political winner, with the potential to split congressional Democrats, but congressional Republicans opted instead for tax cuts weighted toward business and the wealthy, reflecting Republican base

Table 2.1.   Patterns of Control of the Federal Government, 2000–2020

	President	House	Senate	
1.	Republican	Republican	Republican	2002, 2004, 2016
2.	Republican	Democratic	Republican	2018
3.	Republican	Republican	Democratic	2001 (Jeffords)
4.	Republican	Democratic	Democratic	2006
5.	Democratic	Democratic	Democratic	2008, 2020
6.	Democratic	Republican	Democratic	2010, 2012
7.	Democratic	Democratic	Republican	
8.	Democratic	Republican	Republican	2014

orthodoxy—at least the old establishment base. Trump nominated prominent conservatives to the Supreme Court and in other ways supported the social conservative agenda, despite being a "Donny come lately" to such issues. So, in these respects the Republicans followed the recent pattern of overreach. More likely, however, specific policies and appointments mattered less for the off-year elections than did the determined activism of Democrats to right the perceived wrong of 2016, when the loser of the popular vote won the presidency as well as voter fatigue with Trump's personal behavior.

Given the absence of any policy accomplishments between 2018 and 2020, Trump's defeat is not the best illustration of the overreach argument. Of course, absent COVID-19, I suspect that Trump would have won the election. The aftermath of Joe Biden's election, on the other hand, fits the overreach argument pretty well. Biden did not run as a transformational president. Rather, he promised a return to normalcy—responsible adult behavior by an experienced, knowledgeable Washington leader. While he won a clear majority of the popular vote, the heavy Democratic majorities turned in by a few states like California (which accounted for five million of Biden's seven million popular vote majority) give something of a misleading picture. Even more than in 2016, the election turned on some very close margins in a few swing states—about forty-three thousand votes in Wisconsin, Georgia, and Arizona. The congressional results were disappointing—a Democratic gain of only three seats resulted in a tied Senate, and the loss of some twenty House seats resulted in a single-digit majority in that chamber.

Despite this knife-edged control of national institutions, however, the Biden administration acted as if it had won an electoral mandate akin to that of Roosevelt in 1932 or Johnson in 1964, proposing trillions of dollars in new spending and a massive expansion of the welfare state. While Democrats point out that many of the proposed programs polled well individually, the evidence suggests that support is tepid—majorities do not believe that the programs will do much for them personally—and likely not strong enough to outweigh rising concerns about inflation, jobs, and the economy (Ipsos 2021). Other poll data suggest that increasing number of voters see the Democrats' activist agenda as too ambitious (Jones 2021).

From the midpoint of 2021, Biden's approval ratings have fallen about ten percentage points so that his disapproval numbers are now higher than his approval numbers with performance ratings on some issues such as immigration and foreign policy even lower (Stoddard 2021). Independents account for a large share of the drop on Biden approval, consistent with the argument in *Unstable Majorities* that marginal supporters of the electoral majority get a more liberal or conservative policy agenda than they had hoped for (Skelley 2021). Democratic prospects of holding the House in 2022, already low given the historical midterm loss and a Republican advantage in decennial redistricting, now look even bleaker. The Democrats' hopes to retain control now rest on Republican primary voters' demonstrated capacity to shoot themselves in the feet as they did in Senate races in 2010 and 2014, reinforced by Donald Trump's demonstrated willingness to damage his own party's candidates should he be in the mood.[7]

An old saying goes that something that can't go on forever, won't. Electoral chaos and government gridlock in the face of mounting national and international problems eventually will provoke some kind of crisis or other reaction that changes our politics—for better, one would hope, but for worse is always a possibility. It is extremely difficult to foresee when such hinge points will occur and what will follow them, but historically they seem associated with national elections that produce a major victory for one party or the other, which then governs in a manner that solidifies its position.[8]

NEW PARTY COALITIONS?

Social change causes political change; hence, it is natural to imagine a changed politics down the road from observing social changes occurring today. Components of each party have identified social changes they believe can be exploited to construct enduring electoral majorities. In fact, both of their visions are at odds with available facts and both reduce the prospects of moving beyond our present situation.

Democrats: A Multiracial, Multicultural Majority[9]

In 2002, John Judis and Ruy Teixeira published *The Emerging Democratic Majority* wherein they argued that ongoing sociodemographic trends worked to the long-run advantage of the Democrats. These trends included a rising percentage of ethnic minorities and growing percentages of younger voters, unmarried working women, and the college-educated population. Individually and cumulatively these developments suggested a bright electoral future for the Democratic Party.

The 2008 Obama coalition appeared to confirm the arrival of this "new American electorate" or "coalition of the ascendant." In the aftermath of Obama's 2012 reelection, the Republican National Committee recognized the need to adjust the party's positions to the changing country when it issued an "autopsy" of Mitt Romney's loss, concluding that it should become more inclusive and increase its appeal to ethnic and racial minorities, women, and young voters. A few years later the United States Census Bureau put an official stamp on one of the important demographic trends when it issued a report titled "Non-Hispanic Whites May No Longer Comprise Over 50 Percent of the U.S. Population by 2044" (United States Census Bureau 2014). Many official government reports go unnoticed; not this one. The idea of a majority-minority country quickly entered the national political conversation.

There is no downplaying the political impact of what has been called "the browning of America" (Frey 2015). The narrative of the majority-minority nation has become a staple of political commentary, especially on the left side of the political spectrum. Contrary to expectations, however, in the short run—the 2016 elections—some Democrats (e.g., Lilla 2016) believe the party suffered from acceptance of the thesis and its apparent support for an electoral emphasis on identities. Although the contributions of ethnocentrism and racism to Trump's vote have likely been exaggerated (Fiorina 2020), social changes, particularly rapid and cumulative social changes, are unnerving to some elements of the population, with political reaction a natural result (Tavernese 2018). One need not accept far-out notions like "white extinction anxiety" (Blow 2018) to recognize that a rising American electorate logically entails a declining American electorate, and one hardly can fault older, white, married noncollege-educated voters for wondering where or if they fit in the new Democrat majority. As Judis himself noted in 2015, the presumption of *The Emerging Democratic Majority* not only was that rising groups would continue to favor the Democrats in their voting, but also that increased Democratic support from rising groups would not be offset by falling support among declining groups, contra to the movement of white working-class Democrats to Trump in 2016. As Teixeira and Rogers (2001) earlier pointed out, there are still too many whites in the electorate for the Democrats to win without attracting a goodly share of them. Ironically, an emphasis on racial and ethnic identities may have boomeranged by creating a "white consciousness" (Jardina 2019) where little or none existed before. Moreover, the increase in Trump support among Latinos and even African Americans in 2020 suggests that the first assumption of continuing or increasing minority support for Democrats is fragile as well (Teixeira 2021).

Politics aside, however, the simple fact is that the notion of a majority-minority America is empirically false, as shown by academic demographers who have been criticizing the Census Bureau projections for nearly a decade. An important new book by CUNY professor Richard Alba (2020) should be required reading for the intellectual elites of both parties.

The accompanying snapshot of Senator Ted (Rafael Eduard) Cruz and his family provides the best short explanation of the critique. Senator Cruz is the son of a Cuban father and Irish mother. The Census Bureau classifies him as Hispanic, a minority. Cruz's wife, Heidi, is of northern European ancestry.

Figure 2.1.   Sen. Ted Cruz, R-Texas, his wife Heidi, and their two daughters Catherine, 4, left, and Caroline, 6, right, wave on stage after he announced his campaign for president, Monday, March 23, 2015 at Liberty University, in Lynchburg, Virginia. Cruz, who announced his candidacy on Twitter in the early morning hours, is the first major candidate to officially enter 2016 race for president.
Source: AP Photo/Andrew Harnik.

The two daughters also are classified as minority (so long as the parents report their children's Cuban heritage on the Hispanic origin question—see below). Should these girls grow up, marry say, ethnic Norwegians, and have one or two children each, Cruz's grandchildren will be classified as minority, again, as long as whoever fills out the census form acknowledges their Hispanic ancestry. So, if he lives until 2044, Senator Cruz could contribute as many as seven people to the projected nonwhite majority: himself, two children who are one-quarter Cuban, and two to four grandchildren who are one-eighth Cuban. Most people would find such a classification procedure surprising, if not dubious, reinforced by a picture of the current Cruz family.

The projections in the 2015 report are based on questions dealing with race and ethnicity that were first included on the 2010 census. Consider question 8 on the census form, which asks about Hispanic ancestry. Those who report any Hispanic ancestry on this question move into the minority category, regardless of their responses to question 9. Non-Hispanics who check the "white" box on question 9 go into the white category, of course—*unless they write in anything else.* Should they wish to claim say, an American Indian ancestor (fairly common), or recognize a Vietnamese grandmother, they again fall into the minority category despite their white self-categorization. In both cases, descendants stay in the same category as the parent—minority—if they acknowledge the parent's ancestry. In sum, the Census Bureau projection reflects a one-drop rule akin to that used in the Jim Crow South. The white category consists only of people who are 100 percent white.[10] If one adopts a more expansive definition of white, the projection of a majority-minority nation disappears. Myer and Levy (2018), for example, calculate what future American populations would look like if anyone who checks the white box on question 9 is classified as white. With this very liberal classification, the nation is three-quarters white in 2060.

What is actually occurring is that the United States is experiencing a rapid rise in multiethnic and multiracial people. On first hearing about the projected nonwhite majority, many people probably form a mental image that looks

→ NOTE: Please answer BOTH Question 8 about Hispanic origin and Question 9 about race. For this census, Hispanic origins are not races.

8. Is Person 1 of Hispanic, Latino, or Spanish origin?

☐ No, not Hispanic, Latino, or Spanish origin
☐ Yes, Mexican, Mexican Am., Chicano
☐ Yes, Puerto Rican
☐ Yes, Cuban
☐ Yes, another Hispanic, Latino, or Spanish origin – *Print origin, for example, Argentinean, Columbian, Dominican, Nicaraguan, Salvadoran, Spaniard, and so on.*↓

9. What is Person 1's race? *Mark ☒ one or more boxes.*

☐ White
☐ Black, African Am., or Negro
☐ American Indian or Alaska Native- Print name of enrolled or principal tribe. ↓

☐ Asian Indian	☐ Japanese	☐ Native Hawaiian
☐ Chinese	☐ Korean	☐ Guamanian or Chamorro
☐ Filipino	☐ Vietnamese	☐ Samoan
☐ Other Asian- *Print race, for example, Hmong, Laotian, Thai, Pakistani, Cambodian, and so on.*↓		☐ Other Pacific Islander- *Print race, for example, Fijian, Tongan and so on.*↓

☐ Some other race – *Print race.* ↓

Figure 2.2. US Census: Race and Ethnicity Questions
Decennial Census of Population and Housing Questionnaires & Instructions, https://www.census.gov/programs-surveys/decennial-census/technical-documentation/questionnaires.2020_Census.html

roughly like this: four whites, two Hispanics, two Blacks, one Asian, and perhaps one "other." As the preceding discussion explains, however, the picture is much more complex. A "majority of minorities" will not consist of people who are 100 percent Latino, 100 percent Asian, 100 percent Black, 100 percent Native American, or 100 percent Hawaiian or Pacific Islander (the official Census categories). Rather, the majority of minorities will include people of numerous shadings of color. The United States is becoming more racially and ethnically diverse, not only because of the changing relative sizes of the five large groups, but also because of the growing internal diversity within each group as the sizes of their mixed portions swell. Diversity is increasing *within* individuals as well as among groups.

Alba reports numerous analyses using census data, birth certificates, and surveys to describe the increasing occurrence of mixed marriages and the children who are products of such interracial and interethnic unions. Mixed marriage rates have steadily increased and the 2020 census will likely report that nearly one in five new marriages now are mixed. Fully 80 percent of these marriages are between a white and a minority. Forty percent of these involve a white and a Hispanic, with Asian-white unions at 15 percent. Forty percent of Americans report having a close relative who is married to someone of another racial group.

Objective measures of life chances and well-being show that mixed-race children fall between non-Hispanic white and all minority children (with the exception that Asian-white children do *better* than all-white children on some measures). Parental education levels are lower for white-minority children than for white children, but higher than for minority children—except for Asian-white children where education levels are higher than in all-white families. The proportion of multiracial children who live in two-parent families is lower than that of all-white children, but higher than that of all minority children. Family income levels of multiracial children are lower than that of all-white children (except for Asian-whites, whose families have higher levels), but higher than that of all minority children.

On more subjective measures, mixed-race children report more fluid identities than those of single ethnicities, sometimes reporting one part of their parentage and at other times another. Asian-white multiracial identifiers provide a striking example: two-thirds of those included in both the 2000 and 2010 censuses did not give identical answers; at one time they chose one identity or mixture and at the other time made a different choice. Some mixed-race individuals choose to identify as white, some as mixed, some as their minority heritage, and their choices differ at different times and in different contexts.

For the most part, Alba's findings are positive: they replace a white versus minority binary that encourages an us-versus-them orientation among some Americans with a more complex picture where racial and ethnic boundaries are far less clear and constantly shifting—even within individuals—from day to day. The findings about Black-white multiracial children (about 20% of mixed white minority children) provide the one glaring exception to this positive picture. "Multiracials with black and white parentage are the huge exception to this pattern, and their experience is quite distinct. They grow up in less affluent circumstances and are exposed to much more severe discrimination, as evidenced by their frequent complaints of mistreatment at the hands of the police. They are more comfortable with blacks than with whites and usually identify with the black side of their family heritage" (Alba 2020, 136). But Alba (2020, 136) goes on to note, "Yet they too exhibit a level of integration with whites that exceeds that of other African Americans, as reflected in the relative frequency with which they marry whites."[11]

After the 2020 census was completed, the Census Bureau made a major announcement reporting that the white population of the United States had declined by nineteen million people (Bahrampour and Mellnik 2021). Again, this announcement led to an explosion of media coverage and some outbreaks of "white extinction anxiety" on the far edges of the political spectrum (Noble 2021). Alba and his colleagues (2021) have recently shown again, however, that the Census Bureau figure is extremely misleading; it is almost entirely an artifact of a rarely employed way of categorizing whites.

So, the case for a majority-minority electoral coalition rests on bad data. An identitarian Democratic Party almost certainly will be a *minority* Democratic Party—a party that consistently loses elections. Political appeals to various ethnic and racial groupings will be less effective as those groupings become less distinct and their identities become more diffuse, as indications of increased Republican voting by Hispanic and Black voters suggest.

The Republicans: A Populist Nationalist Party?

What about the Republicans? To say that there is any developed vision of a party future on the Republican side certainly would be an exaggeration. As the party's base of support has shifted, the three-stooled Reagan coalition of economic, foreign policy, and social conservatives has fractured. A consensus on neoliberal economic policies has crumbled as major elements of today's party express skepticism about international trade, immigration, and globalization. Eighteen years of inconclusive war in the Mideast have dampened support for an activist role in international affairs championed by the neoconservative wing of the party. Meanwhile the country grows more liberal on social issues other than abortion.

Some activists suggest that the party should embrace the changes evident in the Trump elections and transform into something akin to a populist party with white nationalist overtones, one that would at least delay its inevitable descent into minority status. The same data that impeach the Democratic idea of a majority-minority electorate show the fallacy of such thinking on the Republican side. If 40 percent (and this is number is increasing) of Americans report having a relative of another racial/ethnic group, it seems unlikely that a party will achieve majority status by insulting people's multi-racial relatives. One could embrace populism, of course, without adopting its less savory aspects. A multiracial, multiethnic Populist Party such as some elements of nineteenth-century southern and western populism attempted to build has greater potential and some embryonic arguments in that vein have begun to appear (Hammer 2021). Whether they will become widely adopted by Republicans only time will tell.

Even if the Republicans were to become a more inclusive party in racial and ethnic terms, however, there are contradictions that continued move-ment in a populist direction would find it difficult to escape. The McKinley Republicans managed to construct a multiethnic coalition uniting enough elements of labor with corporate America to dominate politics for a genera-tion. Whether that earlier success can be duplicated is an open question. An "America First" stance on trade, immigration, and globalization pits new working-class Republicans against the older corporate wing of the party, especially the donor base. And the educated neo-conservatives who tempo-rarily left the Republican Party because of Trump may leave it permanently, although it is not clear where they could go (Saldin and Teles 2020). Recog-nizing the importance of Social Security, Medicare, and other components of the social safety net to working-class Republicans will make it difficult or impossible to reform those programs, a goal of the Republican establishment for decades. Meanwhile, a continued heavy emphasis on culture war issues creates tensions between social conservative warriors and more moderate suburban Republicans whose partisan loyalties have been wobbling in recent elections. Republican candidates and strategists will attempt to finesse these contradictions, but they cannot make them go away.

For these reasons, I do not see any end to the Era of Unstable Majori-ties. This raises the question of how long the world's premier democracy can stand nearly paralyzed in the face of major national and international challenges. The one thing that is clear is that the state of our parties must change. This prescription is a desperate hope, but perhaps the contradic-tions and intra-party tensions noted above are a feature not a bug. If "woke" progressives and moderate Democrats cannot resolve their differences, and establishment Republicans and populists cannot resolve theirs, both parties might become engulfed in civil wars. In the short term, such a situation could produce conditions even worse than those of today, but it might also plow up the packed electoral soil and allow the seeds of significant party transformation to take hold and grow.

NOTES

1. Drutman has a much more positive evaluation of the four-party system than Burns did, demonstrating once again that political science evaluations are heavily conditioned by the prevailing political context.

2. This fact immediately brings up the question of leaning independents. Here is not the place to get into that but suffice it to say that there is quite a bit of evidence—generally ignored—that leaning independents are not just "hidden partisans" (Fiorina 2017, chapter 6).

3. This increase in ideological *consistency* generates polarized ideological indices that occur even in the absence of polarization on the individual issue dimensions (Abramowitz 2010, chapter 3).

4. These works disagree somewhat on the proximate causes of the sorting, however. Carmines and Stimson emphasize the primacy of race, whereas Abramowitz and Saunders conclude that race was only one of a number of issues that became ideologically connected.

5. Byron Shafer and Richard Johnston (2006) show that initial Republican gains occurred among the racially resentful but later Republican gains in the south were a result of economic development.

6. Which helps to explain why gun control was not a partisan issue. Remember Democratic Senators like Frank Church of Idaho, Gale McGee of Wyoming, George McGovern of South Dakota, and Mike Mansfield and Lee Metcalf of Montana?

7. In 2010 a Republican Senate candidate had to deny being a witch (Gura 2010). She lost. In 2014 a Republican candidate in a very winnable seat said that in the case of "legitimate rape" a woman's body had the capacity to shut down the pregnancy and another candidate charged that the theory of evolution and climate change "were lies straight from the pit of hell." Both lost (Viebeck 2012). Most recently Trump has suggested that his supporters should boycott the upcoming elections (Palmer 2021).

8. Mayhew (2004) has shown that the classical realignment account is inaccurate in nearly all its particulars. Still, it is difficult to deny that elections like 1896, 1936, and 1980 set a new direction for the country.

9. This section is based on Fiorina (2021).

10. The official category Is non-Hispanic white: "A person having origins in any of the original peoples of Europe, the Middle East, or North Africa." https://www.census.gov/topics/population/race/about.html.

11. On Black-white multiracials see also Davenport (2018).

Chapter Three

Activists versus Voters

Intra-Party Warfare in the Modern World

Byron E. Shafer and Regina L. Wagner

One of the longest-running struggles in American politics, a struggle that has occupied both theorists and practitioners, involves the proper internal structure of its political parties. On the theoretical level, this structure is what facilitates—or impedes—democratic representation. On the practical level, the same structure is central to determining who gets what from elections and legislation. Seen the first way, theoretically, the state of the parties provides powerful comment on the state of American democracy. Seen the second way, empirically, the state of the political parties essentially *is* the central aspect of the character of American politics.

In a sense, contestation over party structure runs all the way back to adoption of the US Constitution itself, many of whose framers hoped that it would effectively forestall the very appearance of parties. That proved to be a forlorn hope: the creation of a working government produced contending partisan coalitions in remarkably short order.[1] A new incarnation of this struggle emerged in the 1820s, with the creation by Andrew Jackson and Martin Van Buren of the mass political party, specifically in their case the Democratic Party. A short-lived conflict between old and new organizational forms ended in total victory for the new mass-based model over the old elite coalitions, a result that was more or less unchallenged for on toward sixty years: new parties appeared, but no new party models (McCormick 1966; Silbey 1985; McCormick 1986).

Yet the war over party structure would be rejoined and recast a generation after the Civil War when party reformers, gathered as Progressives, brought forward a new notion of what a proper political party should be. Their version valorized independent activists—the "better elements of society," with an innate concern for the "public interest"—attempting to wrest politics away from those who pursued it mainly for private gain, along with the unenlightened masses who supported them.[2] That was to be a very long war, though the institutional arguments at its core would be remarkably stable.

- On one side were the champions of what became known as "organized parties," eliciting labor on behalf of these parties through concrete rewards, that is, direct personal rewards for party workers but also public policies based on divisible goods.
- On the other side were what became known as "volunteer parties," eliciting labor on behalf of these parties from independent activists through policy goals and ideological causes, intended to instantiate the public interest.

From the time of the Progressives onward, the most common expectation was that economic development and social modernization would ultimately drive the balance between organized and volunteer parties toward the volunteer model, in fits and starts but ineluctably. Yet when empirical political scientists began to inquire into the situation after World War II, they discovered that organized parties were alive, well, and widely present, especially in the largest and most politically influential states. The share of the American population that did its political business by way of organized rather than volunteer parties had declined, but not nearly to the degree that casual observers suggested.

On the other hand—a wonderful social-science irony—this refocus by scholarly analysts on party structure, really the first serious social science of the matter, was followed in short order by the long-awaited aggregate shift, altering the balance between organized and volunteer political parties decisively. The apparent critical moment of change was 1970, so that is where this chapter must begin. Our approach is to isolate the key structural differences that distinguished proponents of "reform" (volunteer) from supporters of the "regular" (organized) party. This perspective will allow us to create measurable indicators, which is the focus of the next section of the chapter.

We then turn to the question of what happened to the distribution of the two resulting structural types, with a focus on an alleged break-point around 1970. That is the topic of the third section. The heart of the chapter—and the far more challenging section—follows, with questions about the way this change affected democratic transmissions and representational impacts. What emerges is an important contribution to partisan polarization in American politics. This discussion leads to a final substantive section asking how far this contribution has gone and how it operates in the modern day. The presidential nominating contests of 2012, 2016, and 2020 provide the evidence here, pitting party activists and their policy desires *against* the general public and its programmatic wishes.

TWO STRUCTURAL MODELS

The great initial postwar student of party structure was James Q. Wilson, who theorized ideal types of political parties by means of their incentive systems: what was it each required in order to attract the individual actors who would sustain the institutional party? In an early article with Peter B. Clark (Clark and Wilson 1961), the authors argued that the crucial maintenance activity of any organization was to mobilize and distribute incentives; that all such incentives had consequences for individual behavior; and that changing the nature of that behavior would alter institutional and not just individual activity. They then parsed their incentives into three general categories: *material*, the most tangible and fungible; *solidary*, the most social and associational; and *purposive*, the most substantive and ends-related.

A dozen years later, Wilson took the theory onward, to the full range of organizations regularly involved in American politics (Wilson 1973). For our purposes, the crucial elaboration for political parties came in chapter 6, where Wilson tied his three categories of incentives to three types of party structure, "The Machine," "The Purposive Party," and "Solidary Parties." Each came with different patterns of recruitment, different operating priorities, and different contributions to policy outputs. Yet while his analytic scheme left room for all three types, there was an emerging dichotomy to the party universe that Wilson observed, in a world where solidary parties were already merging into one or the other of the polar opposite alternatives:

> The chief consequences of these trends have been a change in the process of candidate selection and in the nature of electoral appeals. Party organizations composed of persons motivated by material rewards have a strong interest in winning an election, for only then will their rewards be secured. Provided there are competitive parties, candidates, at least at the top of the ticket, will be selected and electoral appeals fashioned so as to attract votes from the largest possible number of citizens. When the organization consists of members motivated by purposive rewards, the candidate selected must be one that can attract their enthusiasm, even if he cannot attract voter support, and the appeals issued must be consistent with their preferences, even if voters find them repugnant. (Wilson 1973, 115)

The great empirical application of this framework then came from David R. Mayhew (1986). Using journalistic accounts of the actual operation of political parties in each of the fifty states, Mayhew fashioned a "dataset" that was encyclopedic if still inevitably impressionistic. Asking, "What if the more fundamental policy-related distinction in the American party sphere of the last century or so has indeed had to do with structure rather than competition?" (Mayhew 1986, 7), he turned to imposing a comparative framework, calibrated to distinguish among state party systems. For this purpose, it was the notion of a *traditional party organization* (TPO) that was specified, elaborated, and mobilized.

Such TPOs had substantial autonomy; they lasted a long time; their internal structure had an important element of hierarchy; they regularly tried to bring about the nomination of candidates for a wide range of public offices; and they relied on material incentives and not much on purposive counterparts for engaging people to do organizational work or supply organizational support. In search of the distribution and evolution of these TPOs, Mayhew came to much the same conclusion as the more theoretically oriented Wilson, that the many previous reports of the death of organized parties had been grossly overstated. On the other hand, Mayhew too concluded that the era of his TPOs was coming to a close as the 1960s gave way to the 1970s:

> The late 1960s is a good time to inspect because it both closes and samples fairly well a long 19th century span between the second and third of three major periods of structural change in American parties—the first being the Jacksonian period, the source of the 19th century's characteristic system; the second, the Progressive period, during which national, state, and local parties were substantially overhauled with the effect of producing a hybrid 20th century system; and the third, the last decade and a half or so, during which local party organizations have decisively declined and telecommunications processes, candidate organizations, and capital-intensive party organizations have become central features of distinctive new electoral politics. (Mayhew 1986, 9)

While Mayhew was finishing his impressionistic tour of party structures in the 1960s, he was more or less overlapping with Alan Ware, the third of the scholars who reinvigorated the social science of party structure (Ware 1983). Ware was in the field with a detailed examination of party systems in three major but distinctive geographic places: New York City, the Denver metropolis, and the San Francisco Bay Area. What he discovered was that the picture theorized by Wilson and empiricized by Mayhew was indeed being rapidly rebalanced, with a triumph for the volunteer model. Summarizing the result as the "breakdown" of organized Democratic parties, Ware described an "Indian Summer" for party structure that was finally coming to an end.

The late 1960s and 1970s had thrown up a set of intensified challenges to these continuing party structures, challenges that would ultimately bring about the demise of many old structural arrangements. The leading stressors on this old order still varied from place to place: fratricide in New York, reform in Denver, and extremism in the East Bay. But despite idiosyncratic starting points and regardless of the particular mix of stresses, the result was generalized, sweeping, and qualitatively different, a result shaped in important ways by the explicitly anti-party themes of the time:

There can be little doubt that what happened to the Democratic Parties in America between the early 1960s and the late 1970s was truly extraordinary. Within a few years, most of them were transformed . . . there are two important respects in which issue conflicts did harm the Democratic parties. First, they helped to make issue-oriented activists much more skeptical about the value of party; what emerged in the 1960s was issue-activism which was not party-oriented, as it was in the 1950s, but which was prepared to use party institutions for realizing objectives as, and when, they seemed useful. . . . Secondly, the issue conflicts actually revived long-standing anti-party sentiments in America, sentiments which were minority ones in the amateur Democratic movement of the 1950s, but which became more apparent in the late 1960s. (Ware 1985, 246–47)

In all these views, the year 1970 appeared to be both the theoretical and the practical pivot in the balance between two ideal party types, and that is where we enter the picture. Classifying party structures according to the taxonomy developed by Wilson, Mayhew, and Ware was hardly a conscious activity of party operatives in either organized or volunteer states. Yet very practical operatives did argue consistently and perennially about how to handle the variety of activities that fall to a political party in democratic systems. Moreover, these arguments have assumed common elements and a common pattern over time. So one can certainly use their opposing substances to create specific indicators of party structure.

THE CRUCIAL CHANGE?

The search for relevant indicators of party structure, organized versus volunteer, begins with three evident touchstones. First is that well-developed theoretical framework from Wilson coupled with those rich impressionistic applications from Mayhew and Ware. Next are various histories of intraparty warfare, some focused on the battle over specific reforms, others where this battle was an aspect of some larger story (Ware 2002). Either way, the structural preferences of the two sides, reform versus regular, tend to be clear (Banfield and Wilson 1963). Finally, there have been what were essentially major grocery lists for party reform, assembled by organizations dedicated to the volunteer perspective (Steward 1950). All of which meant that diverse battles in the long war over party structure tended to be pitched on a small set of recurrent battlefields, ten measures including appointment powers, financial regulations, voting strictures, institutional mechanics, and partisan limitations (see table 3.1).[3]

Table 3.1. Organized versus Volunteer Parties: The Indicators

A. Appointment Powers

Merit Systems: The ability to make personnel appointments was central to organized parties. The first direct and most fundamental challenge to this ability was the coming of civil service, that is, of generalized merit systems.

Unionization: The other great constraint on the ability to make personnel appointments came later, from the rise of labor unions specializing in public employees, which became the great institutionalized competitor to the official party in this regard.

B. Financial Regulations

Transparency of Party Finance: Organized parties reliably took the view that management of their resources was an internal matter—they should be judged on their performance—while public openness about political finance was often central to the reform drive.

Regulation of Campaign Contributions: Organized parties took the view that the raising of funds was likewise an internal matter—a natural part of coalition-building—while limitations on contributions from organized interests were often central to the reform ethos.

C. Voting Strictures

Ballot Forms: The traditional party-column ballot was a central product of the strong-party era. The office-block alternative sought to shift public attention away from party attachments and toward candidate qualifications.

Ticket Provisions: If parties could make nominations internally, they naturally wished to follow with a straight ticket—encouraging voters to accept the total product while accepting collective responsibility for it—while the reform approach favored disaggregating offices and encouraging individualized attention to them.

D. Institutional Mechanics

Institutions of Nomination: The classic arrangement for nominations to public office under organized parties involved making those nominations *through* the official party structure, most often in convention. The reform alternative was nomination by public primary election.

Institutions of Policy-Making: Afterward, organized parties wanted it to be (their) elected officials who made the resultant public policy. Reformers continued to want an augmented public role, to the point of permitting citizens to legislate directly by way of the referendum.

E. Partisan Limitations

Partisan Endorsements: The endorsement of candidates was a central activity of organized parties—why else would a party exist?—while a ban on such endorsements was often part and parcel of the drive for party reform, a conflict at its most intense with judicial elections.

Participatory Structures: For organized parties, a concomitant to the fact that nominations should be internal and policy made by their nominees was that political participation should belong to party members. Conversely, volunteer parties wished to use open and participatory processes to recruit both activists and voters.

For all of these, the preferences of supporters of organized versus volunteer parties are immediately clear. Moreover, all ten measures possess simple indicators that are available over a long period. Most of these can be taken directly from the *Book of the States*, first published by the Council of State Governments in 1935 and produced annually since that time, as supplemented and cross-checked through materials from the National Conference of State Legislatures (*Book of the States* 1935, 2017). As it turns out, all ten are positively correlated, while there is no theoretical reason for using them through anything other than a directly additive measure. So the resulting scale becomes the principal measure of party structure used here.

For other purposes, it could be valuable to follow an individual state and its placement within the full national scale. But for purposes of looking for a major break in the flow of organized versus volunteer parties collectively, a simple dichotomy will sharpen subsequent analysis, *if* this dichotomy accords with three widely recognized alternative versions. These previous attempts to get at state party *structures* again begin with Mayhew's TPOs. They are reinforced on the macro side by the classic taxonomy for state political *cultures* produced by Daniel J. Elazar (1966). And they are reinforced on the micro side by the detailed picture of state party *operations* produced by the Commission on Party Structure and Delegate Selection between 1968 and 1972 (Shafer 1983, 281–82).

As it turns out, there is a huge overlap between lists of organized versus volunteer states derived from these prior classifications. Even more importantly, this consensus tracks neatly on our new, transparent, and comprehensive scale. It is not difficult to ask how the distribution of two party types evolved. Ware and Mayhew suggested explicitly that the year 1970 was a pivot point in the long war between dueling party structures. Thus, the first of two critical questions becomes whether this hypothetical sea-change in the distribution of party types actually came off as scheduled. Only with an answer in hand is it possible to address the larger question of how their changing comparative balance shaped democratic representation.

In that light, the first task for this new measure is to confirm (or not) the hypothesis of major change in the balance between organized and volunteer parties around 1970. If there was indeed a "great break" at that point, then this break was implicitly magnifying the impact of structural change for all subsequent electoral contests. In principle, the shift from collected case studies to scaled party indicators allows plenty of room to discover instead that this grand breakdown was overstated. Yet that is not what an aggregate translation shows. Rather, just such a transformation did indeed occur on a very substantial scale in the years around the hypothesized pivot point, a transformation perhaps even larger than earlier observational accounts would suggest.

Table 3.2.   The Great Change? Reform Progress, 1950–1970

A. Movements Toward—and Away From—Volunteer Party Structure

	Toward Organization	No Change	Toward Voluntarism
States	7	8	35*
Population	8%	14%	78%

B. The Aggregate Fortunes of Organized and Volunteer Parties

		1952	1972
States	Organized	20	11
	Volunteer	28	39*
Population	Organized	53%	23%
	Volunteer	47%	77%

*Alaska and Hawaii became states in 1959, both with clear-cut volunteer structures for internal party politics.

Table 3.2[4] confirms the scope of this change around 1970 in two key regards. First, table 3.2.A shows a major shift toward the volunteer model during the previous generation, where the aggregate index of party structures confirms that this broader thrust had reached into the vast majority of American states. There were exceptions: seven of the now-fifty states actually moved toward organized party structure rather than toward its volunteer opposite. Another eight essentially stayed where they had long been, though for most, this stability was because they could go no farther in the volunteer direction. Yet the diagnostic point remains that thirty-five of the fifty states—now counting Alaska and Hawaii (which entered the union with volunteer parties fully in place)—had moved in the direction of the volunteer model between 1950 and 1970.

So the triumph of a long-running reform drift, beginning all the way back in the 1880s, could finally be confirmed around 1970. Few states managed to resist this drift categorically, a result that becomes even more striking if it is considered not just by raw tallies of states, but also by the share of the American public that lived in states on one side or the other of this organized/volunteer divide. Table 3.2.B tells this counterpart story. It was already clear by the time Mayhew began surveying the fifty states that a solid majority had internal party structures that should be classified as volunteer rather than organized. Scale scores now tell the same story. Yet those states that continued to hew to an older organizational model remained on average the larger ones—California was the striking exception—with the result that the American public as a whole in 1950 was still doing a great deal of its practical politics through organized political parties.

Flash forward to 1970, by which time the roster of states with organized parties had been decimated. Only eleven of the fifty retained the old structural arrangements, where twenty of forty-eight had featured those arrangements in the preceding period. Even further to this distributional point, less than one in four Americans now lived in states with organized party structures, where more than one in two previously did. So an old organizational model for shaping practical politics appeared to be passing, and with it an old world whose demise had long been anticipated but whose resilience had defied expectations, until the 1970s.

REPRESENTATIONAL DIFFERENCES
AND REPRESENTATIONAL IMPACTS

An effort to tease out the democratic impact of this change is the analytic heart but also the major analytic challenge in interpreting the impact of the great rebalancing between organized and volunteer parties. This effort begins with its own list of requirements. It must have a dataset that stretches from the opening postwar years to the modern era. This dataset must tap public preferences on the major domains of postwar policy conflict, namely social welfare, civil rights, cultural values, and national security. Within the results, it must be possible to distinguish not just Democrats from Republicans, but also activists, those who do the actual work of the political parties, from their rank and file, whose participation is limited to responding to party programs at the polls.

A dataset capable of meeting these demands was generated for quite other purposes by William Claggett and Byron Shafer, subsequently extended and managed by Regina Wagner. Derived from the American National Election Study (ANES), its measures were a product of comprehensive exploratory and then confirmatory factor analyses, yielding scales for all four major policy domains (Claggett and Shafer 2010). In the central summary table that follows (see table 3.3), the results are presented as standard scores (that is standardized but not normalized). Party attachment is registered by the canonical two-question format introduced by the authors of *The American Voter* (Campbell, Converse, Miller, and Stokes 1964). Activists are distinguished from the rank and file by the battery of questions about political activity long carried by the ANES (Claggett and Pollock 2006).

In order to study change over time while retaining statistical reliability, the postwar years are divided into three aggregate periods with five elections each: an opening period, 1950–1970 (which represents the old world of party balance); a succcssor period, 1970–1990 (reflecting the great break-point in that balance and the simultaneous triumph of the volunteer model); and a third period, 1990–2010 (which is effectively our modern world). Many aspects of the changing structure of American politics could be addressed through this dataset and this arrangement. But for purposes here, four simple measures can capture democratic representation in summary form:

- "Activist Range" is the ideological distance between active parties, that is, the distance from active Democrats to active Republicans as collectivities.
- "Democratic Gap" is then the distance inside the Democratic Party from party activists to their rank and file.
- Just as "Republican Gap" is the distance inside the Republican Party between counterpart activists and their rank and file.
- "Dual Gap" merely sums these Democratic and Republican gaps, yielding the joint distance between activists and their rank and files for the two parties together.
- Finally, those four ideological distances are stratified by organized versus volunteer parties, for an explicit measure of the difference in their representational performance.

Arrayed this way, what leaps out of table 3.3[5] is that volunteer parties are *always* more polarized than organized parties. This pattern holds true when measured through party activists; it is true inside the Democratic Party; it is true inside the Republican Party; and it remains true when the two partisan gaps are summed (see table 3.3.A). Table 3.3 is confined to the modern world, but this pattern also holds true (tables not shown) for each preceding temporal period. So, the key point is that the direction of polarization between party types—and hence the additionally polarizing contribution of a changed balance between them—is omnipresent and consistent. Volunteer parties augment partisan polarization; organized parties constrain it. By extension, those who decry polarization should cherish the remaining organized parties, while those who valorize polarization should continue the push toward volunteer structures.

A noteworthy associated point is that the size of these gaps goes on to vary by policy domain, being smallest with social welfare and civil rights, largest with cultural values and national security. Said the other way around, cultural values and national security appear to be policy domains that *interfered* with the desired focus of organized parties but *serviced* the operational needs of volunteer parties. Which means that those who are dismayed by the rise of cultural and security issues should cherish their organized parties, while those who would privilege cultural values and national security and diminish social welfare and civil rights should seek even more volunteer parties. Accordingly, if the main point here is that the *direction* of the contribution from party types is consistent across domains, the secondary point is that the specific policy substance of those domains does influence the *scale* of this effect.

Table 3.3. Partisan Polarization and Party Structure: The Modern World, 1990–2010

	A. Ideological Range							
	1. Activist Range		2. Democratic Gap		3. Republican Gap		4. Dual Gap	
	Vol	Org	Vol	Org	Vol	Org	Vol	Org
National Security	.82	.59	.23	.12	.14	−.02	.37	.10
Culture Values	.65	.50	.22	.13	.09	.04	.31	.17
Civil Rights	.87	.84	.13	.07	.24	.14	.32	.21
Social Welfare	.85	.81	.11	.07	.23	.15	.34	.22

	B. Organized vs. Volunteer Differences			
	1. Activist Range	2. Democratic Gap	3. Republican Gap	4. Dual Gap
National Security	+.23 Vol	+.11 Vol	+.12 Vol	+.27 Vol
Culture Values	+.15 Vol	+.09 Vol	+.05 Vol	+.14 Vol
Civil Rights	+.03 Vol	+.04 Vol	+.10 Vol	+.11 Vol
Social Welfare	+.04 Vol	+.04 Vol	+.08 Vol	+.12 Vol

	C. Real Impact							
	1. Absolute Impact				2. Proportionate Impact			
	Activist Range		Dual Gap		Activist Range		Dual Gap	
	Vol	Org	Vol	Org	Vol	Org	Vol	Org
National Security	.82	.59	.37	.10	2.46	.59	1.11	.10
Culture Values	.65	.50	.31	.17	1.95	.50	.93	.17
Civil Rights	.87	.84	.32	.21	2.68	.84	.96	.21
Social Welfare	.85	.81	.34	.22	2.55	.81	1.02	.22

Within all this, the two key activist polarizations might in theory have derived their (polarized) preferences largely from polarization in their rank and files (see table 3.3.C). But in practice, activists diverged from—resisted or even countervailed—the preferences of those rank and files. Which means that these representational gaps become a direct measure of how much (or how little) party operatives cater to themselves rather than to their putative constituents in organized versus volunteer parties. The two gaps are then put back together at table 3.3.A.4, where an effect from party structure on internal party representation is immediately evident in all four domains. Workers in volunteer parties are half again as far away from their rank and files as workers in organized parties, even in the domain of social welfare, a situation that reaches its extreme with national security, where volunteer operatives are on their way to being four times as far away from their respective rank and files as organized counterparts.

To cut to the chase one more time: operatives in organized parties, while hardly ignoring the major issues of their day, preferred to stay within reach of their rank and files, while operatives in volunteer parties wished to pursue their *own* policy concerns, often by escaping the desires of rank-and-file identifiers. If these representational coefficients had remained as they were circa 1970, there would be nothing further to say: about half the country lived under organized parties and half lived under the volunteer alternative. But a generation later—and this generation is the one captured in table 3.3—the balance was no longer one to one but rather three to one, volunteer over organized.

So, the coefficients capturing representation inside volunteer as opposed to organized parties, striking enough in absolute terms, were now three times more consequential than those for organized party counterparts. Table 3.3.C attempts to suggest this fact by tripling the coefficients for volunteer parties. On the one hand, by comparison to tables 3.3.A and 3.3.B, this pattern implies a greater representational gap than would be true for any given pair of parties that exemplify the two party types. On the other hand, it serves as a reminder of how strongly the move toward volunteer parties has driven partisan polarization in society as a whole. One final time, then, fans of a polarized politics know how to drive it forward, and table 3.3.C suggests that even more polarization can be achieved through further reform. Just as those who find growing polarization to be the curse of modern politics know what to protect, or even what to reverse.

LOCKING IN THE RESULT

The battle between organized versus volunteer party structures had been a kind of trench warfare from the 1880s into the 1960s, capturing one or another state here, losing an occasional state there, until a much bigger and more focused change shifted the balance in a decisive fashion around 1970. Yet the impact of this shift still obeyed a long-standing—and well-understood—institutional logic. Organized parties remained more focused on direct rewards for their active members, divisible benefits for their rank and files, and extension of existing policy initiatives. Volunteer parties were more focused on fresh lures for active participants, policy promises that were comprehensive or dissident, and the constant regeneration of both proposals and volunteers. Otherwise, what was different initially was just the balance between the two party types, a balance now loaded heavily toward volunteer parties.

Fifty years on, however, the same generic situation has begun to look different in practice: the very scale of the triumph of volunteer parties and their issue activists appears to have altered the operational dynamics of party politics. When Wilson was theorizing the basic differences between party models, reform partisans argued that their triumph would spread policy influence among a broader and more diverse public, while leading to a more rapid turnover—a constant churn—of policy positions. Yet by the 2010s, internal party politics had increasingly morphed in the opposite fashion, one not obviously anticipated by the old arguments. Now, the volunteer triumph had become sufficiently total as to imply sharply increased partisan polarization, catering to party workers on both sides of the partisan divide, while necessitating an escape from—and sometimes explicit rejection of—a broader, more moderate, more diverse, *and more changeable* rank and file.

Yet there was more: in an effect not envisioned originally by either side, the newly empowered issue-based activists became increasingly aware of themselves as a specialized elite, one able to institutionalize its own control of volunteer parties and drive away those with differing or more moderate preferences. It was easy to miss (or deny!) this development, since twenty-first-century parties did not look like their predecessors from the nineteenth or even mid-twentieth centuries. But these new parties had actually re-secured the critical resources and resolidified the operational arrangements that had long allowed an active minority to control internal party politics. In doing so, they had restored a modern equivalent of the machine-type structure that allowed historical predecessors to shape the process of electoral politics and influence the rewards of public policy, often to the exclusion of their own rank and files.

The opening shot in an alternate narrative capturing this impact of party reform was fired by Marty Cohen, David Karol, Hans Noel, and John Zaller in *The Party Decides* (Cohen, Karol, Noel, and Zaller 2008). For them, the changes which had been the focus of Wilson, Ware, and Mayhew had indeed occurred. Moreover, those changes had achieved the operational impacts previously expected of them, valorizing activists over voters and emphasizing program over production. Yet in this modern view, what had looked like a terminal disruption of the filtering power of political parties had been merely an anarchic interregnum, before active party workers—now in the form of a network of issue activists—adjusted their resources and their behavior so as to reassert coordinating power over the official party.

Two central factors had always been (and in this view continued to be) obvious indicators of this mediating power, namely the amassing of internal party resources and the control of nominations to public office. Those recurred under the new institutional arrangements, as they had once recurred under the old. The revisionist examples from Cohen et al. were drawn from the mechanics of presidential selection, the most easily accessible window on party structure but never more than a derivative of overall party structure. Yet shortly thereafter, a serious attempt to put operational detail into this argument more generically, and more importantly to drive it through the entire party system, came from Seth Masket, in a series of analyses beginning most crucially with *No Middle Ground* (Masket 2014).

Taking off from the ideological polarization of the modern political world, Masket attempted to work backward, both empirically and theoretically, to the new but recurrent elements of party politics that had produced it. In his interpretation, the traditional party organizations (TPOs) of the Mayhew analysis, widespread and vigorous into the 1960s but shrinking and withering in the 1970s, had indeed declined on their own terms. Yet along the way, they had morphed into a modern incarnation of the old centrality of party machinery. Masket referred to this modern variant as "informal party organizations" (IPOs), which had implicitly acquired a modern incarnation every bit as behaviorally muscular, every bit as effectively closed to random participants, and every bit as directive—probably even more directive—in shaping public policy.

In pursuit of his demonstration of a renewed intermediary role for parties that were now built around purposive incentives, Masket found its critical element in the modern incarnation of an even older classical notion, namely political ideology. Nothing in our analysis would gainsay his summary:

> Although the shape of the modern party is more of a network than a machine hierarchy, the function is essentially the same: a small group of people operating only barely within the law manages to control elections and thereby the government. The major difference between these modern informal party organizations (IPOs) and their machine forebears is the existence of ideological activists. Machines distrusted ideologues; IPOs rely on them. The result is extreme candidates and highly polarized politics. (Masket 2014, 19)

Reinforced by such a summary, we are driven to ask how activists, once introduced as the structural saviors of a general public, had been able to please themselves and reduce the influence of that very public. And there, a set of institutional reforms, accompanied as ever by the behaviors that they advantaged, became critical. The first tranche of these involved the institutions associated with the great change between organized and volunteer parties around 1970. But a second set was introduced by rising issue activists as they became the dominant force inside political parties, and these helped to move the initial impacts onward. Once more, the easiest window on this sequence of institutional reforms (and its behavioral changes) can be provided by the politics of presidential selection.

The institutional changes alerting the broadest section of an attentive public to this second triumph of party reform did not directly involve the balance between organized and volunteer parties. Rather, they involved the balance among institutions of delegate selection and presidential nomination. That particular balance had swung immediately, sharply, and strikingly away from party conventions and toward presidential primaries. Ironically, many of the reformers, especially from volunteer states, did not really want to multiply the number of primaries at all. Rather, what they hoped was to convert existing state conventions into reformed participatory caucuses, an institutional lure (as well as lightning rod) for issue activists (Shafer 1983, part II).

So, by the logic that James Q. Wilson had decoded more than a decade before, they favored the "quality" of caucus participation over the "quantity" of primary voting. In the process, they favored themselves over a general public, which they already knew to be less ideological and more focused on the fabric of daily life. But what they got, largely courtesy of the states with remaining organized parties, was a proliferation of presidential primaries. Many of these organized parties would have preferred to stay with old-fashioned party conventions, but they quickly came to believe that they could keep newly mobilized activists out of *state* party business by separating that business from delegate selection and presidential nomination, while coming into conformity with an ostensible party-wide mandate.

Thus, a presidential primary was the obvious compromise: what could be more democratic than that? In fact, the surviving convention systems—now participatory caucuses—would function much as reformers expected. Privileging activists and isolating them within a wider public, these caucuses would go on to advantage the candidates preferred by issue activists rather than the voting public. That effect was clear enough. But since only a minority of states stayed with this institutional arrangement, these participatory systems were never enough by themselves to push an insurgent nominee over the top. On the other hand, the search for further institutional devices to help accomplish that goal was hardly over.

Rather, activists within both parties moved on to a very different institutional arrangement, with the same attraction for fellow activists and the same isolation from a general public. This involved a burgeoning sequence of candidate debates among aspiring presidential nominees, most held before any actual convention delegates had been selected, though a few bled over into the real selection period. These debates would prove irresistible to a news media hungry for political events during the period when politics reliably shifted away from legislative maneuvering but had not yet reached presidential selection.

From the other side, more or less immediately and completing this chain of impacts, the new nationally televised debates proved to be a powerful attraction for a burgeoning array of aspiring presidential contenders. If most of them started with no national profile—and these profiles would get only smaller as time passed—such candidates had little to lose. If they could move their initial polling lines by appealing to a small but attentive public, they might hope to expand this support when the real contest arrived. Within three iterations—2012, 2016, and 2020—the result would be another stereotypical (if superficial) triumph of the active parties. By 2020, the direct fallout from creation of this further institutional twist would reach everywhere.

The fields of ostensible candidates would grow so large that there had to be two complete sets of candidate debates for the opening rounds. The composition of these fields would accomplish the dual purposes of privileging politicians whose tiny levels of national support more or less guaranteed their irrelevance to the ultimate outcome, along with financial donors wealthy enough to *purchase* sufficient poll support to get past minimal—and derisory—requirements for poll standing. Issue activists were delighted with their new ability to split hairs among numerous presidential aspirants—twenty-three at the first Democratic predebate of 2020—a delight richly shared with a political press that was itself increasingly a mechanism of activist opinion and not of communication with the general public.

THE FRUITS OF REFORM— AND THE REVENGE OF THE VOTERS

The Republicans, 2012

The sequence of Republican nominating debates in 2011, leading up to the presidential nominations of 2012, provided an early and dramatic testimonial to the temporary power of these pre-presidential encounters, while underlining the way that this institutional theater was dedicated to activists rather than the general public. Figure 3.1 tracks the poll standing of the six candidates who crossed a five-percent national threshold for some extended period.[6] This field produced a series of apparent bandwagons in public preference for the Republican nomination, first for Congresswoman Michele Bachmann of Minnesota, then for Governor Rick Perry of Texas, then for businessman Herman Cain, then for former Speaker of the House Newt Gingrich, and finally for Pennsylvania Senator Rick Santorum.

Figure 3.1 could tell many stories, but the one most relevant to the stimulation provided to party activists and to the tension between these activists and an eventual voting public turns on the ultimate irrelevance of this extended

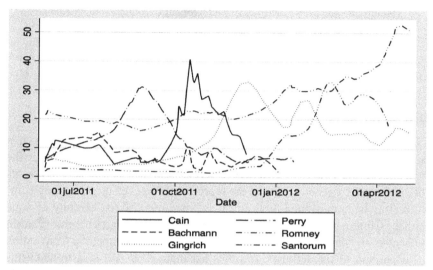

Figure 3.1. Activists versus Voters: The Republicans, 2012

pre-process. For in fact, there was always a serious stable contender, former Massachusetts governor Mitt Romney. Moreover, Romney did not simply survive the onslaught of aspiring challengers and chimerical bandwagons. His victory in the actual contest, while a testament to personal tenacity and campaign quality, was also a remarkable reflection on the shadow-boxing character of the preceding series of prepresidential debates. As expanded, the debates had drawn activist attention at a time when the general public was ignoring an actual contest which, after all, had not begun. These activists, generating one champion after another, had been at best irrelevant, at worst an active distraction—an obvious impediment that ultimately had to be overcome by an awakened public.

More could be said, yet we cannot do better for a summary than the analysis by John Sides and Lynn Vavreck on "The Anatomy of Media Boomlets: Discovery, Scrutiny, and Decline":

The process of discovery began when a candidate who had previously attracted little news coverage did or said something that reporters and commentators judged to be novel, important, and therefore newsworthy. As a consequence, news coverage of that candidate increased sharply.

But this did not last very long. Once a candidate seemed "serious" enough to pay attention to, that candidate was then subjected to increased scrutiny from both opponents and the news media.

This scrutiny took place regardless of what the candidate had done either in the past or in the campaign to that point. It reflected two things: opposing candidates' need to stop the surging candidate from solidifying his or her lead and journalistic norms about vetting candidates.

Having devoted time to writing about a particular candidate, the media had a natural incentive to move on and find a storyline that was novel and more exciting. Unless the candidate did something else that was considered newsworthy, his or her news coverage began to decline, which in turn further drove down the candidate's poll numbers. (Sides and Vavreck 2013, 43–45)

The Democrats, 2016

Not every nominating contest could, even in principle, produce such a striking succession of bogus boomlets. Almost by definition, the fewer the contenders, the greater the limitation on possible outcomes. The Democrats of 2016 were to generate one of the more constrained examples. Many commentators had envisioned this contest as being reduced to Secretary of State Hillary Clinton as the champion of the regular party against Governor Martin O'Malley of Maryland, keynote speaker at the 2012 Democratic Convention as champion of the activists, and thus her main rival. Yet disastrous events in the city of Baltimore, where O'Malley had been mayor before becoming governor, sank his chances early.

That left room for Vermont senator Bernie Sanders, a hesitant entrant and an apparent gadfly when he did enter, to become the champion of the activists instead. Sanders found the pre-nomination debates to be an ideal vehicle for capturing activist attention, and after the practical demise of O'Malley, the 2015 debate series confirmed the front-runner status of Clinton while conveying the activist mantle to Sanders. The preference gap between the two did narrow a bit as the activists came to recognize him as the un-Clinton. (Figure 3.2) The coming of an actual contest for convention delegates would

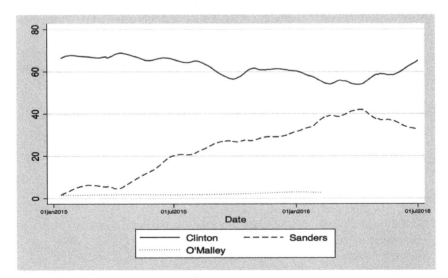

Figure 3.2. Activists versus Voters: The Democrats, 2016

temporarily narrow this gap a bit more, with some initial indication that Sanders might continue to rise—before it began to widen consistently as Clinton began to pick off almost all the major contests.

At no point did Sanders appear likely to overtake her, a nondevelopment that gave some curiosity value to the fact that their personal contest nevertheless continued all the way to the convention. Yet this time, the key to an extended contest lay with a different great institutional gift to party activists, namely the difference between presidential primaries and participatory caucuses. It was these caucuses that were to give Sanders a sufficient string of state-level "wins" sufficient to allow him to continue mobilizing issue activists. In the consequential development, Clinton was to win an overwhelming share of the state contests of any size. But along the way, Sanders was to be even more successful with the smaller states (see table 3.4.A).

Yet that tally understates the further advantages that came with small-state success. To begin with, the states which had retained participatory caucuses were overwhelmingly the small ones (see table 3.4.B). In that environment, Clinton was relentlessly victorious when a state selected its delegates through a presidential primary, while Sanders was even more successful when a state selected its delegates through a participatory caucus. But even more to the skewed advantage that these latter states offered to activists versus voters, there was a huge *statistical* bonus conveyed by the caucus mechanism: it took more than four times as many public participants to convey a delegate in a primary as opposed to a caucus (Table 3.4.C). So, the candidate preferred by the voters had yet another barrier to overcome by comparison to the candidate preferred by the activists.

Table 3.4. Activists versus Voters: Nominating Institutions of Choice

	A. Bias against Large Electorates: Voter Turnout		B. Bias against Primaries: Caucus Outcomes		
	Clinton	Sanders	Clinton	Sanders	
>1,000,000	9	1	28	10	Primaries
>500,000	8	2	2	11	Caucuses
>200,000	10	4			
>50,000	3	6			
<50,000	0	8			
	C. Voters per Delegates				
	In Primaries	8,534			
	In Caucuses	1,886			

The Democrats, 2020

On the other hand, a variant of the 2012 Republican pattern could also sur-
face among the Democrats, as with their 2020 nominating contest. A stable
leader in the person of former vice president Joe Biden would play the role
of Mitt Romney this time. But unlike Romney, Biden would not have to
endure boomlets for an interminable stream of also-rans. Vermont senator
Bernie Sanders would return as the heir apparent for the activists, a standing
that would remain roughly stable through the fall, wobbling only during an
alternative boomlet of the 2020 Democratic contest. Massachusetts senator
Elizabeth Warren would be the reason for that lone wobble, as she challenged
early for the mantle of activist spokesperson. Yet her boomlet would fade
badly before the first real contest began.

Yet this contest did not lack a number of lesser side-shows to the story
of one dominant performance. Modest rises for South Bend mayor Peter
Buttigieg and Minnesota senator Amy Klobuchar were enough to enthuse
personal supporters but not to translate into serious impacts on delegate
numbers once the real contest began. California senator Kamala Harris
gained a mini-boomlet, yet that one always appeared to be primarily a
media phenomenon, as both their attention and her poll showing dissipated
early in the debate sequence. The main role for Harris was just to represent
another truncated version of the discovery/scrutiny/decline dynamic pio-
neered by the Republicans in 2012.

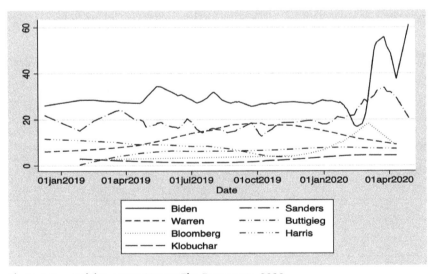

Figure 3.3. Activists versus Voters: The Democrats, 2020

All that said, alternative press fantasies—comprising a kind of opinion poll among reporters—did continue through 2015 and well into 2016:

- "Harris and Warren on the rise," *New York Times*, July 7, 2015: "Interviews with voters in the early primary and caucus states over the last week found that Ms. Harris and Ms. Warren had plainly broken through, drawing on a deep hunger within the Democratic electorate for big ideas and ground-breaking female leadership."
- "It is still within the realm of possibility that Elizabeth Warren can be stopped," *New York Times*, October 1, 2015, "How the Average Joe (and Jane) Could Wind up Stopping Warren."[7]
- "As the debates near an end, Biden is crashing," CNN, October 31, 2015: "But Biden today is in a much weaker position than he was even a few months ago. And this is the time to be peaking, not losing your stride."
- "The real politics of delegate selection makes a pre-convention majority unlikely," "The Democratic Race Is Now Sanders Versus the Field, And a Contested Convention Possibly Awaits," *Washington Post*, February 20, 2020, and "Debate Shows Bernie Sanders Could Win Most Votes But Be Denied Nomination," *The Guardian*, February 20, 2020.

Nevertheless, all the attention to support lines, opinion boomlets, media fancies, and respective crashes during the long unreality of pre-presidential debates were quickly reduced to the status of ephemera by the arrival of a real world (see table 3.5). Activists and their press audience clearly did pay to its prelims; the general public just as clearly did not. So, when the primaries finally arrived, the voting public dispatched both the activists and their press audience; Table 3.5 is one of many ways to tell what was, ultimately, the same story. Biden, the front-runner, stumbled in the opening primary in New Hampshire. He righted himself in the second primary in South Carolina. And in the following round on Super Tuesday, March 3, the contest came to an effective end. Bernie Sanders would stagger on, but he was not to win another primary before even he withdrew in an early April primary in Wisconsin.

Table 3.5.   **The Actual Voters: Primary Outcomes**

	Biden	*Sanders*
February 11	0	1
February 29	1	0
March 3	9	4
March 10	5	0
March 17	4	0
April 7	1	0

The Republicans, 2016

There have been even shorter contests since the explosion of presidential primaries, though mostly just when a sitting president was seeking renomination. The Republican contest of 2020 would add one such. Otherwise, the Democratic nominating contest of 2020 was about as short—and about as lacking in serious challenges—as it is possible to generate in the post-reform world (Sawyer, Shafer, and Wagner 2021). Yet there was one recent nominating contest that was differed from these others, one that, while actively and widely contested, was actually not much affected by the difference between primaries and caucuses or, even more impressively, by any serious distinction between the world of pre-nomination debates and the electoral contests that would produce an actual nomination (Figure 3.4).

For this contest, too, the story ended surprisingly early. Businessman Donald Trump entered only after former governors Jeb Bush of Florida and John Kasich of Ohio had already joined the field, along with current senators Ted Cruz of Texas and Marco Rubio of Florida, plus neurosurgeon Ben Carson, though Trump's entry would hardly have seemed late in previous years. Regardless, the prepresidential debates provided Trump with a forum (and an audience) that he had never previously possessed. He enjoyed it and he began to climb in public support. By the end of the calendar year, he had become the hypothetical front-runner. And from the time of the first actual contests, over delegate selection, he would demonstrate that he could translate poll standing into real support, that is, actual turnout in those delegate contests (Figure 3.4).

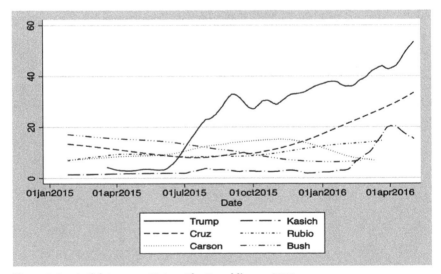

Figure 3.4. Activists versus Voters: The Republicans, 2016

Moreover, when the real contest appeared, there was no latent challenger waiting to emerge. The closest thing to a challenging boomlet had been for Ben Carson in the fall, and he was fading—discovery/scrutiny/decline—by the end of the year. There were lesser associated stories. Jeb Bush, the original champion of the regular party, managed only a long slow collapse. Marco Rubio, argued by many to be the emergent face of the regular party, did not fall away but neither did he enjoy much of a rise. At a distance was Ted Cruz, who began to rise toward the end of the year and continued to do so when the real contest arrived, but never enough to threaten the existing gap with Trump. And John Kasich would enjoy an idiosyncratic bump, though the contest was effectively over before he managed to deny his home state of Ohio to the obvious nominee.

THE ACTIVISTS' REVENGE

The state of contemporary American politics is easily summarized. The general public is closely balanced as between the two parties, perhaps as balanced as it has ever been for an extended period. The activists in those two parties are far apart ideologically and galloping away from each other, on a scale seen occasionally—at the very beginning, right before the Civil War, or in the late nineteenth century—but not on a regular basis. The general public, despite activist efforts as abetted by a news media that is increasingly indistinguishable from these activists, finds itself sitting in between. A majority of this public is always more liberal, much more liberal, than the active Republican Party. A majority of this public is always more conservative, much more conservative, than the active Democratic Party.

In the face of polarized activists inside both parties, the members of this voting public ordinarily have no trouble making a choice between candidate options. One candidate or the other will reliably be closer to any given member of this public. It is just that the same public quickly becomes disillusioned by either Democratic or Republican winners, who can increasingly be counted on to cater to activists and misrepresent voters. Fortunately, American politics offers a simple corrective: respond to programmatic initiatives that you do not like by going with the opposite party next time, thereby redividing control of the institutions of American national government. Given the state of modern American politics, that quickly becomes preferable to allowing unified Democratic or unified Republican government.

Yet it is the state of American *parties* that offers a simple explanation for why this recurrent dynamic surfaces and persists. Though at this point, the analytic story all too often veers off instead into strange territory. Many analysts decry the state of American politics, often on grounds that are shared across ideological lines: parties are too polarized to reflect public wishes; politics is too unstable to deliver policy programs. However, many of these same analysts then go in search of remedies that can only exaggerate those problems. Maybe *gerrymandering* caused all this? Something or someone should make the activists behave in a nonpartisan fashion. Maybe the *filibuster* is at fault? We should find a way to allow narrow majorities of increasingly unrepresentative parties to implement sweeping programs. And all the while, what somehow never re-enters the story is its bedrock, "the state of the parties."

As a nation, we have sought incentives for political activity that give us parties focused not on distributing benefits and encouraging candidates to emphasize a record of policy delivery, but instead focused on abstract programs that allow candidates to emphasize the sweep of their promises and the purity of their positions. This decision is the huge shaping influence that somehow remains hidden in plain view. Even as the most widely repeated criticisms of that politics—it grows only more polarized; it favors staking out positions over delivering programs—follow more or less directly from these "hidden" structural influences.

Having built what is in effect a self-perpetuating activist politics which is in chronic tension with its own putative general public, we have permitted— and the political press has usually encouraged—these activists to attempt to go on and remake governmental institutions and the political process itself in their own image, privileging activism while exiling a public that is only condescendingly represented by these activists, a public that, not very long ago, privileged political brokerage and programmatic accomplishments. And in the end, having successfully done all that—the final irony—we lament not the state of the political parties, but the state of American politics.

NOTES

1. For the original partisan aversion, see the Farewell Address of George Washington. For the partisan world already emerging by the time Washington delivered it, Pasley (2013).

2. For the Progressives as a political movement, Link and McCormick (1983*)*; for a view from the other side, Ford (1898).

3. As assembled in Shafer and Wagner 2019, 11–12.

4. Derived originally as table 1.4 in Shafer and Wagner, *The Long War, Over Party Structure*, p. 24.

5. Drawn from table 4.7 in Shafer and Wagner, 2019, 155.

6. Dropped from the analysis through an inability to draw 5 percent on a regular basis are former Utah governor Jon Huntsman, New Mexico governor Gary Johnson, Minnesota governor Tim Pawlenty, former Louisiana governor Buddy Roemer, and Texas congressman Ron Paul. In order to be complete, Figure 3.1 would add those five roughly flat lines along the bottom of the graph.

7. Though it had occurred to someone that the activists and the voters are sometimes not the same thing:

> In primary after primary, the candidates of the party's left-liberal activists have failed to win the more typical members of the Democratic Party. These voters don't show up at rallies or post on Twitter. They are more moderate. They are disproportionately nonwhite; Southern; and less likely to have graduated from college. But in the modern era, they have usually had the votes to decide the nomination.

Chapter Four

Congressional Primary Challenges and the Health of the Parties

Robert G. Boatright

It is rare for incumbent members of Congress to lose their bids for renomination—or even to come close to doing so. The primary election victory by challenger David Brat over House Majority Leader Eric Cantor in 2014 is one such example; another is the victory of challenger Alexandria Ocasio-Cortez over House democratic caucus chair Joe Crowley in 2018 (Bell, Meyer, and Gaddie 2017; Freedlander 2021). There could be many reasons why these incumbents lost, yet it was tempting in both cases to find lessons in these primary defeats for the incumbents' parties. Such defeats are often taken to be signs of party dysfunction: party elites have lost touch with the voters, that party activists have become more extreme than their representatives, or that factional conflict has broken out. These claims are often hyperbolic, framing primary elections as "civil wars" between progressives and mainstream liberals, or conservatives and moderates (Brooks 2019; Wang 2019).

The premise of this chapter is that variations in the number of challenges to incumbent members of Congress *can* indeed tell us something about the health of the parties.

Primary challenges are by no means bad in themselves—in any given year, some incumbents likely merit defeat, and in places where there is little general election competition, primaries provide a democratic check on legislators' power. There are, however, important reasons to find some primary challenges to be concerning. Instances where incumbent legislators refuse to vote in the interest of their district, defer to powerful interest groups, or fail to seek compromise because of their fear of being primaried suggest that primary elections can do harm to the ability of Congress to deliberate and legislate. In addition, many of the common features of primary elections may exacerbate such problems, including the anemic voter turnout of many primary elections;

the unrepresentativeness of primary electorates; and the even greater unrepresentativeness of primary election donors and independent spenders.

So, when the number of primary election challenges increases substantially, then, the increase is likely to means something. In the 2020 congressional primaries, the number of defeated incumbents was the highest since 1992 and the highest in any non-redistricting year since 1974. These defeats were part of a larger trend—there were more competitive incumbent primaries than in any election years since 1992 as well as a larger number of competitive Democratic primaries than Republican primaries for the first time since 1994.

In this chapter, I summarize patterns in congressional primary challenges to incumbents over the past five decades, paying particular attention to the causes of increased incumbent primary competition since 2010. I then discuss three theories about variation in the number of primary challenges to incumbents over time, followed by the application of these theories to recent primary elections.

The most consequential lesson of this chapter is not that one theory is right and the others are wrong, but rather, the sources of primary challenges vary within the parties over time. Parties may experience surges in primary challenges for similar reasons, but they do not experience them at the same time. In addition, the decline in the strength and capacity of the party organizations that has characterized the past five decades has not been felt equally by both parties.

THREE THEORIES ABOUT PRIMARY CHALLENGES

Figure 4.1 shows all races where the incumbent was held to less than 75 percent of the primary vote (regardless of how many opponents he or she had), broken out by party. This threshold has been useful in my prior work because, on the one hand, almost no challengers who receive less than 25 percent of the vote raise more than a token amount of money, but on the other hand, using some sort of threshold eliminates the variation in the number of primary challengers that one sees across states due to differences in ballot access laws.[1] Studies of general election competition often use a threshold of 60 percent or less; in my judgment this threshold is too low and misses some challenges that might compel the incumbent to campaign, but the time trend when one uses that threshold is similar.

Figure 4.1 shows that primary challenges were common in the early 1970s but declined steadily over the course of that decade and the 1980s. There was a surge in challenges in 1992, driven in party by that year's redistricting and in part by that year's scandal involving incumbents use of the House Bank.

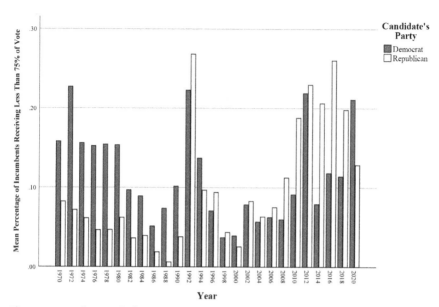

Figure 4.1.   Primary Challenges to Incumbent Representatives, 1970–2020

Challenges then increased steadily beginning in the early 2000s and have remained at levels slightly higher than the 1970s since 2010. During this time, the partisan effects of primary challenges have also been reversed. Before the 1990s they were mostly a problem for Democrats, but they have been substantially more common within the Republican Party in most years since that time. This pattern holds both in terms of raw numbers (as shown in the graph) and in terms of the percentage of incumbents seeking reelection within each party. The number of challenges among Republicans increased substantially during the period from 2010 through 2014 before declining somewhat. Although there was a slight increase in Democratic primary competition around 2006, it was far less substantial than the Republican increase in 2010 or the Democratic increase over the past two election cycles. Democratic challenges increased somewhat in 2016 and 2018, but the increase in 2020 was unique for Democrats. Three theories can help account for these patterns.

Primaries and Partisan Swing

First, Vincent Moscardelli and I (2018) have argued that many primary challengers are opportunistic. When there is a swing for one party or the other in the general election, it is often accompanied by a surge in ideological challenges to centrist legislators in the primaries. For instance, the 2010 Republican gains in Congress were accompanied by an increase in challenges from the right in primaries. Similar increases in primary challenges accompanied partisan swings in the 2006, 1994, and 1974 general elections. These increases in primary challenges also occurred over multiple elections before subsiding; for instance, the 2012, 1996, and 1976 primaries also featured an atypically large number of challenges.

Partisan swings are often driven by two factors: by a measurable sense among voters that the country is headed in the wrong direction, and by a decrease in support for the party that holds the presidency (Abramowitz 1991). It is normal for voters to hold the president's party responsible for the nation's problems. Yet the passage of major pieces of legislation usually requires some level of bipartisan support. When the president is popular or voters are not particularly disenchanted with the state of politics, bipartisanship can often be presented in a positive light—as a means of putting the national good above party. When voters are feeling hostile toward the president, such votes can easily be framed as a betrayal of party principles, or as a sign that one is aiding the enemy. Some representatives have sought to position themselves as moderates, either because of sincerely held political beliefs or out of concerns about winning the general election. But there are in fact many instances of bipartisan legislation, so a prospective primary challenger can usually find some reason to accuse the incumbent of being too moderate.

The partisan surge argument thus has some connection to ideology—we would expect that incumbents who face primary challenges are more likely to be centrists than those who do not face challenges. However, we do not need evidence of this pattern to find instances where partisan surges prompt increased primary election competition—a simple comparison of general election defeats for incumbents and primary election challenges to incumbents across time will suffice.

Pressure from Nonparty Organizations

Second, primaries are an inexpensive forum for interest groups that wish to draw attention to themselves and their causes. Indeed, I have documented how such groups had begun in the mid-2000s to support challenges to centrist incumbents of both parties (Boatright 2013). Such groups were able to use the Internet to solicit small contributions from supporters around the country, and they were able to procure coverage in online political news media to generate a "buzz" about their candidates. The attention they drew was often effective even if their candidates lost—the challenges would force incumbents to raise money or to shift their positions more toward those of the group sponsoring the challenge, and they would serve notice to other incumbents that they, too, might face a primary opponent.

Democratic organizations such as MoveOn.org and Justice Democrats have openly discussed aspects of this strategy, as have Republican groups such as the Club for Growth and several organizations connected to the Tea Party movement. Such groups have been associated with challenges to incumbent senators such as Lincoln Chafee (R-RI), Arlen Specter (R-PA), Lisa Murkowski (R-AK), Joseph Lieberman (D-CT) and Bill Halter (D-AR), as well as to several challenges in the House. During the late 2000s, groups such as these used email lists and Internet advertising to focus national attention on these races, and following the Supreme Court's 2010 *Citizens United v. FEC* decision and the subsequent *SpeechNow.org v. FEC* appeals court decision they were able at times to convince individual wealthy donors to fund independent expenditures (Boatright, Malbin, and Glavin 2016).

Nonparty organizations only can use primaries effectively, however, if their resources are focused on a small number of primaries. The fundraising base for such groups is limited, and groups must show their donors that they are having an impact. At the same time, these groups are effectively targeting the leaders of the party which they support and are likely to provoke a counter-response. As Hassell (2017) has shown, the party campaign committees and their extended network of supporters actively work to discourage primary competition and are usually successful in doing so. A group-sponsored challenge thus requires that the targeted incumbent does not necessarily have the means to respond, or that the incumbent really is out of step with the rest of the party in important ways. The number of such incumbents is rarely very high.

It is easy to identify challenges of this nature. A very small number of organizations have spearheaded these challenges. The challenges tend to come from the partisan extremes, and the rhetoric of the challengers tends to focus on ideology and issues rather than on matters such as the incumbent's age, competence, and so forth. Such challengers tend to raise far more money than the average challenger, and a greater proportion of these challengers' contributions tend to come from small donors from outside of the district or state. Since 2010, ideological primary challengers have often been the beneficiaries of independent expenditures.

Primaries and Presidential Politics

Third, presidents have, at least in theory, the ability to encourage or discourage challenges. It is exceedingly rare for sitting presidents to encourage challenges to incumbent members of Congress, but it has happened. Most notably,

Franklin Delano Roosevelt endorsed challengers in southern Senate primaries in 1938, although there is little evidence that his intervention influenced the election outcomes or that he wanted to do anything more than send a message to incumbents who had not supported the New Deal (Dunn 2012; Grantham 1994, 130; Mickey 2015, 136). Earlier, Woodrow Wilson also endorsed challengers to antiwar southern senators and representatives in 1918 (Bateman, Katznelson, and Lapinski 2018, 339).

In recent decades, presidents have tended to stay away from party primaries, and when they have become involved, it has been to support an incumbent representative or senator with whom they have an existing relationship. Presidents Clinton, Bush, and Obama steered clear of competitive incumbent primaries during their time in office. Obama issued an endorsement of an incumbent in a competitive Senate race in Arkansas in 2010 but did little more (Stein 2011). Some Bush staff members worked on behalf of a successful Senate primary challenger in New Hampshire in 2002, but Bush himself stayed out of the race (Belluck 2002). In fact, recent presidents have seen little advantage to getting involved in primaries; they risk antagonizing fellow partisans no matter the outcome. Presidents must also avoid inadvertently hurting their party's candidate's ability to broaden their appeal in the general election; in the Arkansas case above, support from Obama might have been helpful in a Democratic primary but could be used against the Democratic candidate in a general election. In both the Obama and Bush examples, the presidents had political or personal ties to candidates, but there was little strategic sense in connecting the president's political fortunes to those of congressional candidates.

Donald Trump, however, presents a unique case. As a president who came into office with tenuous ties to the Republican establishment, Trump did not necessarily face the obstacles that other presidents have faced, and he arguably had the power to prompt challenges to legislators who he dislikes. In many ways, he is more like the leader of an organized faction or nonparty group than any other president. It is plausible that other prominent politicians in the future might have or wish to have similar power, but it is certainly an unprecedented development, and it is therefore difficult to measure with reference to any elections before his presidency.

Each of these theories has implications regarding the well-being of the two major parties. One might contend that strong parties will find ways to protect their incumbents from intra-party challenge. This assumption is not always necessary—parties may care little what happens in overwhelmingly partisan districts, and they may in fact benefit from a challenge that removes a problematic incumbent from office. But such circumstances should not vary over time. When primary challenges increase in number, this increase is a sign of a change in the parties' ability or willingness to ensure that they and their incumbents must allocate resources toward the primary which are better used in the general election. Recent scholarship on the rising power of activists and political amateurs in the two parties (Shafer and Wagner 2019), the enhanced power of ideologically extreme small donors (La Raja and Schaffner 2015), and the increased role independent expenditures play in elections (Schatzinger and Martin 2020), all have implications for these theories. That is, one might see each of the above arguments as temporary phenomena: partisan waves recede, nonparty groups come and go, and Donald Trump may well have been a president sui generis. But the relationship between these theories and ongoing changes in political campaigns suggest that these patterns have built upon each other in a way that will continue to reshape electoral politics in an enduring way.

APPLYING THE THEORIES TO RECENT PRIMARY CHALLENGES

These three explanations are not mutually exclusive, but their measurement requires different types of evidence. I consider the evidence for each below, with particular attention to the past three election cycles (2016, 2018, and 2020).

Partisan Swing

The evidence for partisan swing is of a series of correlations between incumbent challenges and incumbents' general election defeats (Boatright and Moscardelli 2018). The number of competitive challenges is higher in years where incumbents of the opposing party fare worse in the general election. For example, in 2010 the number of incumbent challenges within the Republican Party increased, as did the number of defeated Democratic incumbents. Opportunistic conservative candidates in 2010 emerged to run against Democrats, but some conservatives also mounted campaigns against other Republicans.

Indeed, there were significant correlations over the 1970–2014 time period between primary challenges and general election competition were significant both overall, and within each party (i.e., between Democratic primary challenges and Republican general election incumbent defeats, or vice versa). Yet in the past three election cycles, this relationship has disappeared. The correlation between the number of competitive primary challenges and the number of defeated opposite party incumbents for the period from 1970 through 2020 is still significant; a .41 correlation at $p < .05$; as of 2014 it

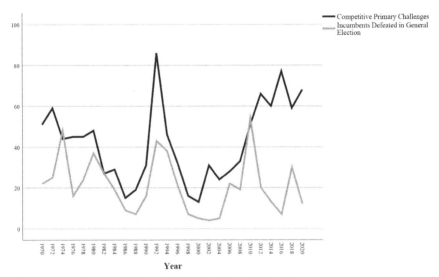

Figure 4.2.   Primary and General Election Competition Compared, 1970–2020

stood at .72 (p < .01). As of 2014 there was a significant relationship within each party as well, but that is no longer the case.

The decay of this relationship is evident in figure 4.2, which shows two trend lines: the number of incumbents defeated in the general election and the number of competitive primary challenges. The two lines move in tandem from 1970 through 2010, with only one or two exceptions, but they begin to diverge in 2010, and in the past three election cycles, they have actually moved in opposite directions. One could perhaps offer ad hoc reasons for the pattern of past three election cycles. For instance, one could argue that many recent primary challenges have occurred in safe partisan districts and thus were insulated from general election trends, or one could argue that due in both years to the perceived unpopularity of Donald Trump, 2016 or 2020 initially appeared to be likely to be higher turnover elections than they wound up being. Still, it remains clear that primary election competition no longer follows the same rhythms as general election competition.

Nonparty Organizations

To find instances where nonparty organizations have played a role in prima-ries, one first must separate out different types of primary challenges in order to see which candidacies might draw the support of groups concerned with influencing the parties. After this sorting, one can look for evidence of group involvement. This precaution is necessary because the more common reasons for primary challenges over time, such as scandal or incompetence on the part of the incumbent, do at times attract some interest group contributions, but such contributions are more likely to be access-oriented in nature—that is, the victory or defeat of an incumbent by a challenger who shares his or her views on policy but is untarred by scandal does not yield policy consequences groups or donors would care about, but it might still attract group or individual donations for other reasons. Groups can only benefit from challenges if they are able to say that the challenge provides a referendum on the popularity of their views.

Figure 4.3 provides two different time series for ideological primary challenges, categorizing challenges according to election retrospectives provided in the *Almanac of American Politics*.[2] The lefthand side bar graph shows changes in the number of ideological challenges by party and year (using the 75 percent threshold mentioned previously). The righthand side bar graph shows the proportion of primary challenges that have to do with ideology. These figures show that ideological challenges have usually been more common in Republican than in Democratic primaries, but that they have increased substantially over the past decade both in number and proportion.

Figure 4.3 shows, even more dramatically than figure 4.1, how primary challenges within the two parties have changed over time. Approximately one-third of Republican primary challenges since the mid-1990s have been ideological, with number of Republican ideological challenges increasing substantially in 2010. It declined somewhat in 2016, but ideological challenges still remained more common among Republicans than among Democrats until 2020. Democrats, as the figure shows, did not have a problem with ideological challenges until 2020. Many observers (including me) have taken this difference as a sign that Democratic Party leaders have been more effective at structuring primary competition than have Republicans. The Democratic Party leadership in both chambers had successively dissuaded candidates in several primaries in 2018, suggesting that something about the Democratic Party leadership or culture made it more able to ward off primary battles. This tendency is reflected in Hassell's (2017) work on party interventions in primaries and in my own work (Boatright and Albert 2021) showing that Super PAC spending in Democratic primaries had been more concentrated than was the case in Republican primaries. It may be time to rethink these assumptions.

However, nonparty organizations do not benefit from large numbers of primary challenges. Hence, it is not just the number of ideological challenges that matters but the concentration of interest group resources among them. In this regard, a comparison of 2020 to 2012 and 2014 is instructive. In 2020, four of the five strongest Democratic primary challenges were challenges

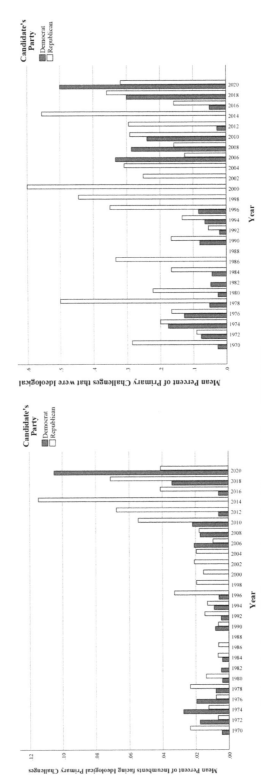

Figure 4.3. Ideological Primary Challenge to Incumbent Representatives, 1970–2020

from the left—including the three successful challenges. Two of these candidates, Jamaal Bowman (who defeated veteran incumbent Eliott Engel in New York), and Marie Newman (who defeated incumbent Daniel Lipinski in Illinois), raised over $2 million, over one-third of which came in the form of donations of $200 or less, and over half of which came from donors who did not reside in these states. Bowman and Newman also were the beneficiaries of over $1 million each in independent expenditures. In contrast, only one of the five Republicans who defeated an incumbent in a primary was an ideological challenger, and that challenger, Colorado's Lauren Boebert, raised only $133,256 in the primary and had only $5,500 in independent expenditures in her favor. Only one Republican primary challenger was the beneficiary of a significant amount of independent spending and that unsuccessful challenger, Texas candidate Chris Putnam, raised little money on his own and instead put over $700,000 of his own money into the race.

This imbalance speaks to the prominence of one major Democratic ideological group, Justice Democrats, and to the willingness of issue-oriented abortion rights, environmental, and civil rights groups to focus their attention on the same Democratic primaries—primaries that took place in safe Democratic districts. Justice Democrats was open about its efforts to learn from Republican challenges of years past and from the political science literature on primary challenges (Boatright 2022). The 2020 primaries were almost the mirror image of congressional primaries from 2012 and 2014: in each of these election years, there was little ideological competition in Democratic primaries but there were over ten ideological challenges among Republicans in each year. In both years, small donations and independent expenditures were focused on a small number of races, including the defeats of Republican incumbents Eric Cantor, Jean Schmidt, and Cliff Stearns. In 2012 and 2014 the effort by Republican groups also included challenges to a number of incumbent senators, including the defeat of Indiana senator Richard Lugar in 2012 and the near-defeat of Senator Thad Cochran in 2014. There was no equivalent Democratic effort in Senate primaries in 2020; the lone competitive Democratic Senate primary, which took place in Massachusetts, was not waged about ideology and in fact the incumbent in the race, Senator Ed Markey, received more support from progressive organizations than did his opponent.

This recent history shows the difficulty of separating interest group activities from partisan wave elections. The surge in Republican interest group activity in primaries coincided with the 2010 Republican wave election and the smaller Republican wave of 2014, yet it was rooted in the desire of a small number of Republican interest groups such as the Club for Growth to show that they could exert power in primaries. One could similarly point to the success of Justice Democrats in aiding Alexandria Ocasio-Cortez in 2018, a Democratic wave year, as the impetus for its expanded efforts in 2020.

President Trump's Role in Republican Incumbent Primaries

The decline of ideological competition within Republican primaries over the past three election cycles may suggest that the party had become sufficiently unified behind Trump that there were not easy targets. If so, however, it is remarkable because threats about primary challenges to anyone who was insufficiently supportive of Trump had become commonplace. There was a perception that Trump had been successful in 2018 and 2020 in using Twitter to interfere in Republican primaries, such as that of his antagonist Mark Sanford (see Isenstadt 2020). Media accounts also tended to frame the retirements of politicians such as Senators Jeff Flake and Bob Corker as responses to Trump. Trump's postelection threats against Georgia governor Brian Kemp and Senate majority whip John Thune also suggest that Trump saw a role for himself in Republican primaries after his presidency. There is little evidence that the Republican Party has as robust a party operation to tamp down primary competition as Democrats do. The fluky nature of primary upsets such as Lauren Boebert's victory in Colorado suggest that Republican primaries continue to have the potential to be more volatile than Democratic ones, but there is clearly nothing left of the organized anti-incumbent efforts of the early 2010s.

The extent of Trump's influence on Republican primaries is subject to debate. In a retrospective on the 2016 election, I found little evidence that candidate Trump's endorsement helped Republicans in primaries (Boatright and Sperling 2019, chapter 4). Trump endorsed a small number of candidates in House primaries, including some primary challengers, but some fared quite poorly, and some of those who won did so comfortably enough that it is doubtful that Trump's endorsement made any difference. Given the widespread expectation during primary season that Trump would lose the 2016 general election, many of the candidates who sought his endorsement were also likely losers who were looking to do something dramatic to draw attention to their struggling campaigns.

Trump's role in 2018 and 2020 is similarly opaque. Several Republican House and Senate members with whom Trump had tangled chose not to run for reelection; these candidates might well have faced an opponent supported by Trump, they might have faced an opponent who claimed fealty to Trump but had little direct support from Trump, and some, of course, might still have won. It is hard also to prove that these incumbents retired because they feared a Trump-inspired challenge, as opposed to retiring because of their dissatisfaction with the direction of the party or for personal reasons. It does seem likely that Trump played a role in Sanford's defeat in South Carolina. However, Sanford had faced strong primary opponents in the past and his open criticism of Trump again makes it unclear whether Sanford lost because Trump campaigned against him, or because voters were unhappy that Sanford criticized Trump (Conroy, Rakich, and Nguyen 2018). Despite the high number of Republican primary defeats in 2020, there are also no obvious cases of Republican incumbents losing or coming close to doing so either because of their views on Trump or because of Trump's views on them.

The effect of Trump on his party's primaries, then, has little to do with his activities as president: as president he spoke more belligerently than is the norm about punishing members of his own party but did little in practice. Trump's postpresidency, however, promises to be different and unique. There has been speculation since January 2021 about primary retribution against House and Senate Republicans who voted for Trump's second impeachment, and Trump himself spoke frequently after the election of seeking vengeance upon these legislators.

In the Senate, only one (Lisa Murkowski of Alaska) will face a primary opponent in 2022, and Alaska's newly adopted top four primary system all but ensures that Murkowski will make it to the general election regardless of that candidate's performance. The real test of Trump's ability to influence incumbent primaries will come in the House, where Republicans' interest in gaining control of the chamber may inspire party leaders to try to quell such conflict (Epstein and Glueck 2021).

The degree to which Republican leaders work to save these candidates may depend on how safe these districts are in the general election. These incumbents are listed in table 4.1. The two Republicans on this list whose seats are safest in the general election appear certain to draw competitive challengers. Two have already announced their retirements (Adam Kinzinger of Illinois and Anthony Gonzalez of Ohio). Even apart from Trump's threatened retribution, both were anticipating running in districts that might be redrawn to their detriment. And the two Republicans from Michigan also hail from a state with a Republican-held state legislature and a declining population, which may mean that these Republicans will also be penalized in the 2022 redistricting. Paradoxically, the safest Republicans on the list may be those who hail from Democratic-leaning states and have not had consistent primary challenges in the past. One factor working against Trump's ability to create any sort of narrative about retribution, however, is the primary calendar. With Gonzalez declining to seek reelection, none of these ten Republicans will be facing a primary until over two months after the primary season has begun, and the one of the ten who appears most vulnerable, Elizabeth Cheney of Wyoming, has the latest primary of any of these candidates.

Table 4.1. Primary Election History for House Republicans who Voted for Donald Trump's Second Impeachment

Representative	District	Year Elected	Republican Presidential Vote 2020	Primary Challenges since 2010 (held to < 75% of vote)	2022 Primary Date
Cheney, Elizabeth	WY-AL	2016	70	2020, 74% 2018, 68%	August 16
Rice, Tom	SC-7	2012	59		June 14
Newhouse, Dan	WA-4	2014	58	2016, 61%**	
Kinzinger, Adam	IL-16		57	2018, 68% 2012, 57%***	June 28
Gonzalez, Anthony	OH-16	2018	56		May 3
Upton, Fred	MI-6	1986	51	2020, 63% 2014, 71% 2012, 67% 2010, 57%	August 2
Herrera Beutler, Jamie	WA-3	2010	51		August 2
Meijer, Peter	MI-3	2020	51		August 2
Katko, John	NY-24	2014	44		June 28
Valadao, David	CA-21	2012*	44	**	June 7

Italics: Not seeking reelection in 2022.
*Valadao lost his seat in 2018 and regained it in 2020.
**Top 2 primary; primary vote calculated from percentage of votes for Republican candidates.
***Incumbent vs. incumbent primary.

Table 4.1 suggests that Trump faces the same incentives and limitations that are confronted by nonparty organizations seeking to be active in primaries. It would be difficult for Trump to seek to defeat all of the Republicans who voted to impeach him, but a victory in one or two early primaries may create a narrative about Trump's relevance and power. This pattern may well be the case even if Trump himself has little to do with the primary defeat. Trump also risks endangering the Republican Party's pursuit of a House majority should he be held responsible for defeating an incumbent in a swing district that is ultimately lost by the Republican nominee in the general election. As has been the case for ideological interest groups in the past, Trump and his allies may care about avoiding such an outcome, or they may find that the threat to harm the party works to their advantage.

IMPLICATIONS FOR THE PARTIES

There are four conclusions about the political parties one can draw from primary challenges in recent elections. First, we really do not know what a "normal" amount of competition is. Although I noted earlier that we should not just assume that primary challenges are cyclical in nature, history suggests that they are at least self-limiting. The data in this chapter cover a fifty-year period; they show that primary challenges were more common in the early 1970s than in the subsequent two decades, but even this fifty-year snapshot does not reveal what is normal. I chose this period in part because of data availability, but it also depicts an era in which political party organizations had begun to undergo substantial change (Herrnson 1988, see chapter 3 in this volume).

We do know, however, that there were periods earlier in the twentieth century when primary competition was higher than it is now (Hirano and Snyder 2019). The few studies of primary competition in the earlier decades of the twentieth century have noted that competition was also higher in areas of one-party dominance and in areas where the party organizations were weak. Some of these circumstances are likely to reappear—for instance, we may face a future where, due to gerrymandering, there are more safe seats. Yet even then most incumbents have continued to win renomination, and reelection. If primary competition were to become more common, it would also become less interesting—and elections might even appear to be more democratic.

Second, we should reject "bothsidesism." The trajectory of primary challenges within the two parties is not identical, nor should we expect it to be. The partisan wave argument suggests that when challenges are surging within one party, they should be declining in the other. The nonparty organizations theory rests on the activity of a very small number of groups. The Republican Party groups that influenced primaries during the late 2000s and early 2010s are largely gone, or at least have toned down their efforts to command news coverage. The Democratic organizations that have supported challengers in 2018 and 2020 may persist, but it is not an inevitability. And there is no reason to believe that Donald Trump's open belligerence toward his party's incumbents is a template that any other president will follow. These asymmetries mean that political observers should exercise caution in making broad claims about any congruence between insurgent primary election victors on both sides of the aisle. The primary challenges on the left in recent election year, such as those of Alexandria Ocasio-Cortez, Jamaal Bowman, and Marie Newman, did not arise for the same reason or feature the same tactics as those that led to the election of the new breed of vocal conservatives.

Third, the media should cover primaries in a less sensationalistic manner. It is natural that journalists and political pundits should find the narrative of primary competition to be attractive. It is worth keeping in mind that most primaries are not competitive, and that the historically high number of incumbents who lost their primaries in 2020—eight—still came to barely over 2 percent of all incumbents seeking reelection. Outside groups can capitalize on the drama inherent in a primary challenge, but the political media are willing participants in this narrative and certainly play a role in framing these elections such that they are purported to be a threat to centrist incumbents of both parties.

And fourth, if one wishes to search for ways to enhance the ability of parties or incumbents to ward off challenges that might pull the party to political extremes, it is important to look at both the national and the state level. At the federal level, changes in campaign finance practices and laws have encouraged primary competition. At the state level, variations in who can vote in a primary, when primaries are held, and how easy it is for candidates to gain ballot access can shape competition. Such variations will not necessarily prevent the over-time variation in competition described above from taking place—nor should they. But some recent changes in state-level elections, such as the new top four primary in Alaska or Maine's adoption of ranked-choice voting, may well alter the nature of primary competition in salutary ways.

For those who would find fault with the nature of congressional primary competition in recent years, these implications all suggest that the primary system itself is not necessarily the problem. Primary election politics is, instead, symptomatic of changes that the political parties themselves have undergone over the past few decades.

NOTES

1. Some states with lower ballot access requirements, for instance, feature large numbers of primary challengers who receive one or two percent of the vote, but such challengers arguably do not pose enough of a threat that we would expect the incumbent to respond in any way.

2. As I discuss in *Getting Primaried* and subsequent work, this method likely misses some lower-profile challenges which could be categorized by using other means, such as candidate websites or media coverage. I use it, however, in order to maintain the ability to do accurate comparisons over the 1970–2020 time period, for which Internet media and other similar information sources are not as easily available.

Part II

PARTISAN VOTERS

Chapter Five

Peak Polarization?

The Rise of Partisan-Ideological Consistency and its Consequences

Alan I. Abramowitz

Political parties and elections in the United States have changed dramatically since the publication of Philip Converse's seminal work on ideological thinking in the American electorate in the 1950s and 1960s (Converse 1964). The ideological divide between Democratic and Republican elites in Washington and in most states has turned into a deep chasm in the twenty-first century. There is no longer any ideological overlap between the parties in Congress as liberal Republicans and conservative Democrats have disappeared and moderates have become an endangered species (Poole and Rosenthal 2007; Theriault 2008; Pearson 2018). At the same time, elections have become highly nationalized with voters increasingly basing their House and Senate choices on their feelings toward the national parties and their leaders, especially the president (Jacobson 2013, 2016; Abramowitz and Webster 2016). As ticket-splitting has fallen to its lowest level in decades, the electoral advantage of incumbency has shrunk considerably (Jacobson 2015).

These changes in the party system and elections have coincided with equally dramatic changes in the political attitudes of ordinary Americans. In recent years, a growing share of Americans has come to see politics as a form of warfare, with elections viewed as contests between the forces of good and evil. Partisans increasingly view supporters of the opposing party not as opponents but as enemies: bad actors who want to inflict harm to the nation and who will stop at nothing to achieve their goals (Iyengar and Westwood 2015; Abramowitz 2018; Iyengar et al., 2019; Finkel et al. 2020).

While Donald Trump did much to encourage this Manichaean view of politics, its growth can be traced back to at least the 1990s and the rise of a new generation of Republicans in Washington led by Newt Gingrich, who introduced a no-holds-barred brand of competition to Congress and the nation. One of the main strategies employed by Gingrich and his allies was to demonize the political opposition by portraying Democrats as dangerous radicals seeking to undermine traditional American values and impose socialism on the nation (Strahan and Palazzolo 2004; Zelizer 2020). The rise of the Gingrich Republicans coincided with another key development—the growth of partisan and ideological media outlets that made it easy for Americans to find news and information aligned with their personal preferences (Levendusky 2013; Smith and Searles 2014). Republicans, especially, have become heavily dependent on one such outlet: Fox News (Jurkowitz et al., 2020).

Democrats and Republicans were deeply divided long before 2016. However, Donald Trump's candidacy and presidency raised the intensity of partisan conflict in Washington, DC, and the nation to a new level (Jacobson 2016). Dislike and mistrust of the opposing party and its leaders set new records during Trump's presidency. So did voter turnout in the 2018 midterm election and the 2020 presidential election. Voters on both sides of the partisan divide sensed that the stakes in these contests were enormous (Nilsen 2018; Galston 2020).

Despite Trump's defeat and banishment from social media and the efforts of his successor, Joe Biden, to tamp down the intensity of partisan conflict, the divide between Democrats and Republicans in Washington, DC, and the nation appears to be as deep as ever in 2021. The former president and many of his fellow Republicans have persisted in questioning the legitimacy of Biden's election—an effort that led to a violent insurrection in the nation's capital on January 6, 2021, and an unsuccessful effort by a large number of congressional Republicans to block the certification of the electoral vote (Yourish, Buchanan, and Lu 2021). In the aftermath of that insurrection, Donald Trump continued to play a dominant role in Republican politics—granting and withholding endorsements based on support for his claims of widespread fraud in the 2020 election (Parker and Sotomayor 2021).

It is common to observe that political conflict in the United States has reached a new level of intensity in the second decade of the twenty-first century. However, what many political observers and scholars have failed to recognize is that the mutual hostility and mistrust that exists between ordinary Democrats and Republicans has an ideological foundation. In this chapter, I will present evidence showing that one of the most important reasons why Democrats and Republicans intensely dislike each other is that they intensely disagree on a wide range of issues, including the size and scope of the welfare state, abortion, gay and transgender rights, race relations, climate change, gun control, and immigration. Moreover, I will show that much like Democratic and Republican elites, ordinary Americans now tend to hold consistent beliefs across these issues. Those who favor liberal policies in one area tend to favor liberal policies in other areas, and likewise, those who favor conservative policies in one area tend to favor conservative policies in other areas. In other words, ordinary Americans have come to view politics through an ideological lens. This development is especially true among those who are the most attentive and politically active, but it true to a surprising degree even among those who only intermittently pay attention to politics and who rarely participate beyond voting. The rise of partisan-ideological consistency is one of the most important developments in American politics of the past fifty years. Growing partisan-ideological consistency has had profound consequences for many aspects of public opinion and political behavior including how Americans evaluate political parties and leaders and how they make their choices at the ballot box.

While recognizing the importance of growing partisan hostility and mistrust among ordinary citizens, with a few exceptions (Jost 2006; Ansolabehere, Rodden and Snyder 2008; Abramowitz 2010) students of American politics have not generally viewed ideological disagreement as an important driver of polarization within the electorate.[1] Many scholars continue to view ideological thinking as largely confined to political elites and perhaps a small minority of activists much as Converse found in his research (Bishop 2004; Kinder 2006; Fiorina, Abrams, and Pope 2010; Kinder and Kalmoe 2017). Indeed, some have argued that policy disagreement has little or nothing to do with growing dislike of the opposing party. Instead, these ideology skeptics view growing partisan polarization as one aspect of the rise of identity politics—a tendency of Americans to views their partisan identity as connected to a larger set of social identities such as race, ethnicity, gender, religion, sexual orientation, social class, and region. According to this social identity theory, a growing association between overlapping social identities and partisanship has led Americans to view the political world as divided into teams consisting of those on our side and those on the opposing side (Green, Palmquist, and Schickler 2002; Iyengar, Sood, and Lelkes 2012; Iyengar and Westwood 2014; Mason 2014, 2018; West and Iyengar 2020).

In this chapter, I present evidence from American National Election Studies (ANES) surveys showing that correlations among ideological identification, issue positions and party identification have increased dramatically within the electorate over the past half century. As a result, the divide between Democratic and Republican identifiers on the ideological identification scale has widened considerably. Then, using the extensive battery of issue questions included in the 2020 ANES survey, I show that a single underlying liberal-conservative dimension largely explains the policy preferences of ordinary Americans across a wide range of issues including the size and scope of the welfare state, abortion, gay and transgender rights, race relations, immigration, gun control, and climate change. I show that the distribution of preferences on this liberal-conservative issue scale is highly polarized with Democratic identifiers and leaners located overwhelmingly on the left, Republican identifiers and leaners located overwhelmingly on the right and little overlap between the two distributions. Finally, I show that location on the liberal-conservative issue scale strongly influences affective evaluations of the presidential candidates and political parties in 2020, and it is a powerful predictor of voter decision-making. Ideologically consistent respondents are far more likely to have polarized evaluations of presidential candidates and parties and to cast a straight-ticket vote than are ideologically inconsistent respondents. These findings suggest the rise of ideological consistency in the American electorate has been a major contributor to the rise of affective polarization, party loyalty, and straight-ticket voting in the twenty-first century.

THEORETICAL FRAMEWORK: PARTISAN-IDEOLOGICAL CONSISTENCY

Partisan-ideological consistency provides a theoretical framework for assessing the political attitudes of members of the public as well as political elites. This theory builds on the work of Converse and other scholars who studied issue constraint and ideological thinking in the American electorate. However, the theory of partisan-ideological consistency views partisanship and ideology not as separate constructs but as interdependent in the current era of American politics. Indeed, the role of ideology in shaping assessments of political leaders and political behavior depends on its close connection to partisanship. This approach reflects findings of recent research indicating that within the American public, ideology now shapes party identification as much as party identification shapes ideology (Chen and Goren 2016).

In order to measure partisan-ideological polarization among members of the public, I identify the liberal and conservative positions on issues based on the positions taken by leaders of the national parties. I identify liberal positions as those adopted by the large majority of Democratic Party leaders and conservative positions as those adopted by the large majority of Republican Party leaders. Thus, I identify support for abortion rights and opposition to building a wall along the US border with Mexico as liberal positions, and opposition to abortion rights and support for building a wall on the border as conservative positions because those are now the positions supported by the vast majority of Democratic and Republican elected officials and party leaders. In contrast, issues such as trade agreements and tariffs on which there are not clear differences between party positions are therefore not included in my measure of liberal versus conservative ideology.

Partisan-ideological consistency is important because it is a key component of partisan conflict. The greater the number of issues on which partisans disagree, the more intense that disagreement is likely to be and the more likely it is to affect other opinions and behavior. When partisans agree with their own party's position on some issues while agreeing with the opposing party on others, they should be less likely to hold extremely negative opinions of the opposing party and to view its leaders as enemies who must be defeated at all costs. In contrast, when partisans agree with their own party on almost all issues and disagree with the opposing party on almost all issues, they should be more likely to hold extremely negative views of the opposing party and to view its leaders as enemies who must be defeated at all costs.

Of course, issue disagreement is not the only reason for dislike and mistrust of the opposing party. In the United States, supporters of the two major parties differ in terms of characteristics such as race, ethnicity, social class, religion, region, and geography. Overlapping differences in social background characteristics can contribute to perceptions of those on the other side of the party divide as different, strange, or even threatening (Iyengar, Sood, and Lelkes 2012; Iyengar and Westwood 2014; Mason 2014, 2018). However, partisan-ideological polarization theory leads to the expectation that ideological disagreement is the most important source of negative opinions of the opposing party and its leaders and therefore exerts a strong influence on voter attitudes and decision-making.

THE RISE OF PARTISAN-IDEOLOGICAL CONSISTENCY

The rise of partisan-ideological consistency within the American electorate is readily observable in ANES surveys conducted between 1972, the first year that a question measuring ideological identification was included in the survey, and 2020. Table 5.1 displays Pearson product-moment correlations among party identification, ideological identification, and four issue questions—government aid to Black Americans, government responsibility for health insurance, government responsibility for jobs and incomes, and abortion rights, at twelve-year intervals between 1972 and 2020. The first three questions were added to the ANES survey starting in 1972. However, the abortion question was not added until 1980.[2]

The results displayed in table 5.1 show that there has been a dramatic increase in partisan-ideological consistency since 1972. As recently as 1984, during Ronald Reagan's presidency, the correlation between party and ideological identification was a rather modest .36 while the correlations of both party and ideological identification with preferences on social welfare issues

Table 5.1. Correlations among Party Identification, Ideological Identification and Issue Positions by Year

Correlation Between	1972	1984	1996	2008	2020
Party ID x Ideological ID	.28	.36	.50	.56	.68
Party ID x Aid to Blacks	.13	.22	.28	.34	.55
Ideological ID x Aid to Blacks	.32	.21	.29	.29	.55
Party ID x Health Insurance	.17	.18	.35	.38	.52
Ideological ID x Health Insurance	.24	.14	.33	.38	.56
Party ID x Jobs/Incomes	.18	.26	.32	.42	.52
Ideological ID x Jobs/Incomes	.26	.24	.29	.34	.53
Party ID x Abortion		.06	.14	.22	.45
Ideological ID x Abortion		.17	.27	.34	.51

Sources: American National Election Studies Cumulative File and 2020 American National Election Study

involving the size and role of government were far weaker, ranging from .14 to .24. Moreover, despite the fact that the Republican Party added a plank opposing abortion rights to its national platform in 1980, the relationships of both party and ideological identification to opinions on legalized abortion were very weak. Abortion was not yet a partisan issue in 1984.

The picture with regard to partisan-ideological consistency was very different in 2020. First, the correlation between party and ideological identification was a very strong .68. In terms of shared variance, the relationship was almost five times stronger in 2020 as in 1984. Likewise, the relationships between both party and ideological identification and preferences on social welfare issues were far stronger in 2020 than in 1984, with correlations ranging from .52 to .56. In terms of shared variance, these relationships were at least five times stronger in 2020 than in 1984. Finally, in 2020 there was a much closer connection between both party and ideological identification and opinions on abortion than in 1984. In terms of shared variance, these relationships were more than five times stronger in 2020 than in 1984. Abortion was clearly an important partisan issue in 2020, dividing Democrats from Republicans and liberals from conservatives.

The dramatic increase in the strength of the relationship between party and ideological identification between 1972 and 2020 indicates that there was a growing ideological divide between supporters of the two parties over those forty-eight years, at least in terms of liberal-conservative identification. Between 1972 and 2020, the gap between the mean locations of Democratic and Republican identifiers on the seven-point ideological identification scale grew from a modest 0.6 points in 1972 to 2.1 points in 2020, which was the largest divide in the entire series.

Moreover, the sharp increase in the size of the ideological identification divide reflected shifts among supporters of both parties with Democrats moving sharply to the left after 2000, and Republicans moving rather steadily to the right. The mean location of Democratic identifiers shifted from 3.9 in 1972 to 3.1 in 2020. At the same time, the mean location of Republican identifiers shifted from 4.5 in 1984 to 5.3 in 2020. At least in terms of ideological identification, the increase in partisan polarization within the electorate was very symmetrical during these years in contrast to the situation in Congress where Republicans shifted much further to the right than Democrats shifted to the left (Hacker and Pierson 2008; Mann and Ornstein 2016).

MEASURING PARTISAN-IDEOLOGICAL CONSISTENCY IN 2020

Our ability to analyze partisan-ideological consistency over time is limited by the number and variety of issues consistently included in ANES surveys. So, while the trends in table 5.1 appear impressive, they are based on a single measure of ideology: liberal-conservative identification. Moreover, some scholars have argued that this question measures ideological identity rather than preferences on public policy. According to this view, for most ordinary voters, thinking of oneself as liberal or conservative is a symbolic identity that has little connection with preferences on policy issues (Conover and Feldman 1981).

Fortunately, the 2020 ANES survey included a large number of questions on a variety of policy issues that allow us to examine the relationships between ideological identification and positions on specific issues as well as the relationships among opinions on these issues. Data from the ANES survey indicate that in 2020 not only was there a very close connection between party and ideological identification, but that both were closely connected with opinions on a variety of issues ranging from the size and scope of the welfare state to abortion, gay and transgender rights, immigration, race relations, climate change, and gun control. In addition, the 2020 data show that opinions across these six policy domains were also closely connected. There was a high degree of consistency in opinions on social welfare issues, racial issues, climate change, cultural issues, immigration, and gun control. Respondents with liberal views in one policy area tended to have liberal views in each of the other areas while those with conservative views in one policy area tended to have conservative views in each of the other areas. Opinions on issues in all of these domains as well as ideological self-identification can be mapped onto a liberal-conservative issue scale with Democratic identifiers located overwhelmingly on the liberal side of the scale and Republican identifiers located overwhelmingly on the conservative side of the scale.

In order to measure liberal-conservative preferences within each of the six policy domains (social welfare, cultural, racial justice, immigration, gun control, and climate change), I conducted a principal component factor analysis of all of the questions that appeared to measure opinions within that domain. The number of questions within each domain ranged from three in the case of climate change to eleven in the case of immigration. For each policy domain, the results of the factor analysis indicated that all of the questions were measuring a single, underlying issue dimension with all of the questions loading strongly on that dimension.

Table 5.2 displays the Pearson product-moment correlations among the six issue scales along with liberal-conservative identification. What clearly stands out in this table is the close connection among attitudes in all of these issue domains. The correlations range from .48 between opinions on gun control and opinions on cultural issues and .76 between opinions on racial justice issues and opinions on social welfare issues. In addition, there were strong correlations between ideological identification and opinions in all of these domains. Those correlations ranged from .49 with opinions on gun control to .72 with opinions on social welfare issues. These results reveal that ideological identification is much more than a symbolic identity. It is closely connected with preferences across a wide range of policy issues.

Previous research has identified two distinct dimensions of ideology within the American public—a social welfare dimension and a cultural dimension (Feldman and Johnson 2014). However, the strength of the correlations in table 5.2 suggests that in 2020, opinions in all six policy domains as well as ideological identification largely reflect a single underlying liberal-conservative dimension just as votes in Congress have been found to largely reflect a single underlying liberal-conservative dimension (Poole and Rosenthal 2007). A principal component factor analysis of scores on the six issue scales along

Table 5.2.   Correlations among Issue Scales in 2020

	Cultural Issues	Immigration	Racial Justice	Gun Control	Climate Change	Social Welfare
Ideological Identification	.61	.63	.64	.49	.59	.72
Cultural Issues		.62	.56	.48	.56	.60
Immigration			.70	.51	.60	.70
Racial Justice				.52	.62	.76
Gun Control					.60	.57
Climate Change						.70

Source: 2020 American National Election Study

with ideological identification supports this conclusion.[3] The first and only factor extracted in the principal component analysis has an eigenvalue of 4.7 and accounts for 67 percent of the shared variance among the issue scales. Loadings on this first factor range from .72 for the gun control scale to .89 for the social welfare issues scale.

I used the results of the principal component analysis of the six issue scales and ideological identification to construct a liberal-conservative issues scale. Scores on this scale are measured in standard deviation units above or below the overall mean of zero. For clarity of presentation, I multiplied these scores by ten and rounded them off to the nearest whole integer. As a result, scores on the adjusted scale ranged from –19 (1.9 standard deviations below the mean) to +27 (2.7 standard deviations above the mean) with an overall mean of zero and a standard deviation of ten.

There are a couple of striking features of the distribution of Democratic and Republican identifiers on this liberal-conservative issues scale. The most important is that supporters of the two parties have sharply divided ideological preferences. Even though these results include nonvoters as well as voters, there is very little overlap between the two distributions. Eighty-five percent of Democratic identifiers are located to the left of center while 86 percent of Republican identifiers are located to the right of center. The average Democratic identifier is located 0.7 standard deviations to the left of center and 40 percent of Democratic identifiers are located one standard deviation or more to the left of center. Meanwhile, the average Republican identifier is located 0.9 standard deviations to the right of center and 49 percent of Republican identifiers are located one standard deviation or more to the right of center.

Another interesting feature of the distributions of party identifiers on the liberal-conservative issues scale is that the share of Republicans on the far right end of the scale is greater than the share of Democrats on the far left end. Only 12 percent of Democratic identifiers were located at least 1.5 standard deviations to the left of center and no Democratic identifiers were located two or more standard deviations to the left of center. In contrast, 19 percent of Republican identifiers were located at least 1.5 standard deviations to the right of center and seven percent were located two or more standard deviations to the right of center. These findings indicate that among the public, just as among members of Congress, the potential impact of the far right on the Republican Party is considerably greater than the potential impact of the far left on the Democratic Party.

Among all respondents in the 2020 ANES survey, the correlation between party identification and the liberal-conservative issues scale is a very strong .76. This correlation provides a striking indication of the high level of partisan-ideological polarization in the overall electorate. However, the extent of partisan-ideological polarization within the electorate should vary depending on a variety of characteristics that are associated with awareness of ideological differences between parties. Three factors in particular would be expected to be associated with ideological awareness among the public: education, political interest, and political activism. In general, more educated, interested, and active citizens tend to be more aware of ideological differences between parties than less educated, less interested, and less active citizens.

Table 5.3 displays correlations between party identification and the liberal-conservative issues scale depending on level of education, interest in politics, and level of political activism. The findings are consistent with our expectations based on previous research on ideological awareness in the public. Partisan-ideological consistency was greatest among those with more years of education, more interest in politics, and higher levels of political activism. What is somewhat surprising, though, is how high the levels of partisan-ideological polarization are even among the least educated, least interested, and least active members of the public. For example, the correlation of party identification with the liberal-conservative issues scale is a very robust .66 among respondents who did not complete high school and .70 among those with only

Table 5.3.   Partisan-Ideological Polarization by Education, Political Engagement and Political Activism

	Correlation of Issue Scale x Party ID	N of Cases
All Respondents	.755	6525
Education		
Some HS	.656	518
HS Grad	.698	1775
Some College	.773	1880
College Grad	.802	1457
Post-College	.792	814
Pol Interest/Attention		
Very Low	.608	1500
Low	.721	2224
Moderate	.793	1519
High	.850	1278
Pol Activism		
Inactive	.524	927
Low	.691	2031
Moderate	.750	1935
High	.833	691
Very High	.877	932

Source: 2020 American National Election Study

a high school degree. Likewise, the correlation between party identification and the liberal-conservative issues is a very strong .69 among classified as low on political activism, a group made up overwhelmingly of individuals who reported voting but not engaging in any other political activities in connection with the 2020 election. In general, the results in table 5.3 indicate that partisan-ideological polarization had penetrated very far into the American electorate in 2020, reaching even less politically aware and active segments of the public.

CONSEQUENCES OF PARTISAN-IDEOLOGICAL CONSISTENCY: AFFECTIVE POLARIZATION

The theory of partisan-ideological consistency provides a framework for understanding two of the most significant changes in public opinion and voting behavior of the past forty years—the rise of affective polarization and the dramatic increase in straight-ticket voting. Feelings of partisans toward the two major parties and their candidates are far more divided now than they were in the past. This trend is very evident when we look at the average difference between partisans' ratings of their own party and presidential candidate and the opposing party and presidential candidate on the 0–100 feeling thermometer scale between 1968 and 2020. The feeling thermometer ratings were introduced for presidential candidates in 1968 and for the two major parties in 1978.

There has been a sharp increase in the average difference between partisans' ratings of their own party and presidential candidate and their ratings of the opposing party and presidential candidate, with most of the increase occurring since 2000. Between 1968 and 2000, the average difference in ratings was generally between twenty and thirty degrees. In 2020, the average difference in ratings was more than fifty degrees for the parties and sixty degrees for the presidential candidates. Interestingly, this increasing divide was almost entirely due to increasingly negative ratings of the opposing party and candidate. Ratings of one's own party and candidate have fluctuated within a rather narrow range, between sixty-five and seventy-five degrees, except for a brief dip in ratings of one's own candidate in 2016—a year in which both Donald Trump and Hillary Clinton received subpar ratings from their own party's supporters. In contrast, ratings of the opposing party and candidate have fallen from the mid- to upper-forties between 1972 and 2000 to below twenty degrees in 2020. Clearly, what is driving the growing divide in affective ratings of the parties and candidates is growing dislike of the opposing party and its candidates (Abramowitz and Webster 2016).

Table 5.4.   Correlation of Liberal-Conservative Identification with Relative Feeling Thermometer Evaluations of Presidential Candidates and Parties, 1980–2020

Year	Presidential Candidates	Parties
1972	.41	X
1976	.34	X
1980	.33	.33
1984	.40	.38
1988	.38	.36
1992	.43	.42
1996	.50	.50
2000	.45	.44
2004	.50	.52
2008	.54	.54
2012	.61	.61
2016	.60	.63
2020	.67	.67

Sources: American National Election Studies Cumulative File and 2020 American National Election Study

The gap between partisans' feeling thermometer ratings of their own party and candidate and the opposing party and candidate has widened considerably in the twenty-first century. Not coincidentally, during these years, the relationship between these feeling thermometer ratings and ideology has become much stronger. This trend is clearly evident in table 5.4, which displays the trend in the correlations between ideological identification and relative feeling thermometer ratings of the presidential candidates and parties since 1972. Between 2000 and 2020, the correlation between ideological identification and relative feeling thermometer ratings of the Republican and Democratic presidential candidates increased from .45 to .67 while the correlation between ideological identification and relative feeling thermometer ratings of the Democratic and Republican parties increased from .44 to .67. In terms of shared variance, these relationships were about twice as strong in 2020 as in 2000.

Of course, ideological identification is an imperfect measure of ideological orientations. It has the advantage that it has been included in every ANES survey since 1972. For the 2020 election, however, we have a measure of ideology, the liberal-conservative issues scale, based on a wide variety of issue positions along with ideological identification. These data show that there was a very strong relationship between feelings toward the parties and candidates and ideology—considerably stronger than the relationship with ideological identification alone. The correlation between ideology and feelings toward the parties is .80 while the correlation between ideology and feelings toward the candidates is a slightly stronger .82.

The 2020 results show that members of the public with scores close to either extreme of the liberal-conservative issues scale had the most divided feelings toward the parties and candidates—rating their own party and candidate far higher than the opposing party and candidate on the feeling thermometer scale. At the far right end of the scale, in fact, the average difference between ratings of Trump and Biden was close to the maximum of 100 degrees. Extreme conservatives tended to rate Trump at 100 degrees and Biden at zero degrees. On the far left, the difference was very large but not close to 100 degrees. While the average rating of Trump by extreme liberals was very close to the minimum of zero degrees, the average rating of Biden was only between 60 and 70 degrees. This pattern was slightly lower than the average rating of Biden by more moderate liberals. Extreme conservatives generally hated Biden and loved Trump. Extreme liberals generally hated Trump but were only lukewarm toward Biden.

Differences in feeling thermometer ratings of the presidential candidates and parties among those near the center of the liberal-conservative issues scale were generally much smaller than among those closer to the left and right ends of the scale. However, the presidential candidate ratings were somewhat asymmetrical: moderate liberals generally rated Biden far higher than Trump while moderate conservatives generally rated Trump only slightly higher than Biden. These patterns suggest that in 2020, Joe Biden had considerably more appeal to middle-of-the-road voters than Donald Trump.

The powerful influence of ideological orientations on affect toward candidates and parties is nowhere clearer than in the case of Donald Trump, perhaps the most polarizing political figure in recent American history. In order to compare the impact of ideology and group memberships on feelings toward Trump, I divided all respondents in the 2020 ANES survey into three groups of roughly equal size based on their locations on the liberal-conservative issues scale: those located at least .5 standard deviation to the left of center, those located between .5 standard deviation to the left of center and .5 standard deviation to the right of center and those located at least .5 standard deviation to the right of center. Table 5.5 compares the mean ratings of Trump on the feeling thermometer scale based on ideology and several politically salient group memberships—first race and then, for white respondents, education, evangelical identification, LGBT identification, and party identification.

The data in table 5.6 show that ideology heavily influenced feelings toward Trump even among members of groups that were generally strongly pro- or

Table 5.5.   Average Feeling Thermometer Ratings of Donald Trump by Ideological Orientation and Group Memberships

	Ideological Orientation		
	Left of Center	*Center*	*Right of Center*
All Respondents	4.5	34.2	81.9
Race			
White	3.3	39.0	84.3
Black	5.1	17.1	45.1
Latino	7.0	34.4	76.1
Asian	6.3	35.5	78.7
White			
College Grad	2.3	33.6	79.8
Non-College	4.6	42.1	85.7
Evangelical	4.2	41.2	88.2
Non-Evangelical	3.2	38.5	81.9
LGBT	4.6	34.9	78.7
Straight	3.1	39.4	84.3
Dem, Lean Dem	2.3	21.5	62.4
Rep, Lean Rep	19.9	55.9	86.6

Source: 2020 American National Election Study

anti-Trump. For example, white evangelicals overall were highly supportive of Trump, giving him an average rating of 69 degrees on the feeling thermometer. However, liberal white evangelicals gave him an average rating of only four degrees. Similarly, LGBT whites were generally quite hostile toward Donald Trump, giving him an average rating of only 21 degrees on the feeling thermometer. However, conservative LGBT whites gave him an average rating of 66 degrees. Most impressively, ideology even had a strong influence on feelings toward Trump among white Democratic and Republican identifiers. Although white Democrats gave Trump an average rating of only 8 degrees on the feeling thermometer, centrist white Democrats gave him an average rating of 21 degrees and the very small group of conservative Democrats gave him an average rating of 62 degrees. Likewise, while white Republicans gave Trump an average rating of 78 degrees, centrist white Republicans gave him an average rating of only 56 degrees and the very small group of liberal white Republicans gave him an average rating of only 20 degrees.

The results in table 5.5 show that group memberships mainly affected feelings toward Donald Trump indirectly—through ideology. Thus, the reason white college graduates rated Trump considerably lower than whites without college degrees was largely because white college graduates were much more liberal, on average, than whites without a college degree: 48 percent of whites with a degree were located to the left of center compared with only 23 percent of whites without a degree. After controlling for ideology there was little difference in feelings toward Trump among whites with and without a college degree. Similarly, the main reason white evangelicals were more supportive of Trump than nonevangelical whites are that they were much more conservative, on average, than nonevangelical whites: 67 percent of white evangelicals were located to the right of center compared with only 34 percent of nonevangelical whites. However, there was little difference between white evangelicals and nonevangelical whites in feelings toward Trump after controlling for ideology.

There was one important exception to this rule, however. Even after controlling for ideology, African Americans had much more negative feelings toward Trump than members of other racial groups including members of other nonwhite groups. Thus, conservative African Americans gave Trump an average rating of only 45 degrees, much higher than the ratings given by liberal and moderate African Americans, but much lower than the ratings given by conservative whites, Latinos, and Asians. African Americans are the one group for which there is clear evidence for the influence of social identity over and above the influence of ideology.

CONSEQUENCES OF PARTISAN-IDEOLOGICAL CONSISTENCY: VOTING BEHAVIOR

We have seen thus far that the rise of ideological consistency in the American electorate has had important consequences for affective evaluations of the presidential candidates and parties—contributing to the growth of affective polarization. Location on the liberal-conservative issue scale powerfully shaped feelings toward Donald Trump and Joe Biden as well as the Republican and Democratic parties. The more consistent were respondents' opinions on ideological identification and a wide range of issues, the more polarized were their evaluations of the parties and candidates.

Along with increasing affective polarization, there has been a marked increase in party loyalty and straight-ticket voting in recent elections. Elections have become increasingly nationalized with votes for the House of Representatives and Senate tied closely to opinions of the national parties and their leaders. According to the partisan-ideological consistency theory, there should be a close connection between straight-ticket voting and the degree of consistency between one's party identification and one's ideology.

Table 5.6.   Percentage Voting for Own Party for President, House and Senate in 2020 by Party Identification and Ideological Orientation

	Ideological Orientation		
	Left of Center	*Center*	*Right of Center*
Dem, Lean Dem	93	66	32
Rep, Lean Rep	18	42	88

Source: 2020 American National Election Study

Democrats with consistently liberal views and Republicans with consistently conservative views should display much higher levels of party loyalty and straight-ticket voting than Democrats with moderate-to-conservative views and Republicans with moderate-to-liberal views.

Table 5.5 displays the relationship between location on the liberal-conservative issues scale and party loyalty among Democratic and Republican identifiers, including leaning independents, in 2020. As in the analysis of affective polarization, I divided voters into three ideological groupings: those located at least .5 standard deviation to the left of center, those located between .5 standard deviation to the left of center and .5 standard deviationsto the right of center and those located at least .5 standard deviation to the right of center.

The data in this table provide strong support for the partisan-ideological consistency hypothesis. Over 90 percent of liberal Democrats and close to 90 percent of conservative Republicans voted for their party's candidates for all three offices. In contrast, moderate-to-liberal Republicans and moderate-to-conservative Democrats were far more likely to defect in at least one of these contests. Although moderates and conservatives made up only 28 percent of all Democratic identifiers, they made up 68 percent of Democrats who defected in at least one contest. Likewise, although moderates and liberals made up only 21 percent of all Republican identifiers, they made up 57 percent of Republicans who defected in at least one contest.

This pattern is even clearer when voter decision-making in the presidential election is examined by itself. According to the 2020 ANES survey, ideologically conflicted partisans made up 30 percent of Democratic identifiers and 25 percent of Republican identifiers who voted for a presidential candidate. However, they made up 91 percent of Democratic identifiers who voted for Donald Trump and 89 percent of Republican identifiers who voted for Joe Biden. Evidence from the 2020 ANES survey suggests that Biden received a disproportionate share of the votes from these ideologically conflicted partisans. Only 11.5 percent of ideologically conflicted Democrats voted for Trump. In contrast, 40.5 percent of ideologically conflicted Republicans voted for Biden. While the ANES survey, like many surveys of the 2020 electorate, substantially overestimated Biden's victory margin, these results suggest that that his appeal to moderate voters was a key factor in his decisive popular vote victory over Trump, whose hard-line conservative positions appear to have alienated many moderate voters in both parties.

DISCUSSION AND CONCLUSIONS

Deep partisan divisions, mutual mistrust, and outright hostility toward opposing partisans are the hallmarks of American politics in the third decade of the twenty-first century. Importantly, mutual mistrust and hostility are widespread among ordinary Americans, not just among members of the political elite and a small minority of activists. Because of this growing affective polarization, party loyalty and straight-ticket voting have set new records in recent elections. Crossing party lines, even to vote for an incumbent officeholder, has become much less common than in the recent past because partisans view any politician on the other side as a threat to their way of life and an enemy to be defeated at all cost.

In this chapter, I show that one of the most important factors in the rise of affective polarization and party loyalty in the American electorate has been growing partisan-ideological consistency. The reason so many Americans intensely dislike those on the other side of the partisan divide is that they consistently disagree with those on the other side of the partisan divide on a wide range of issues. Americans' preferences on issues as diverse as government responsibility for health care, gay and transgender rights, police reform, climate change, immigration, and regulation of firearms are now strongly correlated with each other and with their partisan and ideological identities. On a liberal-conservative issues scale that combines ideological identification with preferences across all of these issues, the overwhelming majority of Democratic identifiers are found on the left while the overwhelming majority of Republican identifiers are found on the right.

When it comes to feelings toward political leaders and parties, ideology dominates membership in social groups. Liberals, regardless of their group identities, tend to view the Democratic Party and Democratic leaders positively and the Republican Party and Republican leaders negatively. Conservatives, regardless of their group identities, tend to view the Republican Party and Republican leaders positively and the Democratic Party and Democratic leaders negatively.

Intense mistrust and dislike of the opposing party and its leaders help to explain another key feature of American politics in the current era: record levels of party loyalty and straight-ticket voting. Like feelings of mistrust and hostility, party loyalty and straight-ticket voting reflect ideological conflict. The reason so many Democrats and Republicans are unwilling to cross party lines in elections is that they disagree with almost everything that the opposing party stands for. However, a minority of ideologically conflicted Republicans and Democrats display much lower levels of party loyalty. In closely contested elections, this relatively small group of center-right Democrats and center-left Republicans can play a crucial role in deciding the outcome. Along with "pure independents," they make up a large share of the true swing voters in American politics and their votes appear to have been a key factor in Joe Biden's popular vote victory in the 2020 presidential election.

The findings presented in this chapter indicate that partisan-ideological polarization is not confined to members of the political elite and a small sliver of activists. It is deeply embedded in the American public. Moreover, while polarization has led some Americans to believe lies and wild conspiracy theories promoted by political leaders, especially former President Trump, it has a rational foundation. Hostility toward the opposing party and its leaders reflects strong disagreement with the policies of the opposing party and its leaders. As long as the parties remain on the opposite sides of almost all of the major issues facing the country, feelings of mistrust and animosity are unlikely to diminish regardless of Donald Trump's role in the Republican Party.

NOTES

1. For a review of this literature, see Carmines and D'Amico (2015).

2. In order to avoid having a large share of respondents with missing data, I have recoded responses on all ANES seven-point scales that include a screening question allowing respondents to opt out of placing themselves on the scale by indicating that they "haven't thought about" the issue. These include the seven-point ideological identification scale as well as the questions on government aid to Black Americans, government responsibility for health insurance and government responsibility for jobs and living standards. Respondents indicating that they "haven't thought about" an issue were assigned to the middle position (4) on the seven-point scale. I chose this approach because simply excluding these respondents from the analysis would have biased the results in favor of finding greater partisan-ideological consistency. I use the same approach in later analyses of data from the 2020 ANES survey that includes a larger number of seven-point issue scales with an opt-out screening question.

3. See appendix B for details.

Chapter Six

Political Identity and Beliefs about Stolen Elections in the American Electorate

Anita Manion, David C. Kimball,
and Adriano Udani

The insurrection at the United States Capitol on January 6, 2021, was a rare event in American politics. It marked the first organized assault on the seat of American government since the War of 1812. In 2021, the insurrectionists were home-grown terrorists rather than a foreign army. According to *The New York Times* (Healy 2021; Schmidt and Broadwater 2021), 5 people died, and 140 police officers were injured in the attack. Those attacking the Capitol on January 6 were fueled by unsubstantiated claims that the 2020 presidential election was "stolen." These claims had been consistently debunked by the courts, invalidated by scholars, and disproven by audits (Kovacs-Goodman 2021; Eggers et al. 2021). How do a significant number of Americans come to believe and act on these false allegations?

We see three crucial elements that drove public beliefs about the legitimacy of the 2020 election. First, the growth of affective polarization means that a large segment of the mass public is susceptible to false claims of a stolen election and motivated to political action. Second, President Trump provided the spark, by turbo-charging Republican claims of voter fraud, taking the frequency and incendiary nature of those allegations to a new level. Third, other Republican political leaders acted as accelerants—rather than correcting the president's false claims of a stolen election, many GOP politicians have amplified those claims. These elements have combined to produce an American public that is bitterly divided over the fairness of the 2020 election and the events surrounding January 6, 2021.

FUEL: GROWING AFFECTIVE POLARIZATION

Partisan polarization is one of the most important features of American politics today (see chapter 5 in this volume). People tend to view the world in "us versus them" terms, often pitting their own party against the opposing party (Tajfel and Turner 1979). Americans develop a party identification at a relatively young age, and it rarely changes over one's lifetime (Stoker and Jennings 2008). In addition, Americans have recently become better "sorted," such that their partisanship has become closely intertwined with other aspects of their identity, like ideology, race, ethnicity, gender, religion, and geography. Increased partisan disagreement among politicians and activists has fostered a more attentive electorate and a stronger sense of partisan identity among the mass public. Polarized politics encourages the public to view party competition in zero-sum terms and to denigrate their political opponents more than in the past. Recent national elections have been heavily contested and produced close outcomes, which increases the stakes for partisan conflicts (Lee 2016). Finally, the growth of partisan news sources, which often describe the opposition in negative terms, contributes to a heightened partisan environment (Levendusky 2013; Lelkes et al. 2017; Bail et al. 2018). These developments have increased the salience of party identification among the mass public.

One indicator of hardening partisanship is increasing expressions of contempt for partisan opponents, often termed "affective polarization" (Lelkes et al. 2017; Iyengar et al. 2019). Disdain for the opposite party has increased substantially over the past few decades. Measures of affective polarization tend to be strongly correlated with strength of partisanship, providing further evidence of construct validity in the original measure of party identification (Campbell et al. 1960). Indeed, among respondents to the 2020 ANES survey, 44 percent identified as strong partisans, the highest share since ANES began measuring partisanship several decades ago. Furthermore, more negative ratings of Democrats by Republicans are concentrated among white Americans and those who oppose government aid to Black people (Mar 2020). As we show below, this pattern is important for beliefs about election integrity.

One by-product of affective polarization is that it increases one's willingness to believe bad things about political opponents. For example, partisans are more likely to believe that politicians of the opposite party are guilty of sexual misconduct than politicians of their own party (Klar and McCoy 2021). Partisans also tend to dehumanize their opponents (Martherus et al. 2021) and view themselves as morally superior to political adversaries (Cassese 2021). Contempt for the opposite party goes a long way.

We also find that partisan biases influence beliefs about the types of people likely to commit voter fraud. That is, partisans suspect the opposition of voter fraud. We test this hypothesis in a conjoint experiment on a module of the 2017 Cooperative Congressional Election Study (CCES) survey. Each respondent was shown profiles of two hypothetical voters and then asked which voter is more likely to cast an illegal ballot. The profile of each hypothetical voter includes eight randomly assigned attributes: sex, race, age, party, citizenship, language, occupation, and whether the person has a criminal record (see table 6.3 in the appendix for a list of each attribute tested). We asked respondents to perform this task four times, each time asking them to evaluate a different pair of hypothetical voters. This design allows us to estimate the effect of each attribute on the probability of being perceived as an illegal voter.

We estimate an OLS regression model with standard errors clustered by respondent. OLS coefficients produce an average marginal component effect (AMCE), which represents the marginal effect of an attribute on the probability of a person being selected as an illegal voter (Hainmueller et al. 2014). Since we are testing for partisan biases, we present the results of the experiment separately for Democratic and Republican respondents. Most of the attributes did not generate statistically significant effects, and for ease of presentation, we report the coefficients for the three attributes that mattered, partisanship, citizenship, and criminal record, in figure 6.1 (along with their 95 percent confidence intervals). These estimated effects are relative to a hypothetical voter who is a white male Democrat, a United States citizen, and has no criminal record.

As figure 6.1 shows, respondents of both parties suspect noncitizens and people with a criminal record of being illegal voters. We also find evidence of affective polarization. Democrats tend to believe that a Republican is more likely than a Democrat to commit voter fraud ($b = 0.11$, $p < 0.001$), while Republicans believe the opposite ($b = -0.08$, $p < 0.01$). There is a rough symmetry to the partisan biases, and the magnitude of the partisan bias in this test is similar to the impact of being a non-citizen or having a criminal record. Although not presented here, these findings only hold for strong identifiers of the two major parties. Weak identifiers and independent leaners do not associate the opposite party with an increased likelihood of illegal voting. Strong partisans on each side suspect the opposition of committing voter fraud.

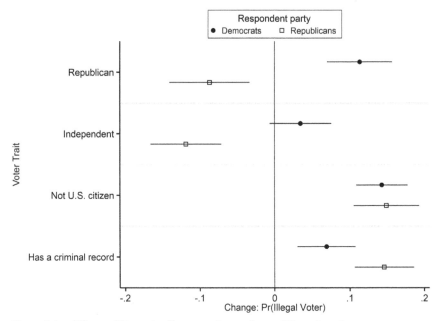

Figure 6.1. Effects of Voter Attributes on Perceptions of Voter Fraud
2017 CCES—UM-St. Louis Module

In sum, the 2020 election took place amid resurgent partisanship in the mass public. Increased contempt for political opponents means that partisans, especially strong partisans, are willing to believe the worst about the opposition and follow cues from party leaders. Members of both major parties are susceptible to the forces of affective polarization. A highly charged electorate provided fuel for the events that came during and after the 2020 election.

SPARK: RACIAL VIEWS OF CRIMINALS AND PRESIDENT TRUMP'S VOTER FRAUD CLAIMS

Voter fraud is a type of crime. As we note above, Americans tend to hold biased images of typical illegal voters. Highly charged debates about voting restrictions in the United States sometimes include explicit or implicit references to race, such as allegations of "inner city" voter fraud (Wilson and Brewer 2013; Dreier and Martin 2010; Ellis 2013). Similar rhetoric links an immigrant threat narrative with concerns about voter fraud (Udani and Kimball 2018). Donald Trump contributed to this rhetoric for several years. During and after the 2016 presidential campaign, Trump made repeated and unsubstantiated claims about voter fraud, often labeling immigrants as perpetrators (Johnson

2016; House and Dennis 2017). President Trump also created a commission to investigate claims of voter fraud in the 2016 election. The commission disbanded without producing evidence of meaningful voter fraud.

It is no surprise that beliefs about voter fraud are shaped by attitudes toward immigrants and Black people in the United States. Resentment toward people of color and anti-immigrant attitudes are strong predictors of public beliefs about voting integrity (Wilson and Brewer 2013; Udani and Kimball 2018; Appleby and Federico 2017). Further research has found substantial differences in the ways that Democrats and Republicans think about this issue. Textual analysis of how partisans define voter fraud (Sheagley and Udani 2021) shows that Republicans appear to ground their views of fraud in concerns about voter actions involving immigrants and "illegal" immigration, while Democrats commonly think of the issue in terms of institutional barriers that impact nonspecific and minority groups.

In our 2017 national sample of US voters, we asked respondents to estimate the share of voter fraud perpetrators belonging to three different groups (immigrants, African Americans, and whites). The exact wording of the question is: "What percentage of people who commit voter fraud in this country would you say are [Immigrants/Black/White]." Once again, the order of the questions was randomized. Responses ranged from 0 percent to 100 percent, and there is considerable variation in estimates across respondents (each item has a standard deviation between 24 and 29). The mean estimate for whites (46 percent) exceeds the mean estimates for African Americans (33 percent) and immigrants (37 percent). We don't have reliable measures of each group's share of actual voter fraud violators in the United States. However, since voter fraud is rare, we might start with each group's share of the US population. Using five-year estimates from the American Community Survey from 2017 US Census data, whites make up a much larger share of the American population (73.3 percent) than foreign born residents (13.5 percent) and African Americans (12.6 percent). Figure 6.2 shows that US voters tend to significantly overstate the immigrant and African American share of illegal voters and underestimate the white share.

Amid Republican leaders' history of voter fraud allegations (e.g., Minnite 2010) and the US mass public's racially biased stereotypes of criminals, Donald Trump's rhetoric was the spark that took voter fraud claims to a new level in 2020. Before he was banned from the site, Twitter was one of President Trump's most frequent means of communication. For example, between Election Day and December 17, 2020, Trump posted 729 tweets, and 69 percent were about the election (Troyer 2020). These messages were frequently spread by his followers—roughly four-in-ten of President Trump's most-liked tweets contained false claims about the 2020 election (Rattner 2021). As we

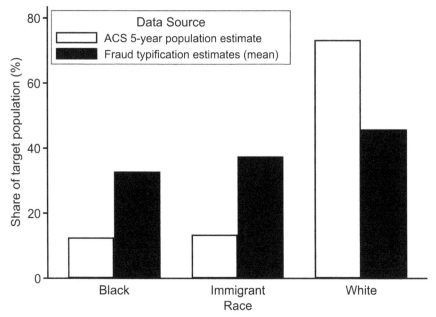

Figure 6.2.   Americans Typify Black and Immigrants as Fraudulent Voters: Typification Estimates Compared to Proportion of US Population
2017 CCES—UM-St. Louis Module

note below, President Trump and his campaign filed dozens of lawsuits challenging the administration and results of the 2020 election. By not accepting the results of the 2020 election, President Trump led many Republicans to believe that the election was not legitimate.

The Republican rally on January 6 ensured that the spark would catch fire. Trump's postelection challenge to the election outcome stoked Republican and conservative beliefs about rampant voter fraud. In addition to President Donald Trump, Eric Trump, Donald Trump Jr., and their significant others all spoke at the rally outside the White House on January 6, where they perpetuated lies about a stolen election, reminded Republicans in Congress that they were watching their votes and encouraged them to "choose wisely," warned lawmakers if they didn't fight for Trump "we're coming for you," and thanked the "red-blooded, patriotic Americans" "for standing up to the bullshit" (Ballhas et al. 2021). It wasn't just the Trump family who was rousing the crowd with inflammatory messages. Their rhetoric was aided by vocal allies in the GOP and the acquiescence of other Republicans. Rep. Mo Brooks fired up the crowd with his words "Today is the day American patriots start taking down names and kicking ass. . . . Are you willing to do what it takes to fight for America? Louder! Will you fight for America?" (Edmondson and Broadwater

2021). And there were the now infamous words from Rudy Giuliani, Trump's personal attorney, "Let's have trial by combat" (Ballhaus et al. 2021).

ACCELERANT: AMPLIFICATION OF MISINFORMATION

The public tends to mimic arguments made by political leaders they trust. If most Republican leaders disavowed or contradicted Trump's baseless allegations of election fraud, then perhaps public opinion would not be so polarized on assessments of election integrity and the 2020 election. However, rather than correcting the president's false claims of a stolen election, many Republican leaders have amplified those claims, acting as accelerants. In a review of congressional electronic newsletters from 2010–2021, Republicans' messages to constituents mentioned voter fraud much more than Democrats, particularly as it related to Trump's election (Brown and Cormack 2021). These messages matter because they provide signals to the public about what to believe.

When it comes to perceptions of voter fraud, partisan divisions are not a new phenomenon. Party identification and ideology are significant predictors of beliefs about voter fraud (Ansolabehere and Persily 2007), and Republicans tend to believe that voter fraud occurs more frequently than Democrats (Wilson and Brewer 2013). But what happened in 2020 was not run-of-the-mill partisan maneuvering. A sitting president refused to accept his electoral loss, and according to reports conspired with others to overturn the results of a free and fair election (Alemany et al. 2021; Sprunt 2021b). Part of that strategy was to convince tens of millions of Americans that the election was "rigged," and in that aspect of the strategy they were effective. The myth of stolen elections moved from the fringes to being accepted by the majority of Republicans who believe that the election was rigged, and that Donald Trump is the rightful President, not Joe Biden (Ipsos 2021). These beliefs persisted even though election officials from both parties spoke out to say the 2020 election was free and fair, allegations of election fraud were found to be unsubstantiated in more than sixty lawsuits (Kahn et al. 2021), and President Trump's own federal agency declared the November 2020 election to be the "most secure in American history" (Cybersecurity & Infrastructure Security Agency 2020). The message from President Trump, other GOP leaders, and conservative media outlets was clear: the 2020 election was stolen from Trump.

Elite rhetoric was especially polarized on how voting processes should adjust to the coronavirus pandemic. Even though he voted by mail in 2020 and many other elections (McEvoy 2021), President Trump and many other Republican leaders criticized voting by mail as fraudulent. In contrast, many

</>

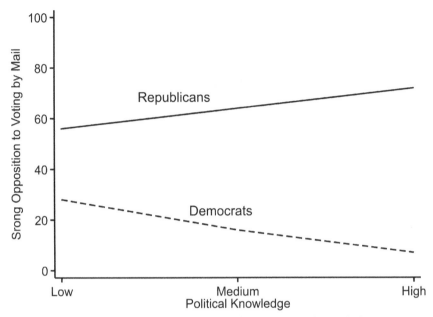

Figure 6.3.   Opposition to Voting by Mail by Party and Political Knowledge, 2020
2020 ANES Time Series Study

Democratic leaders and election officials promoted voting by mail as a way to avoid spreading coronavirus during a deadly pandemic. Indeed, there was a dramatic increase in voting by mail in the 2020 election (Stewart 2020). However, the partisan disagreement over voting by mail polarized public opinion on this feature of election administration. In one survey we fielded in 2015, voting by mail was strongly opposed by 25 percent of Democrats and 43 percent of Republicans, a modest partisan gap in preferences. When we asked the same question in another survey conducted just after the 2020 election, voting by mail was strongly opposed by 11 percent of Democrats and 71 percent of Republicans. Public opinion on voting by mail was so polarized in 2020 that Democrats were twice as likely as Republicans to cast their ballots by mail in the general election (Stewart 2020).

There is further evidence of elite opinion leadership on voting by mail in the 2020 election. Figure 6.3 illustrates the percent of respondents strongly opposed to voting by mail, with the ANES sample segmented by party and political knowledge. The pattern is consistent with John Zaller's (1992) theory of opinion leadership. Among Republicans, opposition to voting by mail increases as knowledge increases. Among Democrats, opposition declines as knowledge increases. Thus, the most knowledgeable respondents are the most polarized by party on the question of voting by mail. A similar pattern exists in public support for laws requiring voters to show photo identification (Gronke et al. 2019), another election policy featuring strong partisan disagreements among politicians.

We examine public beliefs about election integrity more systematically in our next analysis, focusing on three dependent variables from the 2020 ANES survey. One pre-election question asked respondents to indicate how accurately the votes will be counted in the 2020 election on a five-point scale (1 = not at all accurately, 5 = completely accurately). A postelection item asked how often votes are counted fairly in this country's elections (1 = never, 5 = all of the time). The third dependent variable we examine is a pre-election item measuring support for voting by mail on a seven-point scale (1 = favor a great deal, 7 = oppose a great deal).

Our primary independent variables measure group attitudes. The first is a measure of affective polarization (Republican Party thermometer rating minus Democratic Party rating). We expect this variable to be negatively associated with election integrity beliefs. The second is a racial resentment scale, which measures a belief that a lack of work ethic accounts for inequality between Black and white Americans. We measure racial resentment based on four questions that ask respondents the degree to which they agree or disagree with statements about the status of Black people in society (Tesler and Sears 2010, 19). Responses to these four items are averaged together to create the racial resentment index (α = .88). Racial resentment gained potency in public opinion during the presidencies of Barack Obama and Donald Trump (Tesler and Sears 2010; Kimball et al. 2018). Since political rhetoric around voter fraud includes frequent allegations targeting people of color, public beliefs about voter fraud have become racialized (Wilson and Brewer 2013; Appleby and Federico 2017; Udani and Kimball 2018). Thus, we expect racial resentment to be associated with negative assessments of election integrity.

As we show above, beliefs about election fraud have also become closely tied to views of immigrants. The recent growth of and diffusion of immigrants in the United States makes immigration a more top-of-mind consideration in public opinion. In addition, many political leaders, led by President Trump, have made unsubstantiated allegations that immigrants are committing voter fraud in large numbers. Thus, public beliefs about voter fraud have become strongly associated with hostility toward immigrants (Udani and Kimball 2018). We create a measure of hostility to immigrants based on responses to four ANES questions that ask whether immigrants (1) increase crime, (2) harm America's culture, (3) are good for America's economy, and (4) whether immigration levels should be increased or decreased. The four variables were averaged together to form an immigrant attitude scale (α = 0.82). We expect hostility toward immigrants to be correlated with negative evaluations of election integrity. Finally, we include covariates for age (ranging from eighteen to eighty-one years), political knowledge, sex, and white respondents. Each independent variable is rescaled to range from 0 to 1.

Table 6.1 presents the results of OLS regressions with each dependent variable modeled as a function of the independent variables described above. Affective polarization and group attitudes emerge as potent predictors of beliefs about election integrity. Before the 2020 election, respondents at the Republican end of the polarization scale were almost one point less confident about the vote count than polarized Democrats. Those with the most negative views about immigrants were about half a point less confident than respondents with the most positive assessments of immigrants. Contrary to our expectations, racial resentment is uncorrelated with the pre-election measure of voter confidence.

We find even stronger associations between our measures of group attitudes and post-election confidence in the vote count. Strong party identification tends to equate with a strong desire to see one's party win (Mason 2018). Thus, after an election voter confidence tends to increase among supporters of the winning party and decrease among identifiers with the los-

Table 6.1.   **Predictors of Beliefs about Election Integrity**

Independent Variable	Ballots will be counted accurately (Pre-election)	Ballots are counted fairly (Post-election)	Oppose voting by mail (Pre-election)
Affective polarization	−0.87*	−1.50*	2.89*
	(0.06)	(0.06)	(0.10)
Racial resentment	0.03	−0.37*	1.16*
	(0.06)	(0.06)	(0.10)
Anti-immigrant sentiment	−0.54*	−0.84*	0.98*
	(0.08)	(0.07)	(0.12)
Political knowledge	0.21*	0.75*	−0.02
	(0.06)	(0.06)	(0.10)
Age	0.49*	0.40*	−0.10
	(0.05)	(0.05)	(0.07)
White	0.13*	0.13*	−0.14*
	(0.03)	(0.03)	(0.05)
Women	−0.15*	−0.13*	0.02
	(0.03)	(0.02)	(0.04)
Constant	3.30*	4.24*	2.23*
	(0.06)	(0.05)	(0.09)
N	6,907	6,922	6,933
R^2	.11	.32	.35

*p < .05, two-tailed

Source: 2020 ANES Time Series Study

ing party (Sances and Stewart 2015). This pattern was evident in the 2020 election as well. After the 2020 election, affective Republicans were 1.5 points less confident about election fairness than affective Democrats on the 5-point dependent variable. Those with the most negative views about immigrants were almost a point less confident in election fairness than respondents with the most positive assessments of immigrants. We also find that racial resentment is negatively correlated with beliefs about election fairness in the postelection measure. Meanwhile, those with higher levels of political knowledge tend to hold more positive views about the fairness and accuracy of the vote count. Finally, older voters, men, and white respondents tend to report higher levels of voter confidence than young adults, women, and nonwhite respondents.

The final column of table 6.1 shows the strongest association between group attitudes and opposition to voting by mail, while the other covariates register almost no association. A GOP effort to denigrate voting by mail produced an extremely polarized public regarding support for that voting method. On the seven-point scale, the average position of affective Republicans is almost three points more opposed to voting by mail than the average position of affective Democrats. In addition, racial resentment and anti-immigrant sentiment each have coefficients near 1, also indicating strong associations with voting by mail preferences. A Republican who strongly dislikes the Democratic Party and holds high levels of racial resentment and anti-immigrant views is likely to strongly oppose voting by mail in 2020. Meanwhile, an affective Democrat with low levels of racial resentment and anti-immigrant sentiment is likely to strongly support voting by mail. Once we account for partisan and group attitudes, the nonexistent association between political knowledge and voting by mail is consistent with the pattern in figure 6.3 above. This finding is significant since the 2020 election saw record numbers of Americans voting by mail. Affective polarization and other group attitudes are strong predictors of beliefs about the integrity and fairness of the 2020 election. According to another study, among Americans who believe there was widespread fraud in the 2020 election, they attribute the fraud to cities (72 percent), Black communities (39 percent), and mail ballots (77 percent) (Khanna and De Pinto 2021).

While rhetoric over mail-in ballots and other measures implemented to increase access to voting during a pandemic were opposed by many Republicans before the election, it is what happened after the election that was particularly problematic. The majority of Republicans in Congress refused to acknowledge that Trump had lost the election, either outright parroting Trump's claims or avoiding the issue and refusing to clearly state that Biden had rightfully won the presidency. However, this unquestioning fidelity to Donald

Trump was not always the position of mainstream Republicans. When Trump sought the nomination to be the Republican presidential candidate in 2016, he faced strong opposition from within the party and inspired the #NeverTrump movement. GOP lawmakers voiced a variety of concerns about candidate Trump including his lack of experience, policy preferences, controversial statements, and personal characteristics (Johnson et al. 2018). Nevertheless, once Trump was the nominee, almost all Republicans in Congress supported him, even if some were reluctant supporters. Below, we discuss three major factors that contributed to the misperception that voter fraud is endemic and that the 2020 election was stolen.

Party Discipline

Johnson et al. (2018) discussed reasons GOP lawmakers opposed Trump in 2016. Those same motivations seem to apply for why Republicans are going along with unfounded claims of a rigged election: electoral motivations, policy preferences, identity, and establishment dynamics. One concern that would constrain political actors from attempting to overthrow an election would be the concern of the damage it would do to their electoral, financial, and organizational support. However, in recent years Republicans have supported increasingly extreme ideological positions, and seem to have faced little backlash (Hacker and Pierson 2006). And Republicans who supported the baseless allegation about the election results have not suffered negative consequences; to the contrary, they have been able to campaign and fundraise off these false allegations. And the few that have stood up to this unethical behavior have been targeted by Trump and his allies, censured by their state legislatures, had threats on their lives, and have lost the support of the Republican Party (Sprunt 2021).

As a clear example of the party supporting the false claims that were made by Donald Trump, House Minority Leader Kevin McCarthy said two days after the election on Fox News, "President Trump won this election" and went on to warn voters about the potential of a stolen election saying, "Do not be silent about this. We cannot allow this to happen before our very eyes" (Scherer and Dawsey 2021). He was not alone in forwarding these false allegations and undermining faith in elections. Senator Lindsey Graham also went on Fox News to support Trump's allegations, saying, "I don't trust Philadelphia" and "I am here tonight to stand with President Trump" (Crowley 2020). Kelly Loeffler and David Perdue who were in a run-off Senate race in Georgia, put out a statement less than a week after the election, while the Georgia Senate race was still being decided, saying. "The secretary of state has failed to deliver honest and transparent elections" and calling for the resignation of Georgia's secretary of state (Loeffler 2020). Texas lieutenant governor Dan Patrick offered a minimum of $25,000 to anyone who provided information about voter fraud that leads to an arrest and conviction. Nearly a year after this bounty was offered, the only payout was to a poll worker in Pennsylvania who reported a Republican for casting a ballot in his son's name (Feinberg 2021). Perhaps some of the most incendiary comments from an elected official came from Arizona congressman Paul Gosar who repeatedly made false allegations that the 2020 election was stolen. Gosar and fellow Republican representative from Arizona Andy Biggs made unfounded claims that there was rampant fraud in other states including widespread voting by deceased people, Republican poll-watchers being banned, and large ballot dumps and found ballots that almost all went for Biden, and they also called for an audit in their home state of Arizona (Hansen 2020). Among other false comments in an open letter on December 7, 2020, Gosar made claims of "statistically impossible spikes in votes for Joe Biden" and "voting patterns that emerged that could not occur in the absence of fraud," and said, "I will fight to restore the rightful victor, President Trump. Our Constitution, our Republic and our nation demand election integrity. We are not giving up. The President has not conceded and will not concede to a Third World coup d'etat." He also called Biden an "illegitimate usurper" (Gosar 2020).

Another way the false allegations of a stolen election were propagated by Trump and his allies was through a series of unsuccessful lawsuits. Between November 3, 2020, and January 6, 2021, Republicans filed seventy-six lawsuits relating to the presidential election (Kovacs-Goodman 2021). While the plaintiffs had no success in proving any allegations of fraud, they did contribute to an erosion of public trust in the democratic process (Kovacs-Goodman 2021). When Texas filed a lawsuit seeking to overturn the presidential election results in four states Biden won, more than half of the members of the House Republican Caucus signed an amicus brief in support of the suit (ProPublica 2020). In multiple rulings across many states, attorneys who brought forth demonstrably false allegations regarding the 2020 election have faced repercussions. These include having their law licenses suspended, being ordered to complete remedial legal education, and paying costs incurred by states and cities to defend the spurious cases; one judge went so far as to say that if the allegations made by these attorneys were "accepted as true by large numbers of people, are the stuff of which violent insurrections are made" (Helderman 2021).

Conservative Outlets and Social Media

Affective polarization is associated with sharing incendiary information on social media. In a study of Twitter users, Osmundsen and colleagues (2021) find that people who report hating their political opponents are the most likely to share political fake news and selectively share content that is useful for derogating these opponents. A significant minority of Republicans in the House of Representatives used the label "fake news" on Twitter since the election of Donald Trump in 2016; conservative representatives used that term at significantly higher rates than moderate Republicans (Cowburn and Oswald 2020). Research suggests that exposure to liberal views on social media that contradict their beliefs led to Republicans expressing markedly more conservative views (Bail et al. 2018). All of this means that the most politically attentive Republicans, particularly Fox News viewers, those in social media echo chambers, and those most devoted to Trump, may be most likely to believe false claims about voter fraud, that the 2020 election was stolen, and that January 6 participants were justified.

Previous studies suggest that viewers of Fox News were particularly likely to support voter ID laws and that political parties have tried to motivate their voting base by making voter fraud a salient issue (Dreier and Martin, 2010; Wilson and Brewer, 2013). Conservative news sources help fuel the partisan nature of election reform debates (Hicks et al. 2015). Recent polling also indicates an influence of conservative news sources in beliefs about voter fraud, finding that 69 percent of Republicans and 74 percent of Trump voters say there was widespread voter fraud in 2020; for Trump voters who regularly watch conservative cable news such as Fox, One America News Network, or Newsmax eight in ten said there was widespread voter fraud, compared to two-thirds of other Trump voters. When asked how they heard about voter fraud, the number one source for those who believe there was widespread voter fraud was reports on the news (73%), 49 percent said they heard about fraud through social media, 43 percent said Donald Trump was a source, and 39 percent cited politicians in Washington (Khanna and De Pinto 2021). In addition to conservative media outlets, social media has played a significant role in the spread of misinformation about voter fraud. Studies indicate that false information spreads faster than the truth on Twitter and those effects are more pronounced for false stories about political news than other topics (Vosoughi et al. 2018), and that misinformation shared by political leaders is more damaging than if it were shared by ordinary users (Timberg et al. 2021). Trump and his allies were effective at utilizing social media to spread the false allegations of a stolen election and to promote the January 6 rally to #StopTheSteal.

Memorializing January 6

A year after the attack on the Capitol, Congress engaged in discussion on how to commemorate January 6 (Cochrane 2021). Following the deadly riot at the Capitol, 147 Republican members of Congress voted against certifying the

Electoral College vote, sending a message that the election was illegitimate (Kahn et al. 2021). Given that party identification is associated with wanting to see your side win, partisanship heavily colored public reactions to the events associated with January 6, 2021. To illustrate, we summarize data from the Collaborative Multiracial Post-Election Survey (CMPS), which was conducted from April to August in 2021. The survey included several questions about January 6. Since party identification develops and shapes public opinion in different ways across racial groups (Hajnal and Lee 2011), we just summarize evaluations from white respondents. Several of these survey questions were forced choice items, without a neutral or don't know option. Nevertheless, the results reveal a public deeply divided in understanding the actions of political leaders and the insurrectionists on January 6 (see table 6.2).

There are large partisan differences in understanding the events of January 6. Democrats almost uniformly thought President Trump was wrong to challenge the election results, while a plurality of Republicans, and a majority of strong Republicans, thought Trump was right to challenge the results. Democrats overwhelmingly believe that President Trump incited the attack on the Capitol, while very few Republicans hold Trump responsible. Similarly, over

Table 6.2. Beliefs about January 6 by Party ID (White Respondents)

Question	Strong D	Weak D	Lean D	Pure I	Lean R	Weak R	Strong R
There was voter fraud: Trump was right to challenge the election results	1%	4%	2%	19%	42%	24%	59%
GOP members of Congress who tried to stop election certification were protecting democracy	11%	11%	3%	18%	47%	30%	62%
January 6 was a coordinated act of insurrection against the United States	84%	66%	80%	48%	19%	26%	19%
Trump encouraged or incited the attack, and shares blame for what happened	86%	80%	87%	50%	13%	22%	8%

Source: 2020 CMPS primary sample—white respondents (N = 3,002)

four out of five Democrats believe January 6 was a coordinated act of insurrection against the United States, while less than one out of five Republicans share that assessment. Finally, a plurality of Republicans, including a majority of strong Republicans, believe that GOP members of Congress who voted against certifying the election results in some states were protecting democracy—less than 10 percent of Democrats shared that belief. We find the greatest differences of opinion when comparing strong partisans (we find similar, although slightly weaker, partisan differences among non-white respondents).

Strong Democrats and strong Republicans hold diametrically opposed interpretations of January 6. Indeed, the events of January 6 were vivid and difficult to forget. Yet memorializing the attack will have significant rippling effect in American politics: the perpetuation of voter fraud beliefs among mass Republican and conservative beliefs and a crystallization of partisan differences in attitudes toward election administration.

CONCLUSION

When Trump lost the presidential election in 2020, many people hoped that there would be a return to normalcy. There was hope that the former president's undermining of democratic processes was an aberration, and when he left office, the country would return to its previous norms, particularly around elections and other democratic institutions. However, that was not the case. While Donald Trump may have been the spark that ignited the "Big Lie" about rigged elections, similar rhetoric and allegations have spread like wildfire and are being used in races at all levels across the country (Siders and Montellaro 2021). In the wake of the insurrection and failed election audits, these claims have not faded away; instead, they seem to have gained traction among Republican candidates. As of July 2021, of the nearly seven hundred Republicans who filed initial paperwork with the Federal Election Commission to run for Congress in 2022, "at least a third have embraced Trump's false claims about his defeat" (Gardner 2021). The relatively small number of Republicans who broke with Trump after January 6 have faced censure in their home states by members of their own party (Sprunt 2021b). A majority of Republicans want Donald Trump to remain a major political figure, and a plurality want him to run for president in 2024 (Dunn 2021).

A highly polarized electorate, combined with a partisan effort to undermine the legitimacy of elections, has created a dangerous period for American democracy. Affective polarization and anger mobilize people to engage in the political process, but these traits are associated with several troubling behaviors. For example, strong partisans are more likely to endorse the use of unsavory tactics to win an election or policy debate (Miller and Conover 2015). Those with high levels of partisan animosity are more likely to endorse violence as a solution to political conflicts (Kalmoe and Mason 2022). Contempt for political opponents reduces support for democratic values, like support for minority rights and constitutional limits on government authority (Webster 2020; Kingzette et al. 2021). Continuing efforts by Republican leaders to cast doubt on the outcome of the 2020 election may motivate some people to act on these impulses. Election officials at the state and local level, who used to conduct their work in relative anonymity, now are subject to verbal attacks and death threats, causing some to resign (Brennan Center for Justice 2021; Carew 2021). The forces that led some Trump supporters to occupy the Capitol on January 6 have not diminished. Thus, it is worth asking: how much risk is there of another January 6 event?

APPENDIX

Table 6.1A. Attribute Values for Conjoint Experiment
(2017 CCES—UMSL Module)

Attribute	Value
Sex	Male
	Female
Race	White
	Black
	Asian
	Latino
	Middle-Eastern
Language Ability	Speaks English fluently
	Speaks English with an accent
	Speaks limited English
Age	18
	48
	68
Party Affiliation	Republican
	Independent
	Democrat
Work History	Janitor
	Primary School Teacher
	Doctor
Criminal History	No criminal record
	Has a criminal record
Citizenship	US citizen
	Not US citizen

Chapter Seven

Major-Party Factions in a Battleground State

Self-Identified Factional Affiliation among Pennsylvania Voters

Stephen K. Medvic and Berwood A. Yost

"A classic issue in studies of party organizations," Pippa Norris (1995, 29) noted some twenty-five years ago, "is how we explain party division and ideological conflict." This long-standing interest among party scholars notwithstanding, the study of party factions has experienced something of a resurgence in recent years (see, for example, Noel 2016; Bendix and MacKay 2017; Hansen, Hirano, and Snyder 2017; Thomsen 2017; Conger et al. 2019; Clarke 2020; Blum 2020; and Masket 2020). Much of that work, as much of the scholarship on factions generally, focuses on factions among party elites, particularly members of Congress. This study contributes to our understanding of party factions by exploring factional affiliation among voters.

In a series of surveys of Pennsylvania voters, we find that most partisans are willing to identify with one of the factions in their party and that significant differences exist between copartisan groups. Those intra-party differences are demographic, attitudinal, and, as one might expect, ideological. Though our findings are limited to a single state, we believe they are instructive. Pennsylvania is one of a handful of battleground states in presidential elections and was critical to both Donald Trump's victory in 2016 and Joe Biden's in 2020. In addition, races for US senator and governor in the Keystone State are always hotly contested. Pennsylvania's status as a swing state is due, in large part, to the near-perfect balance of conservative, rural parts of the state with the more progressive cities of Pittsburgh and Philadelphia and the surrounding suburbs, particularly in the southeast. The result is a political environment with a diversity of partisan and intra-party interests.

THE STUDY OF FACTIONS

Concern that parts of a polity might organize to advance its own interests, rather than the common good, has a long history. First as "factions" and later as "parties," these "partial" entities have long been viewed skeptically. As Bolingbroke famously wrote, "Party is a political evil, and faction is the worst of all parties" (Bolingbroke 1997 [1738], 257).

Attempting to understand the nature of parties perhaps more dispassionately, political scientists turned their attention to factions in the middle of the twentieth century.[1] In his analysis of factions in the one-party South, V. O. Key (1949, 16) initially defined a faction as "any combination, clique, or grouping of voters and political leaders who unite at a particular time in support of a candidate." He would later use the term, more generally, to refer to an "informal party-system-within-a-party" (Key 1958, 320).[2] For Austin Ranney and Willmoore Kendall (1956, 126, emphases in original), if a political party is "a large-scale organization whose purpose is to control the personnel and policies *of the government*," a faction is "an element inside a party whose purpose is to control the personnel and policies *of the party.*"

Notwithstanding Key's inclusion of voters in his original conceptualization, most studies of factions consider them an elite phenomenon. Richard Rose's (1964) classic treatment is emblematic. A faction, argued Rose, is "a group of individuals based on representatives in Parliament who seek to further a broad range of policies through consciously organized political activity" (37; see also Rose 1974, 313). That is, factions have "membership based in Parliament, rather than in the civil service or elsewhere" (1964, 37).

This focus on elites continues to characterize the study of American party factions. For instance, in his historical analysis of factions since the end of the Civil War, DiSalvo (2012) maintains that factions are "networks that are comprised of officeholders, organizational officers, and outside groups" (26). Perhaps not surprisingly, members of Congress are the most common subject of research in this area. Measures based on roll call votes (e.g., DW-NOMINATE scores) and interest group ratings are often used to identify differences between factions or to determine factional affiliation (see Medvic 2007; Noel 2016; Bendix and MacKay 2017; Clarke 2020; and Blum 2020), but members' decisions to join ideological caucuses in Congress (Thomsen 2017) and self-descriptions of congressional candidates (Kamarck and Podkul 2018) have also been examined. In addition, the factional activity of party officials, staffers, activists, donors, and convention delegates, as well as party-aligned interest groups, has garnered quite a bit of scholarly attention (see Reiter 2004; Koger, Masket, and Noel 2010; Noel 2016; Conger et al. 2019; Blum 2020; Clarke 2020; and Masket 2020).

The few studies that explore voters' factional affiliations tend to distinguish factions based on voting behavior. Hansen, Hirano, and Snyder (2017), for instance, examine county-level primary results for seven statewide offices in four states—Louisiana, Minnesota, North Dakota, and Wisconsin—throughout much of the twentieth century. Each of their cases was a one-party state during the period under consideration, which likely amplified the incentives for factional activity. Their results indicate a clear connection between factional groupings of voters and factional organizations that were active in each state. "In all four states," they write, "the most important work the factions did for voters was identification, attaching labels to candidates and thereby classifying individuals as members of teams" (183).

Several recent studies attempt to explain support for Donald Trump among Republican voters. Rapoport, Reilly, and Stone (2020) utilize a YouGov panel survey that interviewed Republicans two weeks before the 2016 New Hampshire primary and again in March 2018. The authors find three groups of Republicans—those who indicated a preference for Trump from the beginning of the process ("Always Trump"); those who preferred a different Republican nominee but indicated they could support Trump in the general election ("Maybe Trump"); and those who favored a different nominee and could not support Trump in the general ("Never Trump"; 698–99). The analysis seeks to determine factional influence on evaluations of Trump, the Republican Party, and the Tea Party, as well as support for Trump's border wall. The results indicate that the factional structure within the Republican Party had shifted by early in Trump's presidency from one where the Trump nomination candidacy was substantially orthogonal to support for the Republican Party, to one where support for the Republican party was tied more closely not only to evaluations of Trump, but also to his signature policy and to a potential rival faction defined by support for the Tea Party (704–05).

Like Rapoport, Reilly, and Snyder, Barber and Pope (2019) divide Republicans into three groups based on their support for Trump in the primaries and in the general election. They then determine the levels of symbolic, operational, and conceptual ideology of the three groups. Republicans supportive of Trump in both the primaries and the general election were found to have a high level of symbolic conservatism, a medium level of operational conservatism, and a low level of conceptual conservatism. Those who supported Trump only during the general election had high levels of symbolic and operational conservatism and a medium level of conceptual conservatism. "Never Trump" Republicans were low in symbolic and operational conservatism and had a medium level of conceptual conservatism (732).

In seeking to explain support for Donald Trump during the general election in 2016, Ekins (2017) finds five unique types of Trump voters—Staunch

Conservatives, Free Marketeers, American Preservationists, Anti-Elites, and the Disengaged. Levels of support for the Republican Party vary among these groups and "they hold vastly different views on immigration, American identity, race, economics, and moral traditionalism" as well as "different perceptions of justice in the political and economic systems" (30).

Drutman (2017) draws on the Voter Study Group's 2016 VOTER Survey to identify divisions within both parties based on primary vote choice. He finds more internal division within the Republican Party than the Democratic Party. Nevertheless, Clinton and Sanders Democrats were divided on trade, enthusiasm about America and its history, and pessimism about people like them being "in decline." "[T]o the extent that the Democratic Party is divided," writes Drutman, "these divisions are more about faith in the political system and general disaffection than they are about issue positions" (18). For Republicans, "Trump's biggest enthusiasts within the party are Republicans who hold the most anti-immigrant and anti-Muslim views, demonstrate the most racial resentment, and are most likely to view Social Security and Medicare as important" (21).

It is common for party factions to be described in ideological terms (see Barber and Pope 2019). For example, Carmines, Ensley, and Wagner (2016) calculate the contribution of liberals, conservatives, moderates, libertarians, and populists to each party's presidential coalitions in 2012 (see also Carmines, Ensley, and Wagner 2014). The authors classify voters' ideology based on responses to a series of issue questions in the American National Election Study and their resulting "location in the two-dimensional policy space" (389, n1). In the Republican Party, conservatives constituted a majority (54%) of the party's coalition, followed by libertarians (28%; 392). Liberals made up a plurality (37%) of the Democratic coalition, followed by moderates (23%) and populists (20%; 393).

Typically, however, ideological divisions within the parties are reduced to a simple dichotomy. For DiSalvo (2012), "Factions can be roughly divided into two types: those that seek preservation and those that seek change" (11). More commonly, the division is between centrists (or "party regulars") and ideologues (Noel 2016, 171; see also Masket 2020). These dichotomies, it should be noted, are rarely applied to voters. An exception is a recent paper by Groenendyk, Sances, and Zhirkov (2020) on intra-party polarization. Though not a study of factions per se, the findings suggest that, in both parties, "stronger ideological identifiers" and moderates have divergent views of their party, with ideologues having more positive feelings than moderates.

The analysis that follows seeks to understand factions among the voters within each party. We rely on voter characteristics, including demographic characteristics, political and ideological self-identification, economic assessments, and issue preferences rather than vote choice to predict self-identified factional affiliation. In doing so, we believe we offer a unique approach to the study of factions within the electorate.

METHODS

The data presented in this chapter come from three surveys conducted among 1,521 randomly selected registered voters in the state of Pennsylvania. Survey interviews were conducted March 1–7 (269 Democrats, 236 Republicans, and 82 independents), June 7–13 (205 Democrats, 177 Republicans, and 62 independents), and August 9–15, 2021 (207 Democrats, 173 Republicans, and 66 independents). All sampled respondents were notified by mail about the survey. Interviews were completed over the phone and online depending on each respondent's preference. [3]

In each survey, respondents were asked the following series of questions to identify the party faction to which they most closely identify.

PARTY. Regardless of how you are registered in politics, as of today, do you think of yourself as a Republican, a Democrat, or an Independent?[4]

Those who responded "independent" to the *PARTY* question were asked if they lean toward a party and, if so, were asked the appropriate faction question. True independents were not asked a faction question. The faction questions were:

RFact. The Republican Party includes several different wings or factions. In the Republican Party, for example, there seems to be a faction that embraces Donald Trump's brand of politics and another that is aligned with a more traditional brand of Republican politics. Do you think of yourself as a Trump Republican, a traditional Republican, or something else?

DFact. The Democratic Party includes several different wings or factions. In the Democratic Party, for example, there seems to be a faction that embraces a consistently progressive brand of politics and another that is aligned with a more pragmatic, centrist brand of politics. Do you think of yourself as a progressive Democrat, a centrist Democrat, or something else?

One might reasonably ask whether voters know enough about the factions within each party to meaningfully affiliate with one of them. Given the amount of media discussion of factions in recent years, we believe they can.[5] Furthermore, we believe the brief descriptions of the factions used in our questions give voters enough information to make valid choices, and, empirically, the consistency of the responses across all three of our surveys suggests that this approach is reliable. Ultimately, we view our factional affiliation questions as akin to the standard party identification question. Each allows respondents to determine for themselves how they choose to identify politically.

RESULTS

Among the partisan identifiers included in these surveys, the factional break-down for Republicans is Trump Republican 47 percent, Traditional Repub-lican 34 percent, and other Republican 19 percent. The factional breakdown for Democrats is Centrist Democrat 44 percent, Progressive Democrat 39 percent, and other Democrat 18 percent. The distribution of factional choices was consistent for respondents in both parties from survey period to survey period. Table 7.1 displays the distribution of respondents within each party faction by self-described ideology, party affiliation, born-again Christian, gender, age, education, race, income, and rural-urban classification.

We analyze our data with two logistic regression models: one fit to self-identified Democratic respondents and the other fit to self-identified Re-publican respondents. These analyses began with models that incorporated demographic, political, economic, and issue variables to predict the odds of belonging to either the "Trump" faction of the Republican Party or the "Pro-gressive" faction of the Democratic Party.

The full models for members of both parties included veteran status, religious denomination, being a born-again Christian, age, educational at-tainment, employment status, urban-rural classification,[6] labor union mem-bership, race, gender, direction of the United States, ratings of President Biden, political ideology, need for government action on climate change, economic optimism, support for gun control, support for abortion rights, and racial attitudes.

Economic optimism is calculated by summing the responses to evalua-tions of personal finances compared to last year and evaluations of expected personal finances next year, and dividing by two. For each item, those who responded "better off" scored a 1, those who responded "same" scored 0.5, and those who responded "worse off" were scored 0.

The racial attitudes scale included three items ($\alpha = .69$) from the FIRE bat-tery (DeSante and Smith 2020). Respondents were asked to report how much they agreed with each statement: I am angry that racism exists; white people in the United States have certain advantages because of the color of their skin; and racial problems in the United States are rare, isolated situations. A strongly agree response was scored as two points while an agree response

Table 7.1. Distribution of Respondents by Party Faction and Selected Demographics

	Trump R (n=303)	Traditional R (n=221)	Other R (n=120)	Other D (n=99)	Centrist D (n=239)	Progressive D (n=206)
Ideology (%)						
Extremely liberal	0%	0%	1%	14%	4%	31%
Liberal	4%	3%	1%	18%	30%	27%
Moderate	13%	38%	39%	42%	58%	31%
Conservative	36%	28%	32%	13%	5%	5%
Extremely conservative	42%	27%	17%	1%	0%	3%
DK	5%	3%	10%	11%	3%	2%
Party Affiliation (%)						
Strong Republican	64%	41%	30%	0%	0%	0%
Republican	16%	31%	15%	0%	0%	0%
Lean Republican	21%	28%	54%	0%	0%	0%
Lean Democrat	0%	0%	0%	45%	22%	28%
Democrat	0%	0%	0%	17%	19%	16%
Strong Democrat	0%	0%	0%	38%	59%	56%
Identifies as Born-again Christian (%)						
Yes	37%	30%	24%	18%	13%	11%
No	60%	68%	71%	82%	85%	89%
DK	3%	2%	5%	0%	2%	1%
Gender (%)						
Male	62%	54%	68%	36%	33%	41%
Female	38%	46%	32%	64%	67%	59%
Non-binary	0%	0%	0%	0%	0%	—
Age (%)						
Under 35	7%	10%	17%	12%	7%	18%
35–54	34%	32%	47%	26%	27%	35%
Over 55	59%	58%	36%	62%	66%	47%
Educational attainment (%)						
HS or less	33%	23%	17%	26%	14%	15%
Some college	42%	41%	39%	32%	25%	27%
College degree	25%	35%	44%	41%	61%	58%
Racial group (%)						
Non-white	9%	8%	14%	19%	10%	25%
Income (%)						
Less than $35,000	23%	21%	7%	37%	16%	21%
$35–75,000	36%	40%	32%	32%	27%	32%
Over $75,000	41%	39%	60%	32%	56%	47%
Urban rural classification (%)						
Large central metro	8%	13%	10%	31%	24%	38%
Large fringe metro	25%	25%	34%	27%	44%	28%
Medium metro	34%	32%	32%	31%	24%	21%
Small metro	13%	12%	10%	6%	3%	7%
Micropolitan	12%	13%	9%	5%	3%	6%
Noncore	7%	5%	5%	1%	2%	1%

Source: March, June, and August 2021 Franklin & Marshall College Polls (n=1,521)

counted as one point for all items except for the third question, which was reverse scored. The items were summed and divided by six to create a score ranging from 0–1.

Items that were not significant in these original models were removed to arrive at the final reported models. The entire set of variables included in these three surveys and a comparison of the results for the full models to the final models reported in the next section is included in a supplemental appendix.[7]

Republican Factions

Table 7.2 presents logistic regression coefficients for membership in the Trump faction. The odds of identifying as a member of the Trump faction are lower for those Republicans who do not identify as born-again Christian, who are college graduates, and who do not identify as "extremely" conservative. The largest coefficients associated with membership in the Trump faction are for racial attitudes and economic optimism—those Republicans in the Trump faction are less concerned about racism and are less optimistic about their economic circumstances, all else being equal.

Table 7.2. Logistic Regression for Trump Faction, Republicans

Variable	Estimate (Std. Error)
Born-again Christian (No)	−0.588***
	(−0.969, −0.207)
Some college education	−0.214
	(−0.693, 0.265)
College graduate	−0.607***
	(−1.062, −0.153)
Racial attitudes (More concerned w/ racism)	−1.632***
	(−2.342, −0.922)
Economic Optimism	−1.082***
	(−1.783, −0.382)
Ideology (Less conservative or moderate)	−0.806***
	(−1.242, −0.369)
Ideology (Undefined)	−0.254
	(−0.722, 0.213)
Constant	2.050***
	(1.451, 2.649)
Observations	593
Log Likelihood	−365.1
Akaike Inf. Crit.	746.2
Area under the ROC curve	0.71

Note: *** $p < 0.001$; ** $p < 0.01$; * $p < 0.05$

Democratic Factions

Table 7.3 presents logistic regression coefficients for membership in the Progressive faction of the Democratic Party. The odds of identifying as a member of the Progressive faction are higher for union members, those under fifty-five years of age, non-whites, those who "definitely" want more state action on climate change, those who believe abortion should "always" be legal, and those with more economic optimism. The largest coefficient associated with

Table 7.3.   Logistic Regression for Progressive Faction, Democrats

Variable	Estimate (Std. Error)
Member of labor union (No)	−0.435*
	(−0.883, 0.013)
Age 35–54	−0.431
	(−1.297, 0.436)
Age over 55	−1.045**
	(−1.859, −0.231)
Non-white	0.976***
	(0.389, 1.563)
Catholic	0.333
	(−0.258, 0.924)
Other or unaffiliated religion	0.312
	(−0.180, 0.803)
More state action on climate (Yes probably)	−0.914***
	(−1.535, −0.293)
More state action on climate (No probably not)	0.523
	(−0.809, 1.855)
More state action on climate (No not at all)	−0.459
	(−2.887, 1.969)
Abortion support (Sometimes legal)	−0.405*
	(−0.817, 0.008)
Abortion support (Never legal)	−0.125
	(−1.282, 1.031)
Economic Optimism	0.796*
	(−0.137, 1.729)
Ideology (Less liberal or moderate)	−1.674***
	(−2.300, −1.047)
Ideology (Undefined)	−1.184***
	(−1.807, −0.560)
Constant	1.287**
	(0.051, 2.522)
Observations	551
Log Likelihood	−307.852
Akaike Inf. Crit.	645.704
Area under the ROC Curve	0.737

Note: *** $p < 0.001$; ** $p < 0.01$; * $p < 0.05$

membership in the Progressive faction is for ideology; those who identify as extremely liberal are significantly more likely than those who are less liberal, or are moderate, to identify as a Progressive Democrat.

In addition to the items included in our logit models, some of our surveys included scales that provide additional though limited data on characteristics that some have suggested might drive membership in these factions. This section examines the factional differences on four different scales. Details about the construction of these items can be found in the supplemental appendix in endnote 7.

Support for Democracy in Principle and in Practice

We sought to determine respondents' level of support for the principles of democracy and their assessment of how democracy is working in practice. With respect to the principles of democracy, we asked if all citizens deserve an equal say in how our government runs; if a leader may sometimes need to break the rules to get things done; if there should be NO barriers to voting in our country; if citizens should be allowed to say whatever they think even if their views are unpopular; and if it is important to have established rights that protect defendants in civil and criminal trials, including the presumption of innocence. On a 10-point scale, where 10 represents strong agreement with all five democratic principles and 5 represents agreeing "somewhat" with each principle, the average score was 7.1. At the same time, most voters in the state do not believe that American democracy is working as it should in practice. To gauge how respondents think American democracy is working in practice, we asked if citizens think the decisions of federal judges are fair and impartial; if the actions of the US House and Senate represent the collective will of the American people; if elections in the United States are free and fair; if the federal government is corrupt; and if the federal government's operations are open and transparent. The average score on the democracy-in-practice questions was 2.4, which means that respondents disagreed with statements describing a well-functioning democracy. Both Republicans and Democrats support democratic principles (with scores of 6.6 and 7.5, respectively) and both are likely to disagree that American democracy is working well (1.8 and 3.1, respectively). But Republican scores on both scales are significantly lower than Democratic scores.

The essential difference between the party factions is in their assessments of American democracy in practice. Trump Republicans (average score of 1.1) are much less likely than Traditional Republicans (2.4) to agree with all five statements that the American system is working (see figure 7.1). The bottom line is that, while all respondents tend to think that the system isn't

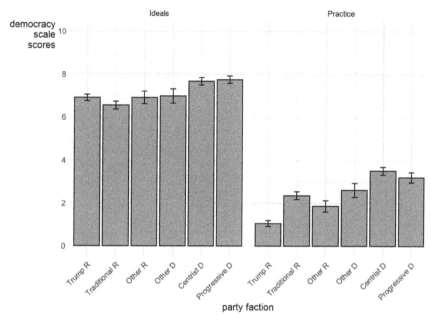

Figure 7.1. Democratic Principles and Practice Scale Scores by Party Factions

working as we'd expect it to, Trump Republicans are especially likely to hold that perspective. The differences among Democrats are not as stark; the differences in these groups' ratings of democratic ideals and democracy in practice do not differ.

Christian Nationalism

Respondents were asked to report how much they agreed with four statements related to Christian nationalist beliefs: the Founding Fathers intended the United States to be a Christian nation; the Founding Fathers were evangelical Christians; the United States' founding documents are based on biblical principles; and America's power in the world is dependent on its obedience to God. A strongly agree response was scored as 2 points while an agree response counted as 1 point for all items. The items were summed and divided by four to create a score ranging from 0–2.

Republicans (mean = 0.91) are more likely than Democrats (mean = 0.39) to believe in Christian nationalist ideals, but members of the Trump faction are much more likely than other Republicans to believe that the United States is a Christian nation (see figure 7.2). Trump Republicans are more likely than Traditional Republicans and all Democratic factions to believe in Christian nationalist ideals. Democrats do not differ from each other on these beliefs.

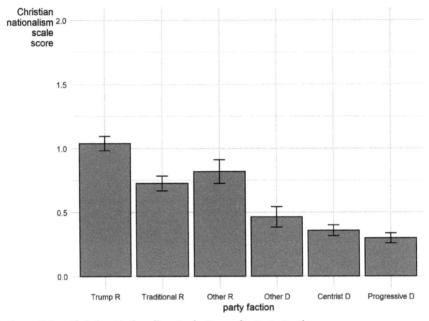

Figure 7.2.   Christian Nationalism Scale Scores by Party Factions

Operational Ideology

The operational ideology scale included five items that asked respondents to choose which of two statements best reflected their personal views (see supplemental appendix for question wording). Responses that reflected a conservative perspective were scored as 1 point and the total scale score could range from 0–5. The operational ideology scale confirms the findings from the logistic regression analysis that the Trump faction of the Republican Party is the most conservative of all the partisan factions and that these individuals are more conservative than other Republicans (see figure 7.3). The operational liberalism scores among Democrats are not significantly different.

DISCUSSION

This chapter has explored voters' sense of where they fit within their own parties using designations that are commonly discussed in contemporary media coverage and political discourse. Based on analyses of an assortment of data, we find that each party has at least three discernable intra-party segments and that these segments are defined by a cluster of ideological, demographic and policy attributes.

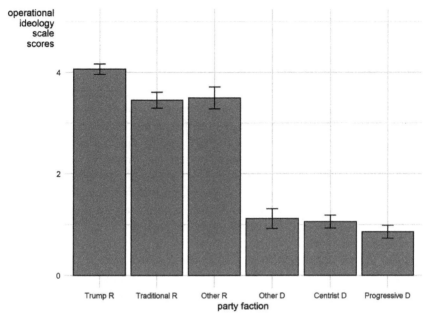

Figure 7.3. Operational Ideology Scale Scores by Party Factions

We should not be surprised that a system that fundamentally relies on just two major parties has discernable factions within each. What we find noteworthy is that the factional distinctions are strongly ideological within both parties, but that attributes beyond ideology help to further differentiate the factions within each party. For Republicans, religion, economic assessments, and attitudes about race produce the major points of division, while for Democrats it is age, race, and policy preferences for government action on climate change and abortion rights that amplify ideological differences.

Our findings have important implications not only for Pennsylvania and other swing states but, indeed, for national electoral politics and the state of the two major US parties. While a plurality of Republicans identify as members of the more ideologically extreme faction in their party, a plurality of Democrats identify with the centrist faction in theirs. The result is likely to be vastly different dynamics in the nomination politics of the two parties in 2022, 2024, and beyond. In the Republican Party, nominations are likely to be dominated by variations on Trump's brand of politics as candidates appeal to the largest, and most active, faction among Republican voters. For Democrats, tensions between those who believe the party should position itself in the center of the ideological spectrum in order to expand the electoral map into territory that is typically unfriendly to Democrats, and those who want the party to offer meaningful change to the status quo (and who have been frustrated by what they perceive to be the party's unwillingness to do so) is likely to intensify.

Factional politics in the Republican Party, as presented in this chapter, have the potential to be disruptive to American democratic practice in the near term. The Trump faction's attitudes about race and their identification with Christian nationalism, along with their pessimistic views of American democracy as it is currently practiced, are potentially combustible. To the extent that future Democratic election victories are viewed by this faction as not only fraudulent but unacceptable threats to an idealized "American way of life," members of this faction are not likely to accept such outcomes. Whether a refusal to accept electoral defeat translates into widespread rejection of the democratic consensus and habits of American democracy as they have been practiced for more than half a century remains to be seen.

Additional research is, of course, necessary to fully understand the factional affiliations of the electorate. In addition to the items included in our logit models, we captured limited data on characteristics that some have suggested might drive membership in these factions as well. We found that some of these items, particularly support for Christian nationalist ideals among Republicans, would be worthy of additional work. Obviously, it would also be useful to ask our faction affiliation questions to a national sample of voters. And, finally, we hope to undertake further analyses of the characteristics of those voters in both parties who did not affiliate with a faction and, instead, selected the "other" category.

One of the limitations of this work is that it is a product of the current political moment. Undoubtedly, the labels given to these factions will change and the core groups will reconfigure themselves in response to signals from political elites and the fusion of broader political and cultural issues. This makes it particularly necessary to chart the feedback loops between elites and voters that should continually reshape these self-defined factional affiliations.

NOTES

1. Sartori (1976) resisted the use of the term "faction" to describe party subunits and maintained that American political scientists were largely responsible for the adoption of the term, which, to his mind, had been done "unfelicitously" (72).

2. Similarly, and more recently, Rachel Blum (2020) describes factions as "miniature parties within parties" (13).

3. Survey results were weighted (age, gender, education, geography, and party registration) using an iterative weighting algorithm to reflect the known distribution of

those characteristics. Estimates for age, geography, and party registration are based on active voters within the PA Department of State's voter registration data. Gender and education is estimated using data from the November 2018 CPS Voter Registration Supplement (data downloaded from IPUMS-CPS, University of Minnesota, www .ipums.org, accessed 12/31/2019).

4. The survey also included a question about actual voter registration since all voters in Pennsylvania choose a party affiliation when they register to vote. Registration and party identification do not correspond perfectly in the state and party identification, as asked in this question, tends to be a superior indicator of current partisanship in the state (Yost 2003).

5. For just a sample of recent journalistic accounts of factions in the parties, see Bacon (2019), Haberman (2021), Olsen (2021), and Balz, Clement and Guskin (2021).

6. Classification based on Ingram and Franco (2014).

7. The supplemental appendix can be found at https://uakron.edu/bliss/docs/State -of-the-Parties-2021/medvic-yost-sop21-appendix.pdf.

Chapter Eight

Blue Metros, Red States

The Geography of the 2020 Vote in the Swing States

David F. Damore, Karen A. Danielsen, and Robert E. Lang

In *Blue Metros, Red States: The Shifting Urban-Rural Divide in America's Swing State* (Damore, Lang, and Danielsen 2021a), we examine how the growing demographic, economic, and sociocultural differences between Democratic-leaning, million-plus metros and the more Republican-voting balance of their respective states affect election outcomes and intrastate policy competition in thirteen swing states that feature a combined twenty-seven million-plus metros.[1] Our analysis of statewide elections between 2012 and 2018 suggests that movement toward the Democratic Party in rapidly urbanizing suburbs characterized by high levels of population density, ethnic and racial diversity, and educational attainment is shifting America's partisan fault line from a long-standing urban-rural divide to an emerging metro-rest-of-state division.

To this end, in 2020 Democratic presidential candidate Joe Biden's vote share in nearly all the million-plus metros analyzed improved relative to Hillary Clinton's presidential run in 2016 (Damore, Lang, and Danielsen 2021b). These effects were strongest in many of the Sun Belt swing-state metros, most of which also delivered a larger share of the statewide vote compared to the 2016 presidential election. In addition to flipping both Rust Belt and Sun Belt swing states, Biden won every conterminous state where a single metropolitan area accounted for half or more of a state's population.[2]

In this chapter we extend the *Blue Metros, Red States* framework to consider the importance of metropolitan scale for understanding the contours of partisan voting patterns. Drawing on classic and recent scholarship, we evaluate the metro-level dynamics shaping political cohesion in large-scale, swing-state metros. Next, we present data examining how geography conditioned partisan support in 2020 and the degree to which within-state shifts in partisan support relative to 2016 were decisive to the outcome of the presidential election in thirteen swing states. We conclude by assessing how growing intrastate geographic partisan divisions and political competition for suburban voters will affect electoral competition in the coming years.

BLUE METROS, RED STATES, AND THE POLITICS OF SCALE

The blue state, red state, swing state trichotomy has been used since at least the 2000 presidential election as shorthand for conceptualizing the country's partisan landscape. Despite its ubiquity, the framework ignores how intrastate geographic tensions and political competition imbue the divisions between red and blue America. Within state differences also anchor the long-standing urban-rural divide, a salient feature of American politics since the nation's founding.

In *Blue Metros, Red States* (Damore, Lang, and Danielsen 2021a), we argue that intrastate variation in partisan voting patterns derives from four interrelated influences: sociocultural factors, often determined by initial settlement patterns, that shape values and attitudes related to diversity acceptance; demographic and economic sorting that has concentrated ethnic and racial diversity and economic productivity in the country's largest metros; sharper attitudinal differences due to rising negative partisanship and the growing saliency of cultural, racial, and other diversity-related issues and the implications these have for perceptions of status loss, particularly among whites; and institutional biases, such as the apportionment of the US Senate and the Electoral College, redistricting, Dillon's rule limitations on local autonomy and state preemption of local government actions, and metro fragmentation that often disadvantage urban and suburban interests.

Collectively, these factors have led to a decoupling of demographic and economic power from political power (Brownstein 2018). In *Blue Metros, Red States* we consider the causes and consequences of these tensions by using a common geographic framework—the million-plus metro compared to the rest of a state's population—to analyze political and policy competition in the swing states that determine the partisan balance of power at the federal level.

The million-plus population threshold distinguishes large, high-density metros from smaller-scale metros that while urban in form, differ from their bigger counterparts in important ways. Million-plus metros generate most of the nation's economic output, foreign trade, and innovation technologies (Tomer and Kane 2014; Muro and Whiten 2018). These metros also support significant infrastructure and transportation networks, deliver extensive public services, and require administrative organizations that can rival those of state governments (Damore, Lang, and Danielsen 2021a).

In developing the "the urban-size ratchet" model, Thompson (1965) argues that large metros are self-sustaining due to their fixed infrastructure, market access, high levels of economic diversification, and ability to attract investment resources and human capital. Once established, large metros typically continue to grow and are insulated from "absolute decline" (Thompson 1965, 24), effectively becoming self-reinforcing "growth-machines." Smaller-scaled metros with narrower industrial bases and less extensive infrastructure are more vulnerable to contraction because they may lack the capacity to adapt to economic and demographic shifts.

Scholars also argue that scale matters politically (Fischer 1984). Large metros typically include numerous counties and municipalities that feature a variety of forms ranging from dense, urban cores to large-lot, single-family exurban neighborhoods. Today, the country's fifty-six million-plus metros are home to most of the nation's population despite comprising less than 10 percent of the U.S. land area. Moreover, since 1940 the number of million-plus metros has increased fivefold and the share of the country's population residing in these metros increased by more than thirty percentage points.[3] In addition to inter- and intrastate migration, since the 1990s urban growth has been powered by immigrants (Frey 2018).

Now consider the long-standing relationship between population density, ethnic and racial diversity, and Democratic voting (Lang, Sanchez, and Berube 2008). Add to that the growing Democratic support among higher-educated voters who are clustered in the country's largest metros (Florida, Patino, and Dottle 2021) and the migration of blue-state voters into large red-state metros such as Austin, Texas that has shifted the Lone Star state from reliably Republican to increasingly competitive (Levin 2020). Thus, it is easy to see how shifts in partisan support in million-plus metros can be so consequential to outcomes in statewide elections. In many states, the metro vote share is so large that if the Democrats win enough urban and suburban voters, there may not be enough Republican votes remaining for the GOP to win statewide elections. As these patterns strengthen over successive election cycles, the urban-rural divide that for generations nourished Republican majorities may be eclipsed by a division between major metropolitan areas and the rest of the state—an emerging dynamic that favors Democrats (Damore, Lang, and Danielsen 2021a).

To be sure, there has always been an acknowledgment that the level of urbanization affects tolerance and political behavior (Tam et al., 2013; Johnston, Jones, and Manley 2016; Gimpel et al. 2020). The idea of testing political tolerance in urban areas began with Stouffer's (1955) idea of "culture shock," where he found that city dwellers are more tolerant of diversity than rural residents due to the "shock" of being exposed to diversity.

He predicted that tolerance would increase as the country urbanized and the populace became exposed to more conflicting values. Stouffer considered the migration of people from rural areas to more urban areas as the mechanism for increased tolerance and acceptance (Stouffer 1955). In a more direct assessment of how geography shapes political identities, Gimpel et al. (2020) find that the physical distance people live from large cities predicts their party affiliation. The more remote the locality, the more likely an individual is to identify as a Republican.

According to some scholars, the migration of people to more urban areas does not always engender more tolerance (Marcus, Piereson, and Sullivan 1980). This premise experienced a revival with the publication of Bishop's *The Big Sort* (2009). Bishop argues that the "sorting" of like-minded individuals into the same geographic spaces foments electoral polarization. Although Bishop suggests that sorting exists at the inter-region, interstate, and inter-community levels, his analysis only considers county election results (Johnston, Jones, and Manley 2016). Counties, of course, vary in size from a few hundred residents to more than ten million in the case of Los Angeles County.

Research at the zip code level suggests that the effects of migration and sorting on political behavior may be indirect. For instance, Tam et al. (2013, 859) argues that "there is ample evidence that partisan considerations are not foremost in relocation decisions." Consistent with Tiebout's (1956) contention that people select where they live based on the level of public services they want and are willing to pay for, relocation decisions are shaped primarily by evaluations of local tax rates and public service provision (Tam et al. 2013). Political factors are normally ancillary and of varying saliency to potential new residents (Gimpel and Hui 2017).

The actual size of the city, or as in our analysis, the size of the metropolitan area, is significant for understanding political outcomes for several reasons. First, metropolitan areas, by definition, have a high degree of social and economic integration. These conditions stimulate interactions among different groups and interests that shape and reinforce broader political predispositions (Lofland 1998; Gimpel et al. 2020).

Second, million-plus metro areas are often polycentric. That is, big metros are composed of a principal city along with several satellite cities or suburbs and may encompass multiple counties, resulting in a more logical economic and social unit that can be substituted for formal jurisdictional boundaries in analyses. Because density and diversity are not evenly distributed within a large-scale metro, these metros feature pockets of partisan support that collectively shape the intra-metro partisan balance of power. For instance, while large metros vote heavily Democratic, residents of these metros account for the vast majority of campaign donations to both parties (Gimpel, Lee, and Kaminski 2006), and given their scale, million-plus metros also deliver large shares of Republican votes.

Further, analyses that use smaller-scale geographies will not necessarily see the same patterns of political behavior that can be detected at higher levels of geographic aggregation. Observations at lower levels of analysis may reflect the effects of local land use policies that determine overall density and housing types. Racial and ethnic segregation at the neighborhood level may also exhibit a similar bias (Trounstine 2018). Thus, relative density, diversity, and their effects on political attitudes and behavior may be best captured at the metro-level scale to overcome selection biases associated with lower levels of analysis (South and Crowder 1998). For example, racial segregation in metropolitan areas can be a proxy for income stratification. Because there are more housing opportunities in larger metros, it is easier for minorities to move from poorer to richer neighborhoods but that can only be observed at a larger geographic scale.[4]

Third, principal cities are interconnected with their suburbs and even to some degree their surrounding rural areas through telecommunications, transportation, and media. Cities influence these surrounding areas through these same economic and social forces (Huggins and Debies-Carl 2015). As Fischer's (1984) subcultural theory posits, "the scale of urban life" allows for the emergence of new innovations in social and economic behavior. His concept of "critical mass" suggests that a population threshold is necessary to change or modify subcultures in urban areas. The larger the number of people or the more urban the area, the more these changes and effects are "intensified." According to Fischer (1984), "intensification" is the mechanism that creates new subcultures, attitudes, and common interests that eventually translate into voting behavior.

Fourth, because large metros are heterogeneous, no single group controls the entire geographic or political space, necessitating collaboration, communication, and by extension, tolerance, and acceptance. This idea is the basis of Anderson's (2011) notion of "cosmopolitan canopies" that provide a more pluralistic model for group engagement. Lofland (1998) suggests that "repeated interactions with others" leads to tolerance.

Huggins and Debies-Carl (2015, 259) also suggest that tolerance can operate at a variety of societal levels, even in rural areas, and they contend that "tolerance should be thought of as a form of acceptance of nonconformity and not just an acceptance of diversity." In their study of forty-eight countries, Huggins and Debies-Carl (2015) operationalize tolerance into two constructs: "tolerance of difference" and "tolerance of threat." Tolerance of difference was measured whether someone would mind having someone as a neighbor based on cultural differences. Tolerance of threat was measured as whether someone would want to live near people who engaged in deviant behavior such as heavy drinkers or drug users among other undesirable qualities. They find that tolerance of difference and threat was more common in larger cities and in places with higher levels of educational attainment. The smaller and less educated the space, the lower the tolerance of threat and less willingness to live near people who behave in "nontraditional" ways.

The million-plus-metro unit of analysis then is appropriate for understanding how geographic density shapes patterns of social interaction and the reinforcement of salient sociocultural and political values. As we assert in *Blue Metros, Red States* (Damore, Lang, and Danielsen 2021a, 40), "Big cities are not liberal just because they are diverse. They are also liberal because they expose white and minority inhabitants to dense and diverse environments that facilitate social integration and reduce bias." Thus, while selection effects may account for the demographic differences between a million-plus metros and the balance of a state's population, "The politically relevant behaviors and opinions manifest in these spaces also are shaped by differing patterns of social interaction" (Damore, Lang, and Danielsen 2021a, 40).

Given the regional variation in swing states with at least one million-plus metro there are reasons to expect variation in these effects. Demographically, a contrast exists between the Sun Belt swing states where the million-plus metros are rapidly growing, diversifying, and attracting higher educated residents, and the Rust Belt swing states where these trends are less prevalent. Among the thirteen swing states considered here, many feature multiple million-plus metros. In contexts where the urban space is splintered, metro residents may perceive themselves as rivals rather than allies and political loyalties may be divided. In other swing states, the metro population may not be large enough to offset the rest of a state's partisanship even if the million-plus metros still vote Democratically.

SWING STATE AND METRO PARTISAN SHIFTS: COMPARING 2020 TO 2016

To assess the effects of scale on geographic patterns of partisan support in presidential elections, we summarize shifts in the presidential vote from 2016 to 2020. The primary unit of analysis is the million-plus metro. We define these metros using the US census-designated Metropolitan Statistical Area (MSA) and refer to the MSA using the leading principal city instead of the formal MSA title. The only exception to this is we use Northern Virginia to label the Virginia components of the Washington-Arlington-Alexandria DC-

VA-MD-WV MSA. For the six MSAs (Cincinnati, Charlotte, Minneapolis–Saint Paul, Northern Virginia, Philadelphia, and Virginia Beach) that extend into multiple states, we only include data for the counties that are in the state associated with the MSA's principal city.

For each of the thirteen states with a million-plus metro and where the 2016 presidential margin of victory was ten points or less, county-level presidential turnout and vote choice data were collected for 2016 and 2020 from secretary of state websites after election results were certified. These data were aggregated for the state and for the counties in the twenty-seven million-plus metros to generate the partisan margins of support. We also use these data to measure changes in the million-plus metros' share of the statewide vote. Data for counties that are not part of a million-plus metro were aggregated to generate the "Rest of State" measure used in figure 8.2.

Table 8.1 summarizes the partisan margin for the 2016 and 2020 presidential election in the thirteen swing states and their twenty-seven million-plus metros, the inter-election shift in partisan support, and the change in the million-plus metro share of the statewide vote. Italics identify states that flipped from Republican to Democratic in 2020. States and metros are grouped regionally using a Sun Belt-Rust Belt framework. For the Sun Belt states, we group Florida and Texas together as "Big Sun Belt" states due to their large scales and the fact that each state has four million-plus metros. The eastern (Georgia, North Carolina, and Virginia) and western "New Sun Belt" states (Arizona, Colorado, and Nevada) are clustered. Table 8.1 also groups the "Rust Belt East" (Michigan, Ohio, and Pennsylvania) and "Rust Belt Central" states (Minnesota and Wisconsin).

Figure 8.1 uses data from the "Difference" column in table 8.1 to order the twenty-seven million-plus metros in terms of their inter-election percentage point shift. Positive values indicate a Democratic shift and negative values indicate a Republican shift. The values in parentheses next to the metro labels summarize the change in the metro's share of the statewide vote from the "Change in Vote Share" column in table 8.1. These data are included to assess the overall magnitude of a shift. If a million-plus metro's share of the overall vote increased, then the impact of the inter-election partisan shift on the statewide vote was even greater. Conversely, if a million-plus metro's vote share decreased, then the effect of the partisan shift on the outcome was less consequential.

As table 8.1 and figure 8.1 indicate, Florida was the outlier. The Sunshine State was the only state where President Donald Trump's margin improved relative to 2016. Trump also improved his performance in three of Florida's four million-plus metros. Only in Tampa did Biden's margin increase relative to Clinton's. In northern Florida, Biden narrowly won Duval County, where

Table 8.1. 2016 to 2020 Presidential Swing State and Million-Plus Metro Vote Shifts

State and Million-Plus Metro(s)	Margin			Change in Vote Share
	2016	2020	Difference	
	Big Sun Belt			
Florida (29 electoral votes)	1.2 R	3.4 R	+2.2 R	
Jacksonville	4.8 R	12.8 R	+8.0 R	–0.1
Miami	27.5 D	16.2 D	+11.3 R	–0.3
Orlando	11.6 D	10.7 D	+0.9 R	+0.1
Tampa	3.0 R	2.5 R	+0.5 D	0.0
Texas (38 electoral votes)	9.0 R	5.6 R	+3.4 D	
Austin	19.5 D	27.2 D	+7.7 D	+0.4
Dallas–Fort Worth	7.1 R	0.5 D	+7.6 D	+0.4
Houston	1.0 R	1.0 D	+2.0 D	+0.2
San Antonio	1.1 R	3.3 D	+4.4 D	+0.4
	New Sun Belt East			
Georgia (16 electoral votes)	5.2 R	0.2 D	+5.4 D	
Atlanta	8.1 D	15.5 D	+7.4 D	+0.7
North Carolina (15 electoral votes)	3.7 R	1.4 R	+2.3 D	
Charlotte	1.5 R	3.6 D	+5.1 D	+0.8
Raleigh	12.0 D	17.3 D	+5.3 D	+0.5
Virginia (13 electoral votes)	5.3 D	10.1 D	+4.8 D	
Northern Virginia	25.8 D	31.6 D	+5.8 D	+0.5
Richmond	9.0 D	14.2 D	+5.2 D	+0.1
Virginia Beach	9.1 D	15.2 D	+6.1 D	–0.3
	New Sun Belt West			
Arizona (11 electoral votes)	3.5 R	0.3 D	+3.8 D	
Phoenix	4.1 R	0.6 D	+4.7 D	+1.5
Tucson	13.8 D	18.9 D	+5.1 D	–1.0
Colorado (9 electoral votes)	4.9 D	13.5 D	+8.6 D	
Denver	15.4 D	25.2 D	+9.8 D	–0.9
Nevada (6 electoral votes)	2.4 D	2.4 D	No change	
Las Vegas	10.7 D	9.3 D	+1.4 R	+1.0
	Rust Belt East			
Michigan (16 electoral votes)	0.2 R	2.8 D	+3.0 D	
Detroit	10.7 D	13.5 D	+2.8 D	–0.1
Grand Rapids	14.2 R	6.3 R	+7.9 D	+0.2
Ohio (18 electoral votes)	8.1 R	8.0 R	+0.1 D	
Cincinnati	12.1 R	7.9 R	+4.2 D	–0.3
Cleveland	15.7 D	14.2 D	+1.5 R	–0.5
Columbus	4.6 D	8.1 D	+3.5 D	+0.3
	Rust Belt East			
Pennsylvania (20 electoral votes)	0.7 R	1.2 D	+1.9 D	
Philadelphia	32.3 D	33.3 D	+1.0 D	–0.5
Pittsburgh	4.8 R	2.3 R	+2.5 D	+0.6

State and Million-Plus Metro(s)	Margin			Change in Vote Share
	2016	2020	Difference	
	Rust Belt Central			
Minnesota (10 electoral votes)	1.5 D	7.1 D	+5.6 D	
Minneapolis–Saint Paul	13.6 D	20.4 D	+6.8 D	+1.2
Wisconsin (10 electoral votes)	0.8 R	0.6 D	+1.4 D	
Milwaukee	7.2 D	9.8 D	+2.6 D	−.06

Note: Italics identify states that flipped from Republican to Democratic in 2020.

Sources: Authors' calculations of data collected from secretary of state websites after completion of ballot certification. Adapted from Damore, Lang, and Danielsen (2021b).

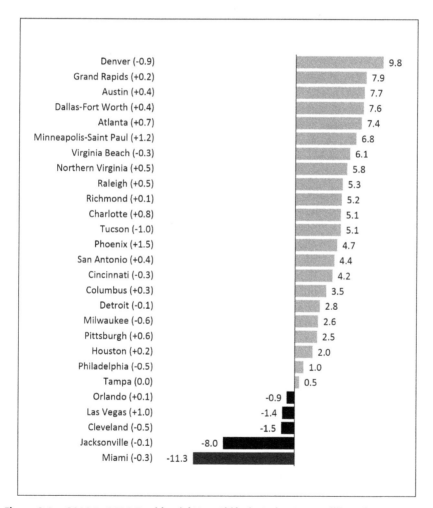

Figure 8.1. 2016 to 2020 Presidential Vote Shifts in Swing-State Million-Plus Metros

Notes: Values are the percentage-point shift in the presidential vote from 2016 to 2020. Positive values indicate a Democratic shift and negative values indicate a Republican shift. Values in parentheses are change in the million-plus metro share of the statewide vote from 2016 to 2020.

Sources: Authors' calculations of data collected from secretary of state websites after completion of ballot certification. Adapted from Damore, Lang, and Danielsen (2021b).

the city of Jacksonville is located (Trump won it in 2016), but Trump carried the metro due to huge margins in the surrounding suburban counties. After Miami, Jacksonville had the largest Republican shift among the swing-state million-plus metros (see figure 8.1). Trump also gained ground in Orlando, but like Miami, Biden won the metro by double digits. Among Florida's four million-plus metros, only Orlando's share of the state vote increased.

In contrast to Florida, Texas and its million-plus metros shifted toward the Democrats, but this shift was not large enough to move the state to the Democratic column. In 2016, Austin was the only million-plus metro that Clinton carried. In 2020, Biden carried all four of Texas's million-plus metros, picking up nearly eight points in Austin and Dallas–Fort Worth, while making more modest gains in Houston and San Antonio. Inspection of figure 8.1 reveals that Biden's gains in Austin and Dallas–Fort Worth were among the largest Democratic shifts in a swing-state million-plus metro. Biden's performance in Texas's four million-plus metros provided him with an even larger bump in support given that each metro's share of the statewide vote increased to account for a combined 70 percent of total turnout. Since the 2012 presidential elections, the Democrats have cut the Republicans' margin in Texas from sixteen percentage points to less than six.

Among the three "New Sun Belt East" states, Biden improved upon Clinton's margin in Virginia and its three million-plus metros. Northern Virginia and Richmond also increased their shares of the statewide vote. Biden's 2020 victory in Virginia is the fourth straight presidential win for the Democrats, last accomplished in the 1930s and 1940s when Virginia voted Democratically in five consecutive presidential elections. In 2020, Trump again carried North Carolina, but Biden outperformed Clinton by nearly 2.5 percentage points statewide largely due to the 5-point increases in each of the state's million-plus metros. Charlotte and Raleigh also increased their share of the statewide vote. By nearly doubling the Democrats' margin in metro Atlanta on his way to a roughly 5.5 percentage point statewide improvement compared to Clinton in 2016, Biden become the first Democratic presidential candidate since 1992 to win Georgia. Among the twenty-seven million-plus metros, Atlanta had the fifth-largest shift to the Democrats (see Figure 8.1). Biden's strong showing in Atlanta was even more significant given the growth in metro Atlanta's vote share.

Out west, Biden won all of the "New Sun Belt West" states. His victory in Arizona was the first for a Democratic presidential candidate since 1996. Biden's Arizona win resulted from strong swings in the Phoenix and Tucson metros. His ability to tip Phoenix was even more potent given the increase in the metro's share of the vote that offset the smaller vote share delivered by more liberal Tucson. Combined, Arizona's million-plus metros accounted for

82 percent of the 2020 vote. Colorado continued trending toward the Democrats. The nearly 10-point swing in Denver was the largest Democratic shift among the twenty-seven metros examined (see figure 8.1). In 2020 Nevada held steady to deliver the Democrats their fourth straight win in the Silver State. As table 8.1 and figure 8.1 indicate, Biden lost nearly 1.5 points in Las Vegas compared to Clinton and Las Vegas's share of the vote increased by a percentage point. Even still, Biden carried Las Vegas by more than 9 percentage points and he offset his erosion in the million-plus metro by cutting Trump's margins in the rest of the state, particularly in Washoe County, Nevada's second most populated county and where Reno is located.

Among the "Rust Belt East" states, Trump's Ohio statewide margin decreased negligibly, and he lost support in two of the state's three million-plus metro. Among Ohio's three big metros, only Columbus's share of the statewide vote increased. Trump again carried Cincinnati and he performed better in Cleveland, but both metros delivered a smaller share of the statewide vote compared to 2016. Modest gains in Detroit and Philadelphia and larger gains in the Republican-leaning Grand Rapids and Pittsburgh metros returned Michigan and Pennsylvania to the Democratic column.

Biden also carried the two "Rust Belt Central" states, flipping Wisconsin and making strong gains in Minnesota. Biden's narrow win in Wisconsin resulted from increased support in Milwaukee and a larger margin in the heavily Democratic Madison metro, the state's second-largest MSA. In 2020, the Trump campaign targeted Minnesota after Clinton narrowly carried the state in 2016. These efforts fell well short as Biden secured Minnesota's ten electoral votes by nearly 6 percentage points due to a Democratic increase of nearly 7 percentage points in metro Minneapolis–Saint Paul. Biden's strong showing in the Twin Cities carried even more of a punch due to the increase in the metro's share of the statewide vote.

To provide additional context for understanding the inter-election partisan swings, figure 8.2 presents the 2016 to 2020 statewide, million-plus metro, and rest of state (all counties not within a million-plus metro) percentage-points shifts. In states with multiple million-plus metros, the "Million-Plus Metro" value combines the data for all such metros. Positive values indicate a Democratic shift and negative values indicate a Republican shift.

The data presented in figure 8.2 illustrate the intrastate partisan differences between million-plus metros and the balance of a state's population. When compared to Clinton in 2016, the increase in the Democratic margin in the million-plus metros exceeded the statewide margin in all of the swing states that Biden flipped except for Pennsylvania. Biden also gained ground outside of the million-plus metros in eleven of the thirteen swing states. His largest "Rest of State" gains were in Colorado and Florida. However, Biden's gains

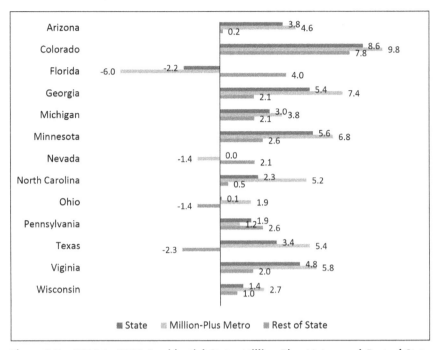

Figure 8.2.   2016 to 2020 Presidential State, Million-Plus Metro, and Rest of State Vote Shifts

Notes: Values are percentage-point shifts in the presidential vote from 2016 to 2020. Positive values indicate a Democratic shift and negative values indicate a Republican shift. In states with multiple million-plus metros, the "Million-Plus Metro" value aggregates data for all such metros. "Rest of State" values are aggregated from all counties not in a million-plus metro.

Source: Authors' calculations of data collected from secretary of state websites after completion of ballot certification. Adapted from Damore, Lang, and Danielsen (2021b).

in Florida's smaller metros and towns were more than offset by Trump's improvements in three of the state's million-plus big metros that resulted in a 6 percent point Republican increase in the "Million-Plus Metro" margin. Ohio and Texas were the only swing states where Trump improved his "Rest of State" margin compared to 2016.

Figure 8.2 also suggests that despite the party's margins in the million-plus metros, Democrats need support in smaller cities and towns to win statewide elections. This is particularly the case in the states where the combined million-plus metro population makes up a smaller share of a state's population. Where these votes come from reflect the uniqueness of each state's political, demographic, and economic history. For example, Pennsylvania, largely regarded as 2020's "tipping point" state, shifted to Biden because of swings in the Philadelphia and Pittsburgh suburbs, as well as stronger showings in places such as Lackawanna County in the west and

Erie County in the east. In the "Rust Belt Central" states, the Twin Ports region of northeast Minnesota and northwest Wisconsin delivered again for the Democrats. In the west, strong support among Native Americans helped Biden cut the Republican-rural advantage in Arizona, while Colorado's high-amenity resort towns in the Rockies fortified Democratic margins in Denver and helped to offset the strong Republican vote in Colorado Springs, the Centennial State's second-largest MSA.

CONCLUSION

Just as the electoral college has an acknowledged "tipping point" state that decides the presidency, a swing state has a putative "swing spot." Located somewhere at the edges of a swing-state big metro is the space where one party or the other runs out of votes, and a state swings red or blue at the ballot box. For the Democrats, long the party of urban America (Rodden 2019), continuing ethnic and racial diversification and population concentration in million-plus metros is positioning the party to expand its support among the growth segments of the electorate (Judis and Teixeria 2002). If Democratic candidates push their support far enough into the suburbs, then the "rest of state" vote may be insufficient to deliver the margins Republicans need to win statewide elections.

By executing this strategy in 2020, Joe Biden was able to regain the Rust Belt states—Michigan, Pennsylvania, and Wisconsin—that delivered the presidency for Donald Trump in 2016 and flip Sun Belt states—Arizona and Georgia—that the party last won in the 1990s. In 2016, Hillary Clinton was caught between diminishing Democratic margins in the Rust Belt and yet to be realized Democratic gains in the Sun Belt (Brownstein 2016; Damore and Lang 2016). Four year later, Biden bridged these regional differences to secure the presidency. Beyond 2020, the analysis presented here suggests that the Democrats' long-term future lies in the rapidly urbanizing and diversifying Sun Belt swing states and their million-plus metros (Damore, Lang, and Danielsen 2021a).

Our analysis also reinforces the importance of scale for understanding the emergence of a pan-metro identity and the consequences this has for partisan voting patterns. In 2020, Biden won every state where a single million-plus metro constitutes half or more of a state's population (see note 2). Moreover, after the 2020 election the Democrats held the ten U.S. Senate seats in the five swing states—Arizona, Colorado, Georgia, Minnesota, and Nevada—where a single million-plus metro comprises more than 50 percent of a state's population. In 2018 and 2020, six of these seats, all in the Sun Belt, flipped to the Democrats—two in Arizona and Georgia and one each in Colorado and Nevada.

The results in states with multiple million-plus metros are less clear cut. In 2020, Biden won Arizona, Michigan, Pennsylvania, and Virginia. Besides Pennsylvania, the other three states have the smallest populations among the eight swing states with multiple million-plus metros. Trump won Florida, North Carolina, Ohio, and Texas, which rank respectively third, ninth, seventh, and second in population among the fifty states.

Given their size, these states feature several medium to large-scale population centers. Although these areas are less than a million residents, combined they are home to substantial shares of their states' populations. Because the urban landscape in these states is less cohesive, the blue metro versus red state tension may be less pronounced. Or put differently, it is easy to understand how Georgians or Nevadans who live outside of Atlanta or Las Vegas may feel alienated from those dwelling in their state's million-plus metro and vice versa. Similar attitudes may be less prevailing in states with multiple big metros, particularly when these metros are geographically dispersed.

Certainly, it is tempting to attribute the 2020 Democratic shifts in million-plus metros to Donald Trump's anti-urban rhetoric and politics. To the degree that Trump's presence wanes and the Democrats struggle to govern, the Republicans should regain some of the suburban turf the party lost since Trump's emergence. Indeed, how these voters swing in future elections will determine if the traditional urban-rural divide is maintained or a division between big metros and the rest of a state emerges. In *Blue Metros, Red States* (Damore, Lang, and Danielsen 2021a, 398), we suggest that different suburb types provide better targets for each party by noting the following:

> American suburbs are now so large-scale and varied that it is impossible to declare that either party maintains a lock on the suburban vote. Republicans continue to hold the line in conventional suburbs that are auto-dominated, mostly white, consist mainly of single-family detached homes on large lots, and lie toward the metropolitan edge. But Democrats are rapidly gaining ground in urbanizing suburbs, especially in the Sun Belt, where multifamily housing mixes with commercial uses that are increasingly served by new transit systems.

In *Boomburbs: The Rise of America's Accidental Cities* Lang and LuFurgy (2007) identify fast-growing cities that fifty years ago were little more than bedroom communities adjacent to large-scale metros. More common in the Sun Belt, these municipalities have now grown by double-digit rates for decades and are socially and economically integrated with their principal cities. In fact, many suburbs have grown so large that they now eclipse the populations of traditional "big cities" (Damore, Lang, and Danielsen 2021a). Consider that more people now live in Henderson, Nevada, than in Saint

Louis, Missouri, or that the population of Arlington, Texas exceeds that of New Orleans, Louisiana.

Over time, many of these suburbs have densified and diversified, often because of migrants from blue states. Decades of double-digit population increases also means that many suburbs can no longer accommodate large-lot, single-family homes. These growth constraints necessitate infilling with mid-rise, mixed-used developments. Increasingly, suburbs are connecting to their urban downtowns via light rail. Light rail often induces changes in land-use patterns and housing types that accelerate suburban urbanization. Through the adoption of some form of rail and vertical infill, many "boomburbs" are urbanizing in form and politics. In the coming years, how partisan support ebbs and flows in these spaces will determine statewide election outcomes across the swing states and ultimately, which party controls the levers of power in Washington D.C.

NOTES

1. States were included if they contained at least one census-defined Metropolitan Statistical Area (MSA) with a population of at least one million residents and a 2016 presidential election margin of ten percentage points or less. The first of these criteria excluded three states that were within ten percentage points in 2016 (Iowa, Maine, and New Hampshire) but lack an MSA with a population of at least one million residents.

2. In 2016, the only such states that Hillary Clinton lost were Arizona and Georgia (Damore, Lang, and Danielsen 2021b). Alaska and Hawaii also have MSAs that account for more than half of their populations but the populations of these MSAs are less than a million residents. Hillary Clinton and Job Biden won Hawaii and Donald Trump carried Alaska in 2016 and 2020.

3. These estimates are derived from Forstall and Fitzsimmons (1993) and from the authors' calculations of census data.

4. For discussions of the issues surrounding the decline and measurement of segregation at different geographic levels, see Denton (2013), Logan (2013), and Vigdor (2013).

Chapter Nine

Turning the Natural State Red

The Rise of the GOP in Arkansas

John C. Davis

The 2020 elections in Arkansas continued to solidify the state's identity as a heavily Republican state. The GOP increased their strongholds in both chambers of the Arkansas General Assembly, made inroads in the few remaining rural pockets of the state where old Democratic loyalties had remained, and President Donald Trump earned an even higher share of the state's overall vote—from just over 60 percent in 2016 to over 62 percent in 2020. Only a decade prior, the Democratic incumbent governor won every county in the state, which had been dominated by the party since the late nineteenth century, and in which Republicans regularly struggled to recruit candidates for elected offices. This chapter reports the factors leading to a historic shift in the partisan politics of Arkansas and serves as a case study of a state that has undergone such a partisan change in a relatively short period[1].

Since V. O. Key's seminal work on Southern politics (1949), in which he wrote, "Perhaps in Arkansas we have the one-party in its most undefiled and undiluted form," (183) the state has fascinated state politics scholars and those who study the region's politics, in particular. For decades, the peculiar situation of Arkansas' politics had been that it remained a solid one-party Democratic state even as other Southern states had begun the transition to reliably Republican. Until recently, the GOP in Arkansas—when the party could claim a victory—would be frustrated by a failure for those wins to result in a lasting momentum capable of large-scale partisan change. The landscape was still heavily Democratic. However, following the 2010 election cycle, the balance of political power in the Natural State changed in a big way. In just three election cycles (2010, 2012, and 2014), Arkansas went from one of the most Democratic states in the country to one of the most Republican. More recently, in 2020, the GOP extended its political dominance in the state.

Arkansas transitioned into perhaps the most ardently Republican state in a matter of a few years. While the dramatic shift in the partisan makeup of Arkansas officeholders may appear to have happened almost overnight, the rise of the Republicans in Arkansas was years, if not, decades, in the making. Changes in voter preference at the top of the ticket in the 1960s, generational replacement in Arkansas' political power structure and systemic changes in the 1990s, party organizational strategies coming to fruition in the 2000s, and a more nationalized and polarized electorate were the culmination of factors that resulted in seemingly sudden electoral success for the GOP. Furthermore, the party's wins in 2012 and 2014 have proven to not be outliers—Arkansas Republicans can now claim sustained dominance in a state that was arguably the most Democratic in the nation as recently as 2008 (Davis, Dowdle, and Giammo 2017; Davis, Dowdle, and Giammo 2021). The following is a study on partisan change in Arkansas, but I contend the findings could also be applied to explain the dynamics of partisan changes in other states, more generally.

THREE GENERATIONS OF THE
MODERN GOP IN ARKANSAS

First Generation, 1966–1992

The first generation of the modern Republican Party in Arkansas began in 1966 with the statewide elections of Winthrop Rockefeller, the first Republican governor in Arkansas since Reconstruction, and John Paul Hammerschmidt to the US House of Representatives. Governor Rockefeller, who first ran and lost in 1964, would be reelected to another two-year term in 1968, only to lose a bid for a third term in 1970. At the time of Rockefeller's historic victory in 1966, and subsequent reelection two years later, the Republican Party's national brand was undergoing a dramatic change following the Civil Rights Act of 1964 and the party's nomination of Arizona senator Barry Goldwater for president of the United States. Rockefeller, a reform-minded progressive, represented a wing within a party that was losing influence. Rockefeller built a party organization in Arkansas in his likeness, with his own personal fortune, which would not be sustained after his departure from the political scene (Urwin 1991).

Nationally, during and immediately following Rockefeller's two terms as governor of Arkansas, the Republican Party began to shift to a more consistently conservative position on issues ranging from civil rights to state's rights, feminism, and abortion. It seems as if Rockefeller was investing his fortune in a progressive movement in Arkansas, his party's brand was moving away from him. In short, Rockefeller's historical electoral success was purely his own, and failed to translate into coattails for others running under his party banner. Meanwhile, the more conservative national positions might well have been in line with many Arkansans at the time, and their approval is reflected in their presidential vote choices beginning in 1972—when Arkansans begin a pattern of favoring the Republican presidential candidate in all cycles—with the exceptions of Carter and Clinton—that continues today. However, the Republican Party of Arkansas largely failed to connect the GOP successes at the top of the ticket to statewide and local races in a state that remained overwhelmingly Democratic.

The 1970s and 1980s for Republicans in Arkansas were—for the most part—bleak. Despite the occasional upset victory—such as the defeat of Bill Clinton in his reelection bid for governor in 1980 to Republican businessman Frank White—the only consistent electoral success enjoyed by Republicans in the state was for the party's presidential nominees. When Republicans were victorious, it was usually in an open seat race. For example, in 1978, Ed Bethune, a Republican attorney and former FBI agent who had previously lost a contest for state's attorney general, sought and won election for an open US House seat that encompassed Little Rock—the state's largest city—and surrounding areas, only to then challenge a Democratic US Senator, David Pryor, and lose in 1984. Such victories were rare and short-lived.

The post-Rockefeller years were a time of transformation for the GOP in Arkansas. The party was wrestled away from Rockefeller loyalists for a more conservative, Goldwater/Reagan-inspired brand, as reflected by changes in party leadership and platform (Blair 1988). Despite Arkansas' voting population being largely white and moderate to conservative, with an already established reputation for favoring Republicans for president, Democrats in the state remained effective at maintaining personal connections with voters in a state accustomed to more parochial, personality-based politics.

The Big Three

The practice of voting for the Republican presidential nominee while still largely favoring Democratic candidates down the ticket, or ticket-splitting, provided a window of opportunity for state Republicans, as Democrats in Arkansas were faced with the challenge of distancing themselves from their national party's stances—a practice the "Big Three" (Democrats Bumpers, Pryor, and Clinton) developed into something of a political art form in the 1970s, 1980s, and 1990s. In her study of these three iconic Democrats who are credited, in part, with stemming the tide of Republican gains in the state until their political ambitions or political retirements pulled them from state politics, Diane Blair (1995) wrote that these three men, at least one of which appeared on the ballot every cycle between 1970 and 1994, helped maintain Democratic political power in the state as its neighbors began the process of historical partisan change in the 1980s and 1990s. The presence of Bumpers, Pryor, and Clinton would be felt well into the early twenty-first century, as their collective brands extended beyond their own names, and their approach of personal politics transcended party for many in the state who otherwise would have likely favored Republicans in state and local races.

While the party had witnessed electoral successes not previously seen in the twentieth century, the first generation of the modern Republican Party in Arkansas fell short of building upon these successes in a way that created a consistent electoral momentum. Rather, this period is filled with a series of triumphs and defeats, victories in fits and starts. Certainly, the party was stronger in 1990 than it was in 1966, but compared to its neighbors in the southern United States, Arkansas remained a strong Democratic state. The "Reagan Revolution" did not transform Arkansas politics (Wekkin 1998) in the same obvious ways seen in other southern states. However, the 1990s would be a decade of opportunities for party building and growth.

Second Generation, 1992–2010

The Second Generation begins with the election cycle of 1992. That general election was a pivotal moment in the state's political history. Arkansas governor Bill Clinton announced his intention to seek his party's nomination for president of the United States in October 1991. Clinton would then go on to secure his party's nomination for president and unseat George H. W. Bush, the Republican incumbent. Clinton's victory is significant to the eventual overtaking of the state's politics by the GOP: it created a political power vacuum by transplanting a considerable amount of up-and-coming state Democratic political talent to Washington, DC—opening the door for more two-party competition.

In addition to favoring their own governor, Bill Clinton, in the 1992 presidential election, Arkansas voters made other impactful decisions for the state's political future. In 1992, Arkansas voters supported a ballot initiative that imposed some of the strictest legislative term limits in the United States. Once enacted a few years later, legislative term limits took away the advantages of incumbency for Democrats in the General Assembly—creating opportunities for the GOP. As expected, over time, term limits did result in more Republican legislators in the General Assembly as longtime Democratic incumbents were forced out of their positions, resulting in open seat contests (English 2003).

Another race in 1992 held significant, if not immediately obvious, ramifications for the partisan balance of the state. One of the state's US Senate seats, occupied by former Democratic governor Dale Bumpers since 1975, was on the ballot in 1992. Bumpers' Republican opponent was a relatively unknown pastor and broadcaster from south Arkansas, Mike Huckabee. Despite losing to Bumpers in 1992, Huckabee's underdog campaign garnered nearly 39 percent of the vote against the popular incumbent in that contest (Secretary of State). Immediately following his Senate bid defeat, Huckabee was recruited by then-GOP chairman Asa Hutchinson to run for lieutenant governor in a 1993 special election to fill the vacancy created when, pursuant to the state constitution, Democratic lieutenant governor, Jim Guy Tucker, succeeded Clinton. Mike Huckabee defeated the Democrat in the race, Nate Coulter, by a narrow margin to fill the position of lieutenant governor in the special election.

Huckabee would assume the role of governor in the summer of 1996 following Jim Guy Tucker's resignation (Wekkin 1998), becoming only the third Republican governor in the state since Reconstruction. The impact of Huckabee's tenure as governor on the Republican Party of Arkansas was significant in many ways. According to Huckabee, appointments were especially crucial to the long-term success of the GOP in the state. The state's constitution affords the governor significant appointment power to state boards and commissions. The governor of Arkansas is responsible for the appointment of approximately 350 boards and commissions—ranging from the obscure to some of the most powerful unelected political posts in the state. According to Huckabee, his ability to serve more than ten years in office and thus fill every board or commission assignment, thereby creating a GOP political bench, was the most significant thing he did to advance his party in the state (Huckabee 2021). Before Huckabee, Republicans had only had three two-year terms in more than one hundred years to exercise appointment powers in ways that rewarded party loyalists, and—most importantly—cultivated hundreds of potential political talents who might one day run as Republicans in the state. Huckabee's more than ten years as governor meant, among other things, he would use appointments to boards and commissions to reward party faithful and cultivate a new political generation of Arkansans who were less loyal to the state's Democratic history.

Another significant event during this time addressed the issue of primary ballot access in Arkansas—a legal challenge would aid the Republican Party's efforts to recruit candidates to run for local elections and make it possible for more voters to participate in GOP primaries. According to Asa Hutchinson, who led the lawsuit on behalf of the GOP in Arkansas, the state had long required parties to fund their primaries. This resulted in the beleaguered GOP, in some cases, being able to afford only one primary voting location in a county, while the well-funded Democrats would have several locations (Hutchinson 2021). In 1995, the 8th Circuit Court of Appeals ruled the practice of partisan-funded primaries were a violation of the Fourteenth Amendment of the US Constitution and resulted in state-funded primaries and polling sites—a significant leveling of the playing field for the party. In a state with open primaries, this change was the beginning of the end of an era when virtually all races were settled in the Democratic primaries as a means of practical necessity.

While Huckabee was reelected in 2002, the GOP picked up the occasional open seat in congressional races, and the state's voters continued to prefer Republican candidates for President, the 2000s highlighted the continued ability of Arkansas Democrats to separate themselves from their national party's more liberal brand. Dating back to at least the early 1990s, Republicans had made attempts to convince Arkansans that their party, at all levels, aligned with the average voter's views and to draw contrasts between the GOP and the Democratic Party (Hutchinson 2021). By 2001, with the conclusion of Clinton's second presidential term, the "Big Three" were no longer serving in elected office. While this could have allowed for the popularity of George W. Bush (who won Arkansas in 2000 and 2004) or Governor Huckabee to create coattails to lower offices, this did not occur in any significant way. By this time, Arkansas politics were unique in how the state remained Democratic as its southern neighbors shifted Republican (Blair and Barth 2005).

While there are likely alternative explanations, it seems the fact that there was no Democratic president at this time, and the Democrats serving Arkansans in Congress were talented at walking a more moderate line than their copartisans from most other states, kept Arkansans somewhat insulated from the more liberal national brand of Democratic politics. Arkansas voters could somehow still disengage from the nationalization of partisan politics in a way that continued to advantage Democrats in the state. Meanwhile, Republicans had their own struggles. For example, as recently as 2008, Republicans failed to field a candidate in a US Senate contest against a one-term incumbent.

Despite mixed results by the GOP at the close of the first decade of the twenty-first century, fundamental changes were occurring that would allow the party to capitalize on a strong election cycle with odds in their favor. Following the 2008 election cycle, wherein the party had failed to nominate someone to run in the cycle's biggest in-state contest and even lost ground in the state's General Assembly, the GOP sought to professionalize their state party and enhance the organization's outreach efforts. In 2009, for the first time in the state party's history, the chair position became a salaried, full-time job. Recalling the state of the GOP in Arkansas when he took over, Chairman Doyle Webb said that "2009 was a difficult year for us. We had trouble fundraising and recruiting candidates, but we could see things happening" (Carter 2019).

The Second Generation concluded with new opportunities for the party through open seats, legal reforms to primaries, and a vacated governorship, resulting in a GOP governor for over a decade, hundreds of recent political appointees now establishing a Republican network within the state, and—later— a state party organization attempting to make strides to capture electoral opportunities. While these components did not yield immediate results (Dowlde and Giammo 2010) on their own, these variables later combined to create an opportunity to seize on a political moment and yield sustained success.

Third Generation—2011 to today

Following the 1992 election cycle, Arkansas Democrats could claim the White House, along with an overwhelming number of positions in the state. However, 1992 also provided opportunities for the GOP. In particular: a special election in 1993 placed Republican Mike Huckabee in the lieutenant governor's seat, while many young Democrats moved on to Washington to serve in or around the Clinton administration, leaving a political vacuum of sorts for the future; and voter-supported term limits created open seats and more competitive contests for GOP candidates. The close of the 2008 cycle, similarly, favored Democrats in the state. The GOP, as noted earlier, failed to recruit a candidate for the highest in-state race on the ballot that cycle, the party organization was struggling, and despite the signs that the party was poised for success from events which occurred the decade before (reforms to primaries, a GOP governor, continued support for Republican presidential candidates, etc.), the future must have looked murky, at best. The election cycle in 2008 may have been a low point—a floor—for the modern GOP, but events quickly put into motion a dramatic and historical shift in voters' preferences in the state, and the party would become poised to not only take advantage of the favorable climate in the short term, but harness sustained success—something that the GOP had never managed to do in the state.

The power of Democrats' personal politics in the state would abruptly end at the close of the first decade of the twenty-first century, at a time when the first African American (and non-Southern Democrat since 1960) is elected president, and the national brands of both parties could no longer be divorced from their state and local levels in Arkansas. Despite success that, up to that point, was unprecedented, the end of the second generation of the GOP in Arkansas saw a party struggling to compete. Following the 2010 election cycle, Republicans picked up one Senate seat (defeating an incumbent Democrat), two open US House seats (one of which had been held by a Democrat since Reconstruction), some state constitutional offices, and several seats in the General Assembly.

The 2010 cycle was a very successful one for the GOP. However, Republicans in the state had seen success before, in short bursts, in the first and second generations previously discussed. The difference post-2010 was the ability of the party to enjoy sustained success. Over the following two election cycles, the GOP would hold all state constitutional offices (including governor), another US Senate seat (again, beating an incumbent Democrat), all four US House seats, majorities in both chambers of the General Assembly, and would even make extraordinary gains in county and local offices. In four years, Arkansas had gone from one of the most Democratic states to one of the most Republican—trading the one-party dominance of one party for that of the other.

While it might be tempting to see Arkansas politics today and say, "Well, it is no surprise that the state's politics are dominated by Republicans. After all, Arkansas is predominately white, rural, conservative, and in a geographic region that, up until recently, has been largely dominated by Republicans for decades," such a cursory glance at the state minimizes the historical significance of the quick and dominating series of political events and conceals the multiple elements that led to the party's growth.

GOP Party Organization

For decades, as Arkansas Democrats enjoyed unparalleled and uncontested dominance in the state, its political structure was loosely built around individuals instead of any organized entity (Key 1949; Blair 1988; Blair and Barth 2005; Dowdle and Wekkin 2007). In 1999, as Democrats continued to be the dominant party in the state, Aldrich, Gomez, and Griffin conducted the "State Party Organizations Study." This survey assessed the self-reported roles and responsibilities of state party organizations. In 2013, Davis and Kurlowski (Davis 2014; Davis and Kurlowski 2017) sought to update and build upon this previous work to evaluate the changes that have taken place with regard to the operations and organizational strength of state parties. Both major-party organizations in Arkansas participated in each study. Taken together, these studies cover a period of significant change in Arkansas politics that allows for comparisons between the GOP organization in Arkansas in the late 1990s and early 2010s.

On the whole, these studies suggest the Democratic Party of Arkansas and the Arkansas Republican Party each enhanced the organizational structure of their respective state parties. However, the Arkansas Republican Party's state organization gains proved to be more impactful as it improved the party's ability to recruit, coordinate, brand, fundraise, and assist its candidates for office. The state GOP made considerable gains between the years 1999 and 2013 that helped the party reach its goals of winning elections and maintaining electoral successes from one cycle to the next—something it had struggled to do in the past (Dowdle and Wekkin 2007). Meanwhile, the Democratic state operation enhanced its capabilities, but also suffered from financial instability (Moritz 2019) and recruitment struggles—having their candidate for the US Senate drop out shortly after the close of the fling period in 2020—while the Republican Party in Arkansas seemed to flourish to previously unknown heights and national prominence as one of the most stridently Republican states in the country (Hebda 2019). Since the 2013 survey (conducted at a pivotal time in the party's electoral success), the GOP in Arkansas has enjoyed historical success and Democrats find themselves in much the same situation Republicans found themselves decades ago—the other party in a one-party dominated state.

The Nationalization of Arkansas Politics

While it might have been difficult to see immediately following the 2008 elections, the GOP was poised to gain significant ground in Arkansas but needed a catalyst to spark the partisan change in the state that many neighboring states had undergone. The election of President Obama that year, and the passage of the Affordable Care Act, led to enormous backlash in Arkansas. While it was well established by this point that a majority of Arkansas voters often preferred GOP presidential candidates, the visceral dislike for Obama and his policies from large segments of Arkansans, for the first time ever, spilled over into the down-ticket races in 2010 and onward. In a PBS story in 2014, Roby Brock, host of a popular business and politics television show who also conducts regular political polls in Arkansas, was quoted as saying, "Obama 'has been toxic for Arkansas Democrats,' that 'there is a cultural disconnect,' and that the unpopularity of Obama and his policies 'have been exploited expertly by Arkansas Republicans'" (PBS 2014). Brock's comments capture the disapproval of President Obama—particularly, it seemed, among some of those voters who had previously voted for Republicans for president, but still preferred Democrats further down the ballot.

While the extent to which President Obama's race played a factor in the negative reactions among portions of white Americans, including many of those in Arkansas, can be debated, it is well-documented that there is a strong relationship between voters' race, attitudes toward people of other races, and their support (or lack thereof) of Obama—particularly in the South (Maxwell

2021; Maxwell and Shields 2019). Among southern states, Arkansas is unique in that it has a larger portion of whites among its population than its neighbors. In Arkansas alone, some of the most dramatic shifts in voting behavior to occur during Obama's presidency took place in the state's whitest counties (Barth and Parry 2018).

At this point, the nationalization of state politics, due in large part to social media and cable news outlets such as Fox News, was poised to overwhelm the state (Vickery 2021). The parochial, personality-based, retail politics that, in many ways, seemed to benefit popular, personable Democratic incumbents were coming to an end as the distinctions between national and state politics began to blur in the state.

The GOP's rise in Arkansas outlived the two terms of the Obama presidency. President Obama was not only the first African American elected to the office, he was also the first nonsouthern Democrat to win a presidential election since Kennedy in 1960. To Arkansans, particularly rural whites in the state, the perception was that Obama was not relatable, in ways that transcended or complicated their previously held personal views on race in America. For many white Arkansans—who had rarely been confronted with issues regarding race and other social equity issues—President Obama may have seemed to be pushing boundaries perceived to be outside of the mainstream for these individuals (Barth 2021). Prior to the 2010s, Democrats in Arkansas were largely successful at convincing voters of their moderation and "common sense" appeals when Clinton was in the White House and were even more successful in perpetuating that narrative when George W. Bush—a Republican—was the most visual partisan in the country.

Whether a native son was in the White House or a Republican, Arkansas Democrats had been able to expertly navigate the political landscape and operate around distinctions from their own party's national brand and the candidate-centered narratives they utilized when seeking reelection. This worked for Democrats until 2010. Obama, in many ways the embodiment of a more diverse and liberal Democratic Party, simply overwhelmed the state and local politics of Arkansas. The state GOP had long been positioning and aligning themselves with their party's national brand, a consistency that has served them well in the last decade with rising conservative sentiment in the state and many other parts of the nation.

Arkansas Democrats could not effectively navigate more nationalized politics in an environment where a majority of voters were not only rejecting the national Democratic politics, but also disavowing themselves of any Democratic attachment down-ticket; the GOP was poised to take advantage. The dam had broken. The partisan shift in the state, beginning in 2010 and

Table 9.1.   Arkansas General Assembly House and Senate Membership by Party, 1992–2020

	Senate		House	
Election Year	Democrats	Republicans	Democrats	Republicans
1992	30	5	89	10
1994	28	7	88	12
1996	28	6	86	14
1998	29	6	76	24
2000	27	8	72	28
2002	27	8	70	30
2004	27	8	72	28
2006	27	8	75	25
2008	27	8	71	28
2010	20	15	55	45
2012	14	21	49	51
2014	11	24	36	64
2016	9	26	27	73
2018	9	26	26	74
2020	7	28	22	78

Sources: Wekkin 2003; Arkansas Secretary of State

becoming more pronounced over time, is perhaps best illustrated by examining the partisan balance in the Arkansas General Assembly.

Table 9.1 reports the partisan makeup of the House in the Arkansas General Assembly from 1992 to 2020. As recently as 2008—a pivotal time in the state's politics, Democrats gained seats. However, in 2010, Republicans picked up a significant number of seats and, since then, have expanded their advantage in the chamber. This table also reports the partisan makeup of the Arkansas Senate. Like to the House, Democrats lose several seats between the 2010 and 2012 cycles as the Republicans now mirror the Democrats' 1990s majorities. Again, as in the House, Republicans do very well in the 2010, 2012, and 2014 cycles, but also continue to expand their majority in the Senate in 2016, 2018, and 2020.

Republicans Gain Among "Independent" Voters

For several decades, polls noted that anywhere from one-quarter to one-third of Arkansans self-identified "Independent" (Ranchino 1972; Arkansas Poll 2020). Political changes had been afoot for some time, particularly in rural "swing" counties that had once been among the most staunchly Democratic (Blair 1988) but had shown a willingness to "swing" to Republican candidates at the top of the ticket over the last quarter of the twentieth century

Table 9.2.   **Partisan Identification in Arkansas**

Year	Republican	Democrat	Independent	Other
2000	23%	36%	35%	9%
2001	27%	33%	32%	5%
2002	28%	33%	33%	3%
2003	24%	38%	31%	4%
2004	30%	35%	28%	3%
2005	23%	36%	33%	4%
2006	23%	36%	33%	3%
2007	24%	39%	30%	3%
2008	24%	35%	33%	7%
2009	24%	33%	34%	7%
2010	21%	28%	42%	7%
2011	26%	31%	34%	6%
2012	29%	31%	33%	3%
2013	24%	30%	37%	4%
2014	28%	31%	33%	3%
2015	27%	32%	32%	3%
2016	29%	25%	37%	3%
2017	29%	24%	35%	5%
2018	32%	28%	32%	6%
2019	35%	23%	31%	9%
2020	40%	21%	33%	6%

Source: 2020 Arkansas Poll

(Barth and Parry 2005). Arkansans stubbornly stuck to their party identifications, as seen in table 9.2. From 2000 to 2020, the portion of those polled who reported being an "Independent" consistently hovers to roughly one-third of the sample while the percentage of those polled appear to decrease among Democratic identifiers and modestly increase for Republicans until more recently, when the GOP began to have a plurality of those identified. Compared over time, the percentage of respondents reporting to identify as Republican in 2000 nearly doubles by 2020 while Democratic identifiers drop by a margin of nearly 15 percent.

Table 9.3 reports the results from a follow-up question from the Arkansas Poll data to determine for which party many of the self-described "independents" lean. Since 2008, Republicans have held the advantage among those who identify as "independents," but lean to a party. The figures in parentheses are the percentage of respondents who were "likely voters." Here, the trend of independents favoring Republicans is more pronounced.

In 2020, a plurality of Arkansans identified as Republican. Furthermore, self-identified independents, long a mainstay in Arkansas politics, also heavily favored the GOP. These polling data track well with the electoral success

Table 9.3. **Independents Leaning to a Party**

Year	Republican	Democrat	Independent
2000	35% (39%)	25% (26%)	35% (30%)
2001	29%	36%	31%
2002	30% (31%)	32% (34%)	33% (33%)
2003	33%	34%	33%
2004	39% (41%)	31% (32%)	30% (26%)
2005	30%	35%	32%
2006	33% (35%)	34% (34%)	30% (23%)
2007	34%	37%	29%
2008	35% (38%)	30% (29%)	33% (31%)
2009	39%	32%	27%
2010	44% (50%)	21% (16%)	33% (33%)
2011	42% (48%)	29% (28%)	26% (22%)
2012	41% (46%)	26% (22%)	28% (27%)
2013	43% (51%)	21% (22%)	31% (22%)
2014	38% (43%)	25% (23%)	30% (28%)
2015	42% (52%)	23% (20%)	30% (25%)
2016	37% (45%)	18% (19%)	40% (35%)
2017	37% (38%)	26% (26%)	32% (31%)
2018	39% (43%)	25% (25%)	35% (32%)
2019	40% (43%)	27% (31%)	31% (27%)
2020	45% (52%)	32% (30%)	19% (15%)

Source: 2020 Arkansas Poll; Note: "Likely Voters" in parentheses

of the Republican Party over the last decade. Clearly, the turning point was in the period between 2008 and 2014, when Arkansas shifted from overwhelmingly Democratic to Republican with arguably no period of strong statewide two-party competition. The 2020 election cycle further illustrates the dominance of the GOP among the state's electorate.

CONCLUSION

In order to understand the more recent shift in the state's politics, this study presents the partisan change in Arkansas in three parts, or generations. From the 1960s to the early 1990s, the GOP's electoral victories were rare, short-lived, and limited to open-seat contests. The success of Winthrop Rockefeller in 1966—while historic—failed to usher in a new Republican era in the state. The first generation of the modern GOP in Arkansas closes with another bruising election cycle for Republicans in 1992. However, that election cycle also brought opportunity and ushered in the next generation of the modern party in the state. Systematic reforms to elections in the state, term limits, and luck provided numerous chances for the GOP to capitalize on the changing political environment in Arkansas in the 1990s and early 2000s, but again, the party found itself on the losing end more often than not. However, the second generation allowed the party to lay a groundwork to eventually seize political opportunity, finally realize lasting electoral success. The election of President Obama, and the subsequent fallout and negative views held particularly by many white Southerners (including those in Arkansas) was the catalyst the Arkansas GOP needed to separate a large portion of voters who had otherwise supported GOP presidential candidates in prior contests, but—up to that point—often still related to Democrats at the state and local levels. This political moment could have simply resulted in one or two positive election cycles for Republicans in Arkansas. However, beginning in 2010, elections in Arkansas became more nationalized. By this time, the GOP had a strong state party organization that was more capable of fundraising, assisting in the recruitment of candidates at the local level, and effectively branding Democrats as out of touch with "Arkansas values." This hastened a steady increase in Arkansans identifying as Republicans and a shift in partisan attachment among the large portion of self-identified independents who began to lean Republican.

The story of partisan change in Arkansas is a story of white conservatives, over a relatively short amount of time, rejecting their generations-old voting habits, and voting more consistently Republican. It may be tempting to see 2010 as the stand-alone watershed moment that set the course for where the state's politics are today, but that would fail to recognize other pivotal points in the state's political history that had previously failed to usher in this level of lasting dominance the GOP now enjoys in the state. The current state of Arkansas partisan politics is the result of a culmination of events and efforts, successes, and failures, dating back decades, that enabled the GOP in the state to finally seize the current political moment in a way that it had previously not been able accomplish.

Today, Arkansas is an overwhelmingly Republican state. Despite a smattering of Democratic pockets, the recent growth of the GOP is undeniable and sustained. While the 2020 cycle highlighted how changing demographics can impact the competitiveness of statewide elections of some Southern states, Arkansas does not, at the moment, appear poised to join the likes of Georgia or Texas anytime soon. The 2020 United States Census revealed only modest growth (3.3%) in the state and much of the overall gain in population was concentrated in one corner of Arkansas. Over the last decade, two-thirds of the state's counties recorded a loss in population (Hightower 2018). Furthermore, the state populace remains relatively rural and largely white at a time when these factors generally favor GOP candidates.

Beyond the state's demographics advantaging the GOP for the foreseeable future, Republicans in Arkansas are now able to take advantage of political processes in the state that once frustrated the party's progress. For the first time ever, in 2021, Republicans enjoyed complete control of the state's reapportionment process. With supermajorities in both chambers of the state legislature, and control of all seats on the Arkansas Board of Apportionment, the GOP was able to protect its gains made within the state and complicate Democrats' attempts to recapture lost ground. In a remarkably short amount of time, Arkansas has gone from a state almost entirely dominated by Democratic politics to one that heavily advantages Republicans—likely for years to come.

NOTE

1. This research is part of a larger project in coordination with David and Barbara Pryor Center for Arkansas Oral and Visual History of the University of Arkansas.

Part III

PARTISAN ACTIVITY

Chapter Ten

Nationalized Congressional Finance

Evidence from 2018 and 2020

Kenneth M. Miller

All ten of the most expensive Senate races in US history as well as all ten of the most expensive House races in US history were in 2018 and 2020 (Gratzinger 2020; Miller 2020). One race among them was especially unusual. In the 2020 Kentucky Senate race, Amy McGrath took on Republican Senate Majority Leader Mitch McConnell. McGrath had never held elective office and her previous campaign experience was a single losing campaign for a US House seat in 2018. McGrath never led in any preelection polls and her campaign was considered a long shot by most observers. The independent expenditure arm of the Democratic Senatorial Campaign Committee, the principal party organization for supporting Democratic Senate candidates, spent nothing on the race. But McGrath's campaign against McConnell took in $96 million in receipts.

Against this backdrop—and in the wake of a sudden spike in Democratic online contributions after the passing of Supreme Court Justice Ruth Bader Ginsburg—Democratic senator Brian Schatz of Hawaii tweeted that Democrats should donate to an independent group run by party veterans: "Don't pick your favorite candidate or the one you've heard of. Give here. I repeat, this money goes directly to the most competitive races, not just the most famous candidates" (Garrison 2020).

The rate of increase in campaign spending has accelerated in the last two election cycles, fueled by a larger scale of both individual donations and organizational independent expenditures. But along with the increase came new inefficiencies in the distribution of funds, as some of the money donated to candidates headed to different races than where independent groups chose to spend.

This study of congressional campaign expenditures in 2018 and 2020 describes three key characteristics of the current campaign finance landscape.

First, the financing of congressional campaigns is a fully nationalized system where candidates are often outspent by outside groups and the campaigns draw on donors from outside of their states and districts. Second, the parties are highly efficient distributors of resources compared to nonparty interest groups, more keenly responsive to the competitiveness of the race. Third, the parties are efficient distributors in another way, drawing back their support from candidates who are well financed by direct donations to their campaigns. Allocating resources according to candidate need has its limits however, as ideologically motivated donors have made more "negative" contributions to challengers of incumbents the donors dislike and some overfunded candidates in Senate contests remain as a result.

EXPENSIVE AND NATIONALIZED CAMPAIGNS

Total spending in congressional campaigns has increased dramatically in the past two election cycles (see figure 10.1). Even after adjusting for inflation, increases in congressional campaign spending in the 2018 and 2020 cycles have dwarfed the rise in spending first attributed to the effects of the *Citizens United* and *Speechnow.org* decisions in 2010. In inflation-adjusted dollars, congressional campaign spending in 2018 jumped by 40 percent compared to the previous midterm cycle. Total spending in congressional races in 2020 nearly doubled (up 95%) compared to the previous presiden-

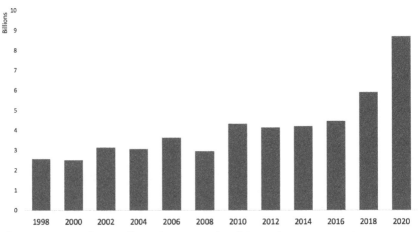

Figure 10.1. Total Expenditures in Congressional Campaigns, 1998–2020

Note: Yearly totals represent all spending in US House and US Senate campaigns by candidate committees excluding candidate-to-candidate transfers, all spending by party committees and other 527 committees, and all other independent expenditures reported to the FEC. Figures expressed in 2020 constant dollars.

Center for Responsive Politics (opensecrets.org) accessed June 21, 2021.

tial cycle in 2016. By contrast, the previous change in midterm spending (2010 to 2014) was slightly negative by 3 percent and the previous change in congressional campaign spending in a presidential cycle (2012 to 2016) was a modest increase of 8 percent.

The expenditures in congressional elections are made by a wide array of increasingly national actors. The central actors in campaign spending are a candidate's authorized committees. Candidates are narrowly focused on their own (re)election and typically spend every dollar they take in on their own race unless victory is certain (Jacobson 1985–1986). Safe incumbent candidates will serve a broader interest by transferring funds out to party candidates in greater peril, but these transfers are usually done only by the safest senior incumbents (Heberlig and Larson 2005). While candidates are almost entirely focused on their own race, their funding is often national in scope. House and Senate incumbents receive much of their individual itemized donations from outside of their states and districts, often more than three-fourths coming from outside of their constituencies (Canes-Wrone and Miller 2022; Crespin and Edwards 2016; Gimpel, Lee, and Pearson-Merkowitz 2008).

The most venerable actors besides candidate committees in campaign spending are the formal party groups through the national "Hill Committees" for each major party: the Democratic Congressional Campaign Committee (DCCC), National Republican Congressional Committee (NRCC), Democratic Senatorial Campaign Committee (DSCC), and National Republican Senatorial Committee (NRSC). Hill Committees have two separate components: first, a coordinated campaign component that gives strategic advice and makes limited coordinated expenditures with candidates; and second, an independent expenditure component that produces and distributes political messages in races. To remain compliant with FEC rules, the independent expenditure arm of the Hill Committee cannot communicate nor coordinated with the candidate or the campaign. The independent expenditure arms of Hill Committees are responsible for far more direct spending than the coordinated campaigns.

The parties have additional, substantial independent spending vehicles for campaigns beyond the Hill Committees. Informal party groups are Super PACs closely aligned with House and Senate leaders, created in the immediate wake of the *Speechnow.org* decision. These groups include the Senate Leadership Fund and Congressional Leadership Fund on the Republican side and Senate Majority PAC, House Majority PAC, and Priorities USA Action on the Democratic side. These groups are important tools for the parties because they are able to accept unlimited contributions.

Independent expenditures controlled by the parties, whether formally via the Hill Committees or informally via the Super PACs closely tied to party leadership should most closely allocate their resources according to a seat-maximizing strategy to win as many races as possible (Damore and Hansford 1999; Jacobson 1985–1986; Snyder 1989). Groups controlled by party interests generally pay little attention to candidates' policy positions, ideological extremity, or even past loyalty to party leadership on floor votes, and instead base allocation decisions almost entirely on the candidate's electoral chances (Cantor and Herrnson 1997; Kolodny and Dwyre 1998; Nokken 2003). Within similarly competitive races, parties additionally consider candidate financial need, spending more on similarly competitive races where their candidates have less resources of their own (Miller 2017).

Nonparty independent groups include the independent expenditures by other Super PACs and tax-exempt groups (501c and other 527 groups organized under the Internal Revenue code) that, while in most cases support exclusively Democratic or Republican candidates, are most often formed around policy or ideological goals, and are not directly connected to the parties. Examples include the Chamber of Commerce, National Rifle Association, and Next Gen Climate Action. In addition, single candidate groups formed to independently support a single candidate in a single election have become increasingly common in congressional races.

Nonparty independent groups, whether candidate-specific or interest-group centered, pursue objectives that can deviate from a seat maximizing strategy. The former simply backing a specific candidate and the latter steering resources to members most friendly to their policy goals. A typical classification scheme such as in Magleby (2014) divides groups making independent expenditures into candidate-specific, party-centered, interest-group-centered groups. These are important differences, but because the interest in the analyses that follow is the difference in the attention groups pay to a seat-maximizing objective, independent expenditures are grouped into two categories: formal and informal party groups, and nonparty independent groups.

When interest groups that make up the bulk of nonparty independent group spending choose to directly spend on a race it is with the goal of replacing policy opponents and installing policy champions (Dwyre and Braz 2015; Franz 2011; Issacharoff and Peterman 2013; Sorauf 1992). When independent groups pursue a replacement strategy, even groups formed around a single issue or group interest will target close contests. After all, backing their most ardent policy champions running in hopeless contests would be a waste of resources. But programmatic policy interests can cause such groups to deviate from a purely pragmatic seat maximizing strategy pursued by formal and informal party groups: for example, the Sierra Club will support Democrats over Republicans, but when choosing which of several Democrats to support, the group could choose the stronger environmental advocate instead of the candidate running in what they believe is the closest race.

SPENDING IN THE 2018 AND 2020
HOUSE AND SENATE CAMPAIGNS

To measure the state of spending by these actors and describe the interplay between candidates and independent expenditure groups in this landscape, candidate receipts and expenditures were obtained from the FEC candidate summary files and independent expenditures from independent expenditures summary files (Federal Election Commission 2021a, b). These data capture the finances of November general election candidates for US House and Senate seats who filed receipt and expenditure reports for that campaign cycle (Georgia Senate special election candidates are excluded from these analyses).[1]

About three-fifths of all spending in Senate campaigns and almost three-quarters in House campaigns came from the candidates own committees, but aggregate spending totals obscure the real impact of independent expenditures in campaigns. Candidates in more competitive contests both raise and spend more in their campaigns compared to candidates in safe seats or pursuing hopeless challenges (Jacobson and Carson 2019). But independent expenditures can be freely allocated across races and even more efficiently compared to the distribution of candidate receipts. Since much of the independent spending is guided by organizations expected to be mostly pragmatic in their allocation decisions–that is, interested purely in maximizing the number of seats won for the party—independent spending overall should be more heavily weighted toward the closest races than the spending by candidates.

To illustrate this difference in responsiveness to competition, the average levels of spending in races by the degree of competitiveness as rated by Rothenberg & Gonzales Political Report are shown in figure 10.2. These race ratings represent the assessments of congressional candidates and other political professionals as well as polling data available prior to the election (Gonzales 2015).[2] In addition to displaying the level of spending by each category of actor in legislative campaigns, the graphs also provide the percentage of spending controlled by candidates on average in each category of competitiveness.

In the House (top of figure 10.2) average candidate spending in noncompetitive races was $1.2 million. After the jump to $3.3 million in candidate spending in the next category of competitive races, the increase with each level of competition was modest up to $5 million in toss-up races. On the other hand, outsiders far more heavily skewed spending toward the closest races. As a result, House candidates were responsible for less than half of the spending in the contests truly in doubt, those rated as tossup (44%) or tilting (48%).

In Senate campaigns (bottom of figure 10.2) it was a slightly different story. Like in House races, Senate candidates in noncompetitive campaigns

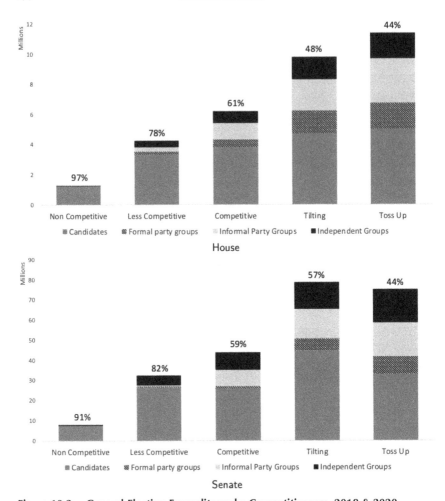

Figure 10.2.   General Election Expenditures by Competitiveness, 2018 & 2020

Note: Totals represent the average spending post-primary by campaigns within each category of race competitiveness. Percentages at top of bars indicate the average percent of total spending in the campaign
made by candidates within each category of race.

spent far less than other candidates. And also like in House campaigns, the
more agile independent expenditure assets flooded into the most competitive
races, reducing candidates to minority spenders in toss-up contests and less
than 60 percent in the next two categories of competitiveness. But in Senate
campaigns in 2018 and 2020 candidate spending was higher on average in
tilting races than in toss-up contests.

The higher average spending by Senate candidates in tilting races was the
result of several 2020 contests where Democratic challengers (and usually
their Republican opponents in turn) attracted massive windfalls into their

campaigns. In Arizona, Democratic challenger Mark Kelly received $101 million in his race against incumbent Republican Martha McSally, who took in $74 million. Democrat Sara Gideon received nearly $76 million to try to unseat Maine incumbent Republican Susan Collins, who received slightly less than $29 million for her campaign. Most impressive, Democrat Jaime Harrison took in $132 million in his campaign against South Carolina incumbent Republican Lindsey Graham, who brought in $107 million. To put these totals in context, the average receipts for all other Senate candidates in the tilting category was under $23 million and the average candidate receipts in toss-up races was $33 million.

But the largest outlier was in Kentucky. Even though the race was considered noncompetitive by professionals (rated as safely Republican by both Rothenberg & Gonzales and Cook Political Report), Democratic challenger Amy McGrath took in over $96 million for her campaign against incumbent Republican and Senate Majority Leader Mitch McConnell who took in $68 million. The average receipts by all other Senate campaigns in this category of competitiveness in the 2018 and 2020 cycles was just $6 million. It is perhaps not surprising then, that there was no independent spending by the formal party groups and almost none by informal party groups in South Carolina and Kentucky in 2020.

What drove these unusually high levels of receipts into these races? Profiles of the motivations of campaign donors have typically settled on some variation of three categories that are not mutually exclusive: those pursuing individual material benefits, individuals seeking expressive ideological benefits, and those pursuing the solidary rewards of group membership (Clark and Wilson 1961; Francia et al. 2003). To this typology Magleby, Goodliffe, and Olsen (2018) adds the factor of candidate appeal, both positive and negative.

In these Senate races negative candidate appeal appears to have been the likely driver of these surprising fundraising hauls. Approximately 90 percent of the individual donations to these campaigns came from out-of-state donors (Geng 2020). It is unlikely that liberal donors around the country were familiar with and personally drawn to Mark Kelly, Sara Gideon, Jaime Harrison, and Amy McGrath. More likely is that Democratic national donors were attracted to the potential of removing Martha McSally, Susan Collins, Lindsey Graham, and Mitch McConnell and donated to whoever presented themselves as the alternative. Further, these negative donations were only somewhat sensitive to the probability of victory. Collins and McSally were thought to be behind in their bids to return to the Senate, but Democrats Theresa Greenfield in Iowa and Steve Bullock in Montana were in races rated as pure toss-ups by Cook and Rothenberg & Gonzales. In terms of expected closeness of the races, Greenfield and Bullock were better uses of liberal donors' funds than

the candidates facing Collins and McSally. McGrath was not considered a serious threat to McConnell, and Graham in South Carolina was considered by
political professionals to be fairly secure. And yet these were the candidates
who attracted the largest amounts from individual donors.

An important feature of these ideological donors who direct money into
the opponents of high-profile incumbents in the opposite party is their lack
of coordination. The pure strategy for a donor motivated to remove a nationally recognized face of the opposing party is to contribute to that incumbent's
challenger. But when these donors become numerous enough and all pursue
this simple strategy to contribute to the same small set of Senate challengers, the result is a small group of oversupplied candidates. A coordinated
and more efficient donation strategy among individual donors would have
directed far more to the Iowa and Montana contests instead. But because individual donations are not efficiently coordinated, it becomes incumbent upon
the parties and independent groups to counter this inefficient distribution
of resources across the party's candidates in Senate contests. Tellingly, this
inefficient distribution of uncoordinated ideological money was not a major
phenomenon in House contests, where individual races are far less likely to
attract attention at the national level.

COMPENSATING FOR OVERFUNDED CANDIDATES

To test whether independent expenditures were distributed differently in
House and Senate contests, regression models are estimated to assess the
effect of a candidate's total receipts on the level of outside spending support in the race. The unit of analysis is the general election campaign for a
given candidate for a Senate or House seat. Only major-party candidates are
included, and the analysis is limited to spending after the state's primary. The
dependent variable is the total independent expenditures in support of the
candidate measured in millions of dollars, that is all independent expenditures
reported to the FEC as supporting the candidate or reported as in opposition to that candidate's general election opponent. The independent variable
of interest for these models is the candidate committee's receipts, also in
millions of dollars.[3] The competitiveness of the race is represented in these
models with Rothenberg & Gonzales race ratings included as a set of dummy
variables with the noncompetitive category excluded. Because campaigns
that are similarly competitive will attract different levels of spending, total
opposing spending in millions of dollars is included combining spending
from the candidate's opponent as well as outside spending in support of that
opponent. Party of the candidate is included as well as an indicator variable

Table 10.1. Outside Spending in House and Senate Campaigns, 2018 & 2020

	Senate	House
	[1]	[2]
Candidate receipts (millions)	−0.008**	0.053**
	(0.003)	(0.019)
Opposing spending (millions)	0.019**	0.076**
	(0.002)	(0.010)
Incumbent	−0.487**	−0.034
	(0.102)	(0.070)
Democrat	0.350**	0.178**
	(0.111)	(0.073)
2020	0.036	0.178*
	(0.176)	(0.073)
Less competitive race	1.432**	2.776**
	(0.517)	(0.210)
Competitive race	2.530**	3.593**
	(0.408)	(0.210)
Tilting race	2.611**	4.033**
	(0.473)	(0.211)
Toss-up race	2.876**	4.113**
	(0.452)	(0.217)
Intercept	−0.400	−3.643**
	(0.357)	(0.179)
Pseudo R^2	.83	.71

Note: Dependent variable is the outside spending in support of the candidate, in millions of dollars. Robust standard errors in parentheses below Poisson regression coefficients.
*p<.05, **p<.01, two-tailed tests

for incumbent candidates. Finally, a dummy variable for year is included to account for the increased spending in 2020.

The coefficients are estimated using a Poisson model because the dependent variable, outside spending, is bounded at zero and positively skewed. Model results are presented in table 10.1. Estimates for Senate campaigns in Column [1] indicate that holding other features of the campaign and candidate constant, as the amount of money received by a Senate candidate increases, outside groups spend less in support of that candidate. The story is quite different in House campaigns, shown in Column [2], where outside groups spend more where candidates spend more, that is, outside groups allocate resources in parallel to the flow of resources flow to candidates.

The intensity of the race has the expected strong association with outside spending, reflected in the increasingly large values of the coefficients for more competitive races. Interestingly, Senate incumbents received less

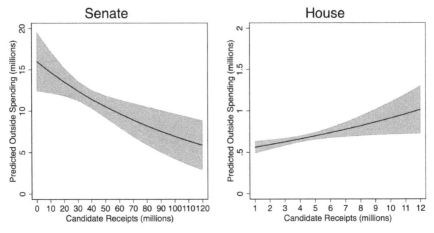

Figure 10.3.   Marginal Effects of Candidate Receipts on Outside Spending

Note: Plots on left are the marginal predicted levels of independent expenditures in campaigns by parties at different levels of race competitiveness. At right are the marginal predicted levels of independent expenditures in campaigns by independent groups at different levels of race competitiveness. Margins calculated with all other covariates held constant at their means.

independent expenditure support than challengers in the 2018 and 2020 election cycles. And in a reversal of trends from prior election cycles, in both the House and Senate models, Democratic candidates were associated with greater independent expenditure support than Republican candidates.

Estimates of the substantive effects of candidate receipts on outside group spending are shown in figure 10.3. Holding other covariates at their mean, in Senate campaigns an additional $10 million in candidate receipts is associated with approximately $1 million less in outside group spending in support of that candidate. Contrast this with the House where an additional $1 million in candidate receipts is associated with approximately $31,000 more in outside group spending for the candidate.[4]

These results show that holding constant measures of the competitiveness of the race, incumbency, party, and year, in Senate campaigns outside money plays a compensatory role where it avoids the candidates who have taken in the most contributions and spends more where the candidates have less resources of their own. Conversely, in House contests outside money plays a complementary role, simply going to the same contests where the candidates have received the most in donations.

PARTY AND NONPARTY SPENDING STRATEGIES

A second set of models are estimated to determine whether formal and informal party groups respond differently than nonparty independent groups to the perceived prospects of candidates. Holding other factors constant, formal and informal party groups should bias their support more strongly toward the closest contests compared to nonparty independent groups. For these models formal and informal party independent spending is considered separately from nonparty independent spending, with one category of outside spending the dependent variable in the model and the other category included as an independent variable. That is, when predicting party spending in support of a candidate, the level of spending in support of that candidate by nonparty independent groups needs to be considered along with the other covariates, and vice versa.

Column [1] in table 10.2 estimates formal and informal party group spending in Senate campaigns as a function of each of the covariates included in the previous models as well as a separate independent variable of the spending by nonparty independent groups. Column [2] estimates independent group spending while including party group spending as a control. In these models,

Table 10.2. Party and Independent Spending in House and Senate Campaigns, 2018 & 2020

	Senate Party	Senate Independent	House Party	House Independent
	[1]	[2]	[3]	[4]
Candidate receipts (millions)	−0.017**	−0.001	0.028	0.091**
	(0.005)	(0.004)	(0.021)	(0.019)
Independent spending (millions)	−0.007	—	−0.036	—
	(0.015)		(0.035)	
Party spending (millions)	—	0.001	—	−0.060
		(0.007)		(0.058)
Opposing spending (millions)	0.019**	0.021**	0.086**	0.067**
	(0.006)	(0.005)	(0.010)	(0.022)
Incumbent	−0.417	−0.617**	0.082	−0.207
	(0.176)	(0.182)	(0.085)	(0.133)
Democrat	0.543*	0.224	0.131	0.383**
	(0.220)	(0.184)	(0.091)	(0.122)
2020	0.481	−0.466**	0.459**	−0.111
	(0.263)	(0.180)	(0.075)	(0.160)
Competitiveness ratings	included	included	included	included
Intercept	−2.624**	−0.326	5.071**	−3.878**
	(0.877)	(0.322)	(0.300)	(0.221)
Pseudo R^2	.81	.70	.72	.48
N	131	131	1,553	1,553

Note: Dependent variable in columns [1] and [3] is the formal and informal party group spending in support of the candidate, in millions of dollars. The dependent variable in columns [2] and [4] is the nonparty independent group spending in support of the candidate, in millions of dollars. Robust standard errors in parentheses below Poisson regression coefficients.

*p<.05, **p<.01, two-tailed tests

greater candidate receipts are associated with reduced party spending but not
with reduced independent group spending, indicating that the compensatory
spending strategy of directing money away from the most well-funded Senate
candidates (while holding factors of competitiveness constant) was an effort
by party groups but not independent groups.

Independent spending in support of House candidates by party and nonparty groups is estimated in columns [3] and [4], respectively. Greater candidate receipts are not associated with reduced independent support by formal
and informal party groups in the House, and greater candidate receipts are
associated with more support from nonparty independent groups.

Across all models, spending by the opposing side was positively associated
with greater spending. For both party and nonparty groups, money follows
money. In addition, the coefficients for the dummy variable for 2020 illustrate
that party spending on legislative races was higher in the presidential election
year while nonparty group spending was lower.

Figure 10.4 illustrates the predicted spending by party groups (at left) and
independent groups (at right) at each level of race competitiveness in Senate
campaigns (top row) based on the models in columns [1] and [2] of table
10.2 and House contests (bottom row) based on the models in columns [3]
and [4] from table 10.2. Holding other factors constant, formal and informal
party groups spend nearly zero on noncompetitive races then increase spend-

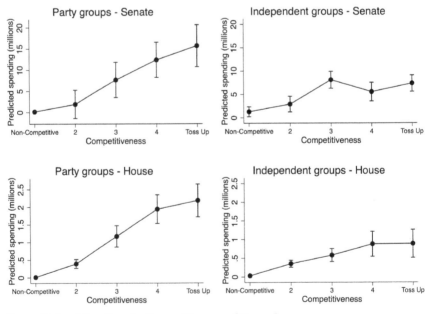

Figure 10.4.   Allocations by Competitiveness of Campaigns

ing at a linear rate from about $1 million for less competitive races up to $16 million for toss-up Senate races and from $0.5 million to $2 million in House races. Nonparty independent groups' increase of spending in response to competitiveness is more muted and little difference is seen across the top three categories of competition in both Senate and House contests.

More formally, these models are also estimated treating the competitiveness variable as a single ordered categorical variable in each model to test the equivalence of the slopes between party and independent group spending in response to competitiveness. A chi-square test of the coefficients finds that the slopes are not equivalent across the Senate models ($\chi^2 = 9.96$, $p = .002$) or House models ($\chi^2 = 3.87$, $p = .049$), indicating that parties allocate more strongly toward the most competitive campaigns. In sum, the results from these models demonstrate that in both House and Senate campaigns in 2018 and 2020, holding constant other race features, nonparty independent groups spread their resources more thinly across a larger number of races, while parties more heavily concentrate their spending in the closest contests.

NATIONALIZED FINANCING OF CONGRESSIONAL CAMPAIGNS

This picture of the 2018 and 2020 congressional campaign spending landscape identifies three trends. First, the financing of congressional campaigns is a fully nationalized system. Candidates in truly competitive races directly control less than half of the money spent in their contests, with most expenditures being made by national organizations. Even most of the money under candidates' control is sourced from national PACs and from a national donor pool that reside outside the candidates' states and districts. Second, formal, and informal party vehicles for independent expenditures distribute their spending according to the closeness of the contest and candidate need, but nonparty independent groups are less responsive to the state of races and spread their spending more broadly. Third, the national donors that finance candidates are a large but uncoordinated force in campaigns. Individual donors appear to be roughly pragmatic, that is, mostly targeting closer races, but important deviations arise when some races (i.e., Senate races with nationally recognized and polarizing incumbents) attract extra attention from ideological donors.

In the first election cycles where independent spending expanded as a result of the *Citizens United* and *Speechnow.org* decisions national actors came to the rescue of underfunded candidates in competitive races (Miller 2017). More recently a new dynamic has taken hold. In 2018 and especially in 2020 independent expenditure groups still distribute their spending with sensitivity to candidate war chests but shift their allocations away from Senate candidates overfunded relative to the true probability of the seat flipping. This pattern is an important change to the compensatory dynamic between candidates and independent expenditure groups. It is fairly easy for fully mobile outside dollars to fill in for an underresourced candidate, but outside groups cannot remove superfluous money from a candidate with resources beyond their needs. As a result, outside money cannot as easily compensate for the funding inefficiencies of a campaign finance system where ideological individual donors concentrate their contributions into a handful of high-profile campaigns.

And what should these overfunded candidates do? Candidates benefiting from the attention of large numbers of national donors could in theory act in the best interests of the party overall. The candidates could redistribute some of this money out of their own coffers and into the hands of the party or into the hands of candidates in more promising races, but there are several barriers to such a move: First, the candidates likely believe that they can win. Their race has attracted national attention, they have out-raised their incumbent challengers, and early polls in some cases offered rays of hope. Second, when one side attracts a deluge of donations the opposing candidate often attracts substantial money in response. Even if projections suggest that the race is not truly up for grabs, any candidate would be unlikely to move extra money out to party allies if the campaign has rough parity of funds with the opponent. Third, in the case of challengers, they are not yet fully integrated into the party networks with leadership PACs and established relationships with party incumbents. Fourth, redistributing some of these funds or holding on to the money and waiting for a better opportunity later risks angering the donors. For example, Democratic Senate candidate Sara Gideon spent $64 million in her effort against Susan Collins in Maine (an extraordinary level of spending for a state with small media markets) but was later criticized for not spending all she had and donating some of her $10 million in leftover money to the state party.[5]

Federal elections were party-centered in the early twentieth century, then became candidate-centered affairs in the 1960s and 1970s (Maisel and Brewer 2010; Wattenberg 1991). These recent high-profile Senate campaigns awash in individual donor money signal a new variety of candidate-centered campaigns that exist in a mostly party-centered system. Parties have returned to prominence in campaigns by adjusting to a system that advantages independent expenditure groups that can receive unrestricted donations. But some candidates have been able to leverage donor antipathy toward opposing party incumbents to attract funds well beyond what other comparably competitive candidates bring in. In doing so, these candidates effectively remove themselves from the system of party support.

Finally, is uncoordinated, national, less pragmatic ideological money a feature of Democratic donors, or is it a feature of the behavior of the donor base of the party out of power? The largesse of donations to relatively unknown Senate challengers suggests that this activity was driven mostly by Democratic donors frustrated with the faces of the opposition party in control. Will Republican donors behave the same way when the tables are turned? Narrow, but still unified Democratic control of federal government in 2020 offers a chance to observe in 2022 whether national less pragmatic money again pours into Democratic challengers when Republicans are in the minority, or if we instead see a groundswell of ideological and less pragmatic money more on the Republican side as conservative national donors seek to dislodge the highest profile legislators of the opposing party in control.

NOTES

1. The FEC page states that the candidate summary files contain "information for each candidate who has registered with the FEC or appears on an official state ballot for an election to the U.S. House of Representatives, U.S. Senate or U.S. President." However, comparing these files with election results from the MIT Election Data Lab revealed that a small number of candidates were missing from the FEC's reporting. These candidates in all cases were extreme long shots or unopposed by a major-party candidate.

2. Race ratings issued on the first week of October in each election year are used instead of election returns because what is of interest are political actors' expectations at the time they make their donation and spending decisions. In addition, preelection expectations that drive allocation decisions can at times not match final results. Susan Collins (R-ME) was widely expected to have a difficult time in her 2020 reelection campaign, and it was rated "tilting Democratic" by Rothenberg & Gonzales. Collins seems to have agreed with this assessment spending $29.2 million from her own coffers and received $46.4 million in independent support (and this in a state with very low media costs). Collins's opponent Sara Gideon spent $64 million and received $54.2 million in outside support. But in the end Collins won by a comfortable margin, 51 percent to 42 percent.

3. In these models, candidate receipts instead of disbursements are used on the expectation that outside groups allocate resources in response to the size of these candidates' war chests, not candidates' expenditures.

4. Mean candidate receipts for Senate candidates in 2018 and 2020 was $17.5 million (s.d. = $24 million) and for the House $1.9 million (s.d. = $2.6 million)

5. For example: "Ten Months After Senate Election Loss Sara Gideon Still Has $10 Million in Unused Campaign Funds," The Intercept, Sep. 24, 2021; and "Gideon Campaign Still Sitting on $10 Million from 2020 Bid for U.S. Senate," *Portland Press Herald*, Oct. 31, 2021

Chapter Eleven

The Ground Game in 2020

Party Contacts as Reported by Voters

Paul A. Beck

From the very beginnings of electoral politics, politicians have valued direct contacts with voters as a resource in their campaigns. Face-to-face contacts on the doorstep and other places where people congregated have been important components of their campaign arsenals. In more modern times, political campaigners have reached out directly to voters through the mail, telephone, twitter, and increasingly the Internet. Although not all have the intimacy of face-to-face contacts, all of them can be subsumed, with some allowance for evolving technologies, under the heading of the more labor-intensive "ground game." What unites them is that the voter is identified personally as a recipient of the campaign message. By contrast, with the advent of the mass media, campaigns also have tried to reach voters through mass-media advertising in newspapers, radio, and television, with the latter often labeled the "air war."[1] Its campaign message is just "put out there" without an attempt to identify and target any specific recipient personally, though particular groups may be reached through micro-targeting. A more capital-intensive way of reaching large numbers of voters, use of the mass media is less personal and probably less effective.[2]

MEASURING THE GROUND GAME

Researchers have measured the ground game in several different ways. First, relying upon survey reports by voters, across elections as early as 1956 from American National Election Studies data, they have assessed personal contacts made directly by political parties and candidates during the election campaign (Rosenstone and Hansen 1993, 162–77; Beck and Heidemann 2014a and works cited therein). The advantage of these reported party contacts is that they directly measure campaign contacts from the perspective of those who receive them. One disadvantage of these reports is that often they are unclear about how these contacts were made. In some cases, they are the product of face-to-face contacts between party workers and candidates and voters through the traditional party canvas. In other cases, they may result from phone calls, emails, or mailings, which vary in how personal they may be. Another disadvantage is that it is indeterminant how accurate are these respondent perceptions of contact. Over the course of a long political campaign, voters may not remember whether they were contacted and how. Unfortunately, there are no easy ways to validate survey reports of party contacts.[3]

A second measure of ground game effort is often indirectly inferred from the presence of local campaign field offices through which they often are managed (Darr 2020; Masket, Sides, and Vavreck 2016; Darr and Levendusky 2014; and the works cited therein). The advantage of using campaign offices is that they typically are known and thereby measurable. These offices organize the activities of party workers at the local level, pinpointing where and how often to contact particular voters. They operate telephone banks that can reach out to voters, with the up-to-date knowledge of whether they are registered and (with early voting) have not yet voted, prompting follow-up efforts to mobilize them on behalf of party candidates. Increasingly, even personalized efforts have been directed from centralized locations rather than the local arena through campaign field offices, however, so relying on identification of field offices may underestimate ground game effort.

Third, classic studies of party contacting relied on party leader reports at the local level to determine their campaign efforts, which in turn were connected to voting results (Gosnell 1927; Cutright and Rossi 1958; Katz and Eldersveld 1961; Cutright 1963). Local party machines are legendary for their contacts with voters. In machine cities, it was the responsibility of local precinct captains to maintain contacts with their residents and to make sure those known to be supportive of the party were mobilized in election campaigns. They were most assiduous in these efforts in support of local candidates, whose victories were necessary for a continuation of machine control. Their canvassing efforts also carried over to presidential campaigns, especially when the presidential election was coterminous with local elections.

This chapter relies on the first type of measure: how ground game efforts reached voters in the 2020 presidential election campaign as reported by survey respondents. It draws upon surveys conducted under the aegis of the Comparative National Elections Project (Gunther et al. 2016)[4] that asked respondents to report party contacts by candidate representatives and their parties during the presidential campaign. What is unique about the questions from these surveys is that they asked separately about personal and other kinds of party contacts, which enables analysis of each kind of contact.[5]

The following analyses begin with the frequencies of reported party contacts in 2020 overall by party and then separately by personal versus other kinds of contact. For purposes of comparison, they are presented and discussed along with frequencies from earlier CNEP US surveys in 2016, 2012, and 2004 in which the same questions were asked.[6] To test the hypothesis that ground game efforts were focused, strategically, on the swing or battleground states in that campaign, this analysis was replicated for those two types of states as they emerged in each campaign. The chapter then goes on to identify key characteristics of respondents who were contacted in 2020, with occasional references to how they had differed from earlier years.

OVERALL PARTY CONTACTS IN 2020 AND BEFORE

Figure 11.1 shows the percentages CNEP survey respondents who reported having been contacted by representatives of political parties and candidates during the 2020 presidential campaign—and, for comparison, in 2004, 2012, and 2016. These results can be employed to test several hypotheses about party contacting.

First, even in these times of huge presidential campaign spending on the air war, grassroots party contacts have been an important part of campaign strategies. Modern campaigns have focused on mobilizing their voter base, assiduously contacting their supporters to make sure that they turn out at the polls. Particularly with the prevalence of early voting, many of us have personally

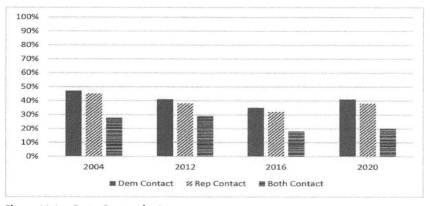

Figure 11.1. Party Contact by Party

experienced personal contacts from the party we are registered with that suddenly end once we have cast an early vote, which is recorded regularly in the official voter data base. Figure 11.1 shows that about 40 percent of respondents reported being contacted by either the Democrats or Republicans during the 2020 campaign. Contacts by both parties were greater than four years before, at similar levels to 2012, somewhat lower than in 2004.

Second, a prominent feature of modern campaign ground game strategies is that they are directed toward their voter base. This hypothesis will be tested more fully later, but a surprising percentage of voters reported having received contacts from both parties. That this percentage is significantly lower in 2016 and 2020 suggests that base mobilization strategies, directed only to a party's supporters, may have become more common in recent years.

Third, it is presumed that Democrats pour more effort into grass roots contacts than do Republicans. Since the 1930s at least, their strength has been concentrated in big cities, where local machines and their campaign efforts were most prevalent. Although the Democratic base is still largely urban, it is doubtful that the political machines are as strong as they were in the past and, therefore, are not as dedicated to mobilizing loyal voters. These expectations are borne out in figure 11.1. While Democratic contacts were slightly more frequent in every year, the differences fall short of significance. In short, both Democratic and Republican efforts were substantial.

Fourth, according to the conventional wisdom, 2016 and 2020 differed sharply in presidential campaigns' attention to the ground game. The Trump campaign in 2016 eschewed traditional ground game activities, especially the opening of local field offices, to concentrate on twitter in particular in reaching supporters directly. The ground game then was widely seen as a strategic advantage for the Clinton campaign (Francia 2018; Sides, Tesler, and Vavreck 2018). In 2020, the tables were turned, with the ground game advantage attributed to the Trump campaign. It invested much more heavily in field offices (Darr 2020), and the ground game effort that they supported, than did the Biden campaign. The reason, it was widely noted, is that the Biden camp was much less inclined to expose its campaign workers to personal contacts, with voters or even among themselves, to minimize their COVID-19 exposure. The great disparity in field offices between the two campaigns reflects this strategic decision (Darr 2020).

The figure 11.1 data belie these impressions. The Trump campaign reached more voters through ground game activities than was immediately apparent in 2016, dramatically eating into what was supposed to be a Clinton advantage (Beck et al. 2018). In 2020, there was an upsurge in reported party contacts on *both* sides. The Biden campaign seems to have been able to overcome its dearth of field offices, and the grassroots efforts they supported, by alternative ways of contacting voters. The differences in reported contacts between the two parties were not statistically significant. One lesson to be learned from these results is that there are alternative ways for the ever-resourceful campaign organizations to contact voters beyond field offices and the grassroots efforts they facilitate. The lesson the Trump campaign learned, despite its electoral win in 2016, is that ground game efforts are worth the investment—even if they did not prove to be sufficient to carry Trump to victory four years later. And the lesson that the Biden campaign learned is that the absence of field offices does not doom the ground game to ineffectiveness

PERSONAL AND OTHER TYPES OF PARTY CONTACTS IN 2020 AND BEFORE

Overall party contacts of course are only part of the story. The advantage of the CNEP measurements of party contacts is that they distinguish between those that are personal, or face-to-face, versus the Internet, telephone robocalls, twitter, and mail. Telephone banks have been valuable resources in reaching out to voters in recent decades. The Internet has become more and more important in various ways. Campaigns directly email campaign messages and fundraising appeals to voters. They rely on twitter to maintain regular contact with their followers. They insert campaign advertisements into social media posts. Their creativity in finding ways to reach voters, especially their supporters, is impressive. These methods must be captured as well to paint a complete picture of party contacting.

The CNEP US surveys asked separately about personal versus other types of party contact (see appendix A for the question wording). The distinction proves to be instructive in several important ways.

Figure 11.2 shows how infrequently respondents report having received a personal contact from a representative of a political party or candidate. Even though personal contact has been shown to be more effective in achieving the desired result, whether it is a donation to a charity or turnout in an election (Green and Gerber 2008), it is challenging for political campaigns. It depends upon labor intensive face-to-face interactions between party workers and voters at the doorstep or in public settings such as shopping malls, county fairs, and other congregate settings. It is hardly surprising that no more than 16 percent of respondents reported having been contacted personally in any year across the 2004 to 2020 period. Nor is it surprising that Democratic contacts were more frequent than Republican. Because they are younger and less educated minorities, with a lower propensity to vote, potentially Democratic voters are more in need of a "nudge" to induce them to vote, and Demo-

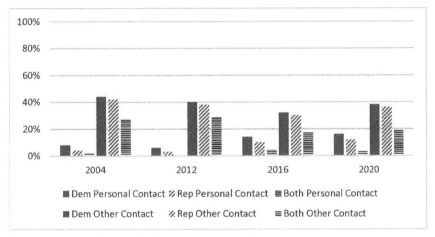

Figure 11.2. Personal and Other Party Contacts by Party

cratic campaign organizations are more dedicated to providing such a nudge through personal contacts (Arceneaux and Nickerson 2009).

What is surprising, considering the ground game strategies of the Trump campaign in 2016 and the Biden campaign in 2020, is that personal contacting rose from less than 10 percent in the two earlier elections to 10 percent and more in 2016 and 2020. The hypothesized drops in personal contacting of the Trump campaign in 2016 and the Biden campaign in 2020 did not materialize. As hypothesized, however, reported personal contacts by both parties were infrequent.

By contrast, figure 11.2 also shows that party contacts through the Internet, mail, and telephone (including twitter most recently) were much more likely to be reported by voters—and at essentially the same levels for the two parties. By this measure, party contacting fell off in 2016 by both parties, but it was restored almost to previous heights in 2020. However, in the two most recent elections, significantly fewer respondents reported receiving other types of contact from both parties, suggesting that the campaigns were more selective in their targeting.

PARTY CONTACTING IN BATTLEGROUND STATES

It is an inefficient usage of scarce party resources, of both labor and capital, for campaigns to devote their attention to all places that choose presidential electors. Most states are not competitive in presidential elections, and presidential campaigns virtually ignore them. Field offices are not established there, candidates "fly over" but do not visit them, and campaign ads do not flood their television markets.[7] The ability to reach potential voters via the Internet and telephone mitigates this strong tendency to ignore the noncompetitive states, however, as messages can be communicated virtually cost-free without regard to where a recipient lives. Indeed, in fundraising, dollars from donors in a noncompetitive state are just as valuable as those from people in competitive states.

Presidential elections are won by candidates with the electoral college majority rather than popular votes. In recent years, the number of states that are truly competitive for these electoral college votes has dwindled to about a dozen. Campaigns develop their own strategies about where to concentrate their resources, but the overwhelming tendency is to focus them on these so-called battleground or swing states. The election will turn on how well candidates do in them. Their importance is well illustrated by the states that were battlegrounds in the 2016 and 2020 presidential contests. Arizona, Florida, Georgia, North Carolina, Michigan, Nevada, New Hampshire, Pennsylvania, Texas, and Wisconsin were targeted by both campaigns in 2016 and 2020. By winning most of them, Trump captured the presidency in 2016. By losing Georgia, Michigan, Pennsylvania, and Wisconsin, which Trump had won in 2016, the 2020 electoral college victory went to Biden.

This chapter defines battleground states as those that turned out to be the most competitive in presidential popular votes: specifically, where the margin between the two major-party candidates was 6 percent or less. This measure employs the same objective standard across the four presidential elections rather than depending upon subjective assessments by campaign experts of what states were battlegrounds. Using a competitiveness margin of 6 percent has the added advantage of including more states in the battleground category than a smaller margin might.

Alternative designations of battleground states are not easy by any subjective measure. The presidential campaigns are not always transparent about where they choose to invest their resources, wanting to hide their strategies from the opposition. And their strategies can change over the course of the campaign, as states they thought were safe for one party become competitive and previously identified swing states emerge as solid for one party or the other.[8] As it turns out, the competitiveness measure overlaps considerably with the subjective designations. The results of this chapter's analysis were essentially unchanged by alternative designations of battlegrounds.

Previous research, primarily based on American National Election Study data, has documented that a battleground state effect emerged in the 2000s. For both Democratic and Republican campaigns in 2000, 2004, and 2008, the difference in overall party contacts between competitive and noncompetitive states was sizable (Beck and Heidemann 2014b). This gap persisted into the 2012 and 2016 elections (Beck at al. 2018). For both parties, the gap was much smaller, usually insignificant, from 1956 through 1996. By most accounts, the disproportionate effort in the electoral college battlegrounds reflected a change in presidential campaign strategies to concentrate primarily on mobilizing the party's base where the competition was most intense.

The CNEP surveys enable a comparison of party contacting between competitive and noncompetitive states in 2020, also drilling down into the types of contacts. As stated earlier, face-to-face personal contacts, albeit infrequent, have been found to be the most effective in mobilizing people to donate to charities and support candidates for office. Where a battleground strategy is employed in presidential campaign, it should be expected to show up most clearly in personal contacts. Other ground game activities, on the other, should not differ as much between the two types of states.

Using the CNEP data, figure 11.3 tests the hypothesis that overall party contacting was more frequent in the competitive battlegrounds than in the noncompetitive states. The differences were as expected in 2004, 2012, and 2016 (see Beck and Heidemann 2014b; and Beck et al. 2018). For both parties, more contacts were reported in the battlegrounds. By contrast, the gap was not nearly as large in 2020 for both parties, falling far short of significance for the Democrats.

Why did a pattern that persisted for almost two decades virtually vanish in 2020? The focus on mobilizing the base had not disappeared, if anything it had grown, even if overall party contacting did not reach earlier levels. It is hard to explain the vanishing battleground effect with any confidence, but two possibilities are plausible. First, the pandemic may have constrained

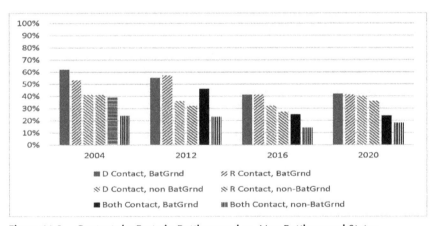

Figure 11.3. Contacts by Party in Battleground vs. Non-Battleground States

some ground game activities. The Biden campaign decided not to establish as many field offices as the Clinton campaign had in 2016 and seemed to be more reluctant to send its volunteers personally into homes and crowded events (Darr 2020). Second, riding the tide of technological advances, both campaigns also relied more extensively on tweets and online appeals, flooding the Internet and social media with campaign messages. They were cheap and could be easily targeted to base supporters, identified through various email and Twitter lists of followers and by demographic characteristics, in battleground and nonbattleground states alike. The focus on these kinds of messages over traditional ground game canvassing may not be only a product of the pandemic, but also it exploits opportunities provided by new technologies that will become even more attractive in the future.

CNEP survey data separating personal from other types of party contacts, presented in figures 11.4 and 11.5, allow us to explore these possibilities. As figure 11.4 shows, reported personal contacts by the Democrats did not differ between the battleground and non-battleground states. The Biden campaign consciously had avoided traditional ground efforts due to the pandemic, and it reduced to insignificance the gap between the two kinds of states. On the Republican side, however, this gap remained, even though voters continued to report less contact from its campaign than from the Democrats in both types of states. As figure 11.5 shows, differences in reports of other types of party contact beyond the personal were insignificant for both parties in the battleground versus nonbattleground states in 2020 in sharp contrast to their divides in the earlier years.

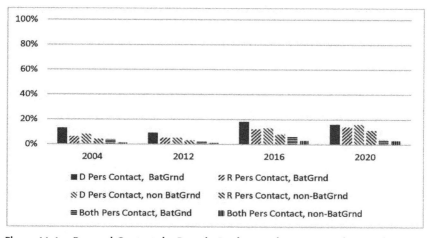

Figure 11.4.   **Personal Contacts by Party in Battleground vs. Non-Battleground States**

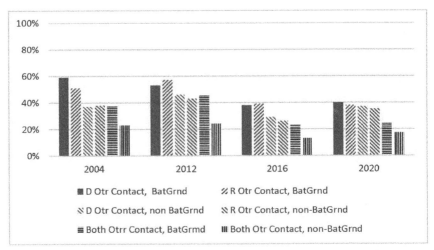

Figure 11.5. Other Contacts by Party in Battleground vs. Non-Battleground States

WHOM DID THE PARTIES CONTACT?

Our attention now turns to whom the parties contacted through their ground game efforts. The conventional wisdom is that they have been targeting their base supporters in recent decades, mobilizing them to vote in the upcoming election (Panagopoulos 2016; Beck et al. 2018). The hypothesis, then, is that reports of contact should be significantly higher among those in the party's base than it is for others. Research drawing upon CNEP surveys of previous elections (Beck et al. 2018) also shows that some demographic characteristics were related to party contacts beyond a party's base supporters. They are best thought of as "low-hanging fruit" that a party ground game should target, especially fellow partisans among them, because of their high propensity to vote.

Table 11.1 presents the Pearson product-moment correlations between the various reports of party contact and a variety of demographic and political characteristics of survey respondents. As before, party contacts are measured by the presence (=1) or absence (=0) of contact and separated into personal and other types, with the two combining into a measure of overall contact. With only a few exceptions,[9] the respondent characteristics are similarly measured in dichotomous terms as either the presence (=1) or absence (=0) of the particular characteristic. To simplify the presentation, cell entries in table 11.1 are provided only for correlations that are significant at the .95 level of confidence. When the cell is empty, the relationship is not statistically significant.

Table 11.1. Demographic and Political Correlates of Party Contacts

	Dems Overall	Dems Personal	Dems Other	Rep Overall	Rep Personal	Rep Other
Income	0.08		0.10	0.11		0.12
Income lower 3rd			0.12	−0.09		−0.09
Income middle 3rd						
Income top 3rd	0.09		0.09	0.12		0.12
BA degree	0.11		0.12	0.10		0.09
BA degree women	0.09		0.10	0.06		0.06
Female				−0.05	−0.06	−0.05
White		−0.18		0.16	0.05	0.17
Black	0.05	0.17		−0.09		−0.09
Hispanic		0.07	−0.06	−0.13		−0.14
Minority		0.18		−0.16	−0.05	−0.17
Age		−0.09	0.07	0.19		0.21
Age 18–30	−0.06		−0.08	−0.15	−0.07	−0.15
Age 31–59		0.07			0.09	
Age 60 & older		−0.10	0.05	0.15		0.15
City resident		0.07		−0.12		−0.12
Suburban resident						
Rural resident	−0.11	−0.08	−0.09	0.07		0.07
White Wkly Church		−0.07		0.17	0.11	0.17
White born-again	−0.07	−0.07	−0.05	0.18	0.09	0.19
Union member	0.08		0.10	0.07	0.09	0.06
Internet elec news	0.24	0.07	0.24	0.12		0.12
Internet sharer	0.20	0.10	0.20	0.15	0.09	0.15
Strong PID	0.11	0.06	0.12	0.08		0.08
Republican PID	−0.19	−0.15	−0.17	0.27	0.14	0.27
Democratic PID	0.33	0.18	0.33	−0.13	−0.13	−0.12
Hi Interest	0.21		.023	0.21		0.23
Rep Activist				0.12	0.16	0.11
Dem Activist	0.21	0.15	0.22			
Clinton Vote	0.35	0.22	0.33	−0.32	−0.19	−0.30
Trump16 Vote	−0.34	−0.19	−0.32	0.30	0.20	0.27
Biden Vote	0.36	0.26	0.31	−0.33	−0.24	−0.30
Trump20 Vote	−0.36	−0.25	−0.31	0.33	0.26	0.31
Dem Primary Vote	0.42	0.28	0.38	−0.06	−0.10	
Rep Primary Vote	−0.17	−0.13	−0.15	0.29	0.26	0.28
Registered	0.17	0.06	0.18	0.20	0.07	0.20
No PID	−0.17		−0.18	−0.16		−0.18
Regular Voter	0.36	0.22	0.34	0.15		0.15
Used party website	0.26	0.13	0.25	0.19	0.12	0.18

It is hypothesized that the parties will target their partisan supporters in the ground game, and the evidence is clear that they did in 2020. Most notably, both types of Democratic party contact are reported by Democratic party identifiers (the signs are positive and significant) and Republicans are not likely to report them (the signs are negative and significant). The reverse is the case in reports by Republican party identifiers: both types of Republican party contact were received by them, whereas both types of Democratic party contact were not. This base-mobilization pattern is repeated for how respondents had voted in the 2016 and 2020 general elections and (with the single exception for other types of Republican contact for Democratic primary voters) in which party's primary they had participated. Similarly, Democratic and Republican party activists are more likely to report contacts of both types from their own parties, but not from the opposite party. These relatively robust correlations indicate substantial concentration of contacting effort on the party's partisan base.

Typically, these base-mobilization patterns are more pronounced for other types of party contact than they are for personal contacts. Personal contacts are difficult to achieve in any election campaign, especially one waged during a pandemic. In 2020, as shown earlier, personal contacts were less reported by survey respondents compared to the contacts by telephone, mail, and Internet. Interestingly in light of the Biden campaign's reluctance to launch an aggressive ground game, however, these personal contacts were not significantly less likely to be reported by Democratic voters and activists than by their Republican counterparts.

Several other political characteristics are significantly correlated with party contacts that at most only indirectly reflect the base-mobilization strategy. Respondents who were highly interested in the political campaign, who had regularly voted in the most recent elections, and who consulted party websites on the Internet were targeted by both parties. When controlled by party identification, however, it becomes clear that in most cases the parties were contacting partisan supporters who possessed these characteristics, not people on the other side. Again, the relationships are typically stronger for other types of party contact than for personal contacts, where they fail to reach significance for people with high levels of campaign interest.

Finally, there are the voters who are not an identifiable part of a party's base. Chief among them are nonpartisans, who were less likely to report contacts from either party, both overall and for other types of contacts. Even though their support often spells the difference between winning and losing, mobilizing them through party contacts may be counterproductive without additional information about their preferences.

A different picture from one of extensive base-mobilization emerges when one looks at the demographic correlates. First, fewer of them attain significance, signifying that the contacting levels do not diverge often by party on them. Second, the coefficients of many of the significant ones are generally weaker, indicating less party difference between contacts and non-contacts. Third, there is evidence that both Democratic and Republican parties sometimes targeted the same groups: higher-income voters, college graduates and even college degreed women, union members, and social media users. Controls for party identification show that their targets, though, are sometimes but not always partisan supporters within these groups.

Two correlations in table 11.1 are of particular note. Union members reported receiving contacts from both parties in 2020. Traditionally an important part of the Democratic base, this seems indicative of the realignment of the party constituencies that was particularly pronounced in the two Trump elections. Union leaders still typically lined up on the Democratic side of the aisle in 2020 and encouraged their rank and file to support Biden. But a significant number of the rank and file resisted their leaders' appeals and supported Trump. Realizing this, the Trump campaign had targeted them. The youngest group of voters, aged eighteen to thirty, were less likely to report contacts from either party. They always have been more difficult to track down, partly because of their greater residential mobility, compared to older voters. With college campuses closed due to the pandemic, 2020 was an especially challenging year for Democrats to mobilize this important voting base, and they underperformed in reaching out to them.

The base-mobilization pattern reappears for several key demographic groups: minorities and white Christians. Both Black people and Hispanics, and minorities overall, were generally more likely to have received Democratic contacts and less likely to have received Republican contacts in 2020. Contrastingly, other types of contact were noticeably absent from the Republican campaign where these groups were concerned. Personal contacts by the Democratic campaign were especially pronounced for these minorities and less likely or insignificant by the Republican party. What is perhaps unexpected is the weakness of this pattern for groups that were an essential component of the Democratic voter base. Clearly, the Democratic campaign in 2020 underperformed in its mobilization of Black people and Hispanics, as had been the case also in 2016 (Beck et al. 2018).

The results of table 11.1 also show evidence of Republican mobilization of its voter base. Whites who identified as born-again Christians reported more personal and other contacts from the Republican campaign—and correspondingly less from the Democratic campaign. Whites who attended church at least weekly reported more Republican attention of both types, but less from the Democrats at least for personal contacts. The GOP also was more likely to contact rural residents, the Democratic campaign less likely.

CONCLUSION

The ground game traditionally has been an important part of a presidential election campaign. This chapter has explored ground game efforts by the 2020 presidential campaigns through the lens of survey respondents as to whether they had been contacted by one or both of the major-party campaigns. It measures these efforts separately for direct personal versus other types of contacts, which combine into an overall contacting measure. To provide some perspective on the 2020 campaigns, its results are compared with earlier election campaigns for which we have parallel survey evidence.

The parties' ground games were active in 2020, as they had been in earlier years. Almost 40 percent of voters reported having been contacted by party representatives, with contacts from Democrats slightly more than those from Republicans and slight increases in both after a dip in 2016. Surprising numbers of voters reported contacts from both parties, suggesting that they may have reached beyond base mobilization strategies. Personal, face-to-face contacts were rare compared to other types of contact in 2020—and before. Despite the Biden campaign's reluctance to commit its workers to personal encounters due the pandemic, it still practiced them more than the Trump campaign.

What was unique about 2020 compared to previous years is that the parties did not concentrate their contacts disproportionately on the small number of battleground states. After a persistent emphasis in contacting in the battlegrounds earlier in the 2000s, the presidential campaigns gave equal attention to battlegrounds and non-battlegrounds in 2020. Why is not clear, but one possibility is that the ease of reaching voters via telephone, twitter, and the Internet made contacting less dependent on state campaign organizations. Moreover, if not to mobilize the party base in key states, such efforts may be directed universally to raise campaign funds. The COVID-19 pandemic also may have figured into these efforts, and earlier patterns may be restored after it has ended.

Both of the 2020 campaigns targeted their base supporters in their contacting efforts, especially when identified by partisan rather than by demographic characteristics. Understandably, Democrats were devoted to mobilizing likely Democratic voters while Republicans were reaching out to likely Republican voters. Both party campaigns targeted some demographic groups in relatively equal measure, probably because they were the "low-hanging fruit" in ease of contact, hoping to reach voters within them who were party supporters. Democrats underperformed in their efforts to reach eighteen- to thirty-year-olds in 2020, though they did better in reaching Hispanic voters than they had in earlier elections. A distinctive characteristic of 2020 was that union members were more likely to report contacts from both campaigns, perhaps capitalizing on the appeal of candidate Trump to white working-class Americans.

American presidential elections in recent years have been highly competitive in a hyperpolarized political world. A shift of fewer than eighty thousnad votes in only a handful of battleground states would have swung the 2016 election to Clinton and the 2020 election to Trump. Consequently, party strategies seem to have focused more than before on mobilizing their base of supporters through, among other things, direct party contacts rather than persuading nonpartisans to vote their way. The presidential candidates and their campaigns understand that a ground game disproportionately favorable to one party rather than its opponent can spell the difference between winning and losing. Following this logic, both parties have devoted considerable attention to mobilizing their voter bases. This chapter has not undertaken the challenging effort to estimate the vote gains that can be achieved from a ground game advantage. Previous research at the local level found substantial gains from effective grassroots organizing at the local (Cutright 1963; Cutright and Rossi 1958) and presidential levels (Beck et al. 2018) over and above the major predictors of the vote. The presidential campaigns too seem to appreciate that, even if the advantages of an effective ground game are marginal, it is at the margins that close elections are won and lost.[10]

APPENDIX A: THE CNEP US SURVEYS

This chapter is based on four national online surveys conducted in the United States under the aegis of the Comparative National Election Project (CNEP). The 2020 survey, which is the centerpiece of this chapter, was conducted online by YouGov, with 2,000 respondents. The 2016 survey also was conducted online by YouGov, with 1,600 respondents. The 2004 and 2012 surveys were conducted online by Knowledge Networks/GfK Knowledge Networks, with 1,816 and 1,289 respondents, respectively. The survey samples for each survey firm were drawn from preexisting respondent panels. YouGov used propensity scores to match respondents to the national electorate. Knowledge Networks relied on random selection from its panel. All four surveys employed weights to make their respondents demographically representative.

The advantage of these CNEP surveys is that they relied on the same pair of proximate questions to elicit reports of direct party contacts, both personal and of specified other types. The two were then combined to into a measure of overall contacts, with the more frequent "other types" contributing the most to the sum. The questions were:

> "Did a representative of any of the following political parties or candidates contact you *in person* during the campaign?"

> "Did a representative of any of the following political parties contact you in any other way such as mail, phone, email, text message, social media, etc. during the campaign?"

The 2020 questions explicitly allowed for multiple selections from the following list: Joe Biden / Democratic Party, Donald Trump / Republican Party, Jo Jorgensen / Libertarian Party, Howie Hawkins / Green Party, Some other party, and None of the above. The earlier surveys also allowed for multiple selections among major and minor party candidates in that contest.

APPENDIX B: THE BATTLEGROUND STATES

2020: Nine states met the 6 percent or less major-party-vote margin criterion: Arizona, Florida, Georgia, Michigan, Nevada, North Carolina, Pennsylvania, Texas, Wisconsin. Survey respondents resided in all 9, N=691, 35 percent of total.

2016: Thirteen states met the 6 percent or less major-party-vote margin criterion: Arizona, Colorado, Florida, Georgia, Maine, Michigan, Minnesota, Nevada, New Hampshire, North Carolina, Pennsylvania, Virginia, Wisconsin. Survey respondents resided in all 13; N=537, 34 percent of total.

2012: Eight states met the 6 percent or less major-party-vote margin criterion: Colorado, Florida, Iowa, New Hampshire, North Carolina, Ohio, Pennsylvania, Virginia. Survey respondents resided in all 8; N=294, 23 percent of total.

2004: Twelve states were decided by a margin of 6 percent or less in the major-party-vote: Colorado, Florida, Iowa, Michigan, Minnesota, Nevada, New Hampshire, New Mexico, Ohio, Oregon, Pennsylvania, Wisconsin. Survey respondents were drawn from all twelve; N=528, 29 percent of total.

NOTES

1. On the distinction between the air war and the ground game, see inter alia the study by Zhang and Chung (2020).

2. For an insightful study of modern ground game techniques and their effectiveness, see Issenberg (2012).

3. An indirect form of validation comes from the contacts reported from each party by party's base groups. Democrats should be more likely to receive Democratic contacts, Republicans to receive Republican contacts; and so forth.

4. CNEP surveys have been conducted in over sixty elections in twenty-nine countries, almost always employing the same questions to ask about party contacts. For more on the project, see u.osu.edu/cnep.

5. The other leading US survey asking about party contacts, the American National Election Studies, does not separate personal from other kinds of contacts.

6. Appendix A contains descriptions of these surveys and their party contact questions.

7. See Darr (2020) on field offices and https://www.nationalpopularvote.com /map-general-election-campaign-events-and-tv-ad-spending-2020-presidential-candi dates for FairVote's data on concentration of presidential campaign resources on the 2020 battleground states.

8. A thoughtful illustration of this comes from Shaw (2006, 57). In his analysis of the 2000 and 2004 campaigns, he distinguishes among the Bush campaign's twenty-nine publicly listed targeted states, twenty-three "real" targeted states, and the "real real" list of fifteen states. The Democrats' priority list presumably did not exactly replicate that of the Bush campaigns.

9. Income is measured in categories of actual dollars; age is in years; Internet election news in days per week; and regular voter in number of times (from 0–3) voting in 2016 and 2020 general election and 2020 primary.

10. I am grateful for contributions that made this work possible from Richard Gunther, Erik Nisbet, Tom Wood, Chip Eveland; my colleagues with the Comparative National Elections Project; and the staff of YouGov, especially Ashley Grosse and Alexander Marsolais.

Chapter Twelve

From Tea Party to Trump Party

W. Henry Crossman and Ronald B. Rapoport

Since its inception in 2009, the Tea Party movement has shown significant success in shaping electoral outcomes for Republican candidates, defeating establishment candidates, and serving as an important engine for Republican general election victories. Yet in the first presidential contest after the Tea Party's inception, establishment candidate Mitt Romney captured the 2012 Republican nomination, defeating candidates with greater appeal to Tea Party supporters, such as Newt Gingrich and Herman Cain.

The 2016 Republican primaries looked more promising for Tea Party supporters as Ted Cruz, Rand Paul and Marco Rubio, early entrants to the race who "each rose to power with support from the Tea Party movement," outperformed establishment favorite Jeb Bush (Hook 2015). Tea Party optimism appeared well-founded until Donald Trump declared his candidacy on June 29, 2015. Within three weeks he had taken the lead, which he never relinquished. Trump was neither establishment nor Tea Party. Though his outsider status and commitment to disrupting the establishment political system would seemingly resonate with Tea Party supporters, Trump's pledge to spend heavily on infrastructure, his disregard for deficits, and his support for tariffs differentiated him from the typical Tea Party candidate.

From its beginning, the Tea Party has been an identifiable and relatively cohesive faction in the Republican Party, as evidenced by Tea Party–endorsed candidates defeating multiple establishment Republicans in primary elections as well as journalists' and scholars' frequent identification of candidates as either Tea Party or establishment. As the 2016 Republican nomination contest began, and until Trump declared, Cruz seemed the likely Tea Party favorite. Jenny Beth Martin, president of the Tea Party Patriots organization, dismissed Trump's candidacy at the 2016 CPAC conference, declaring, "He loves himself more than our country, he loves himself more than the Constitution. Donald Trump has no business thinking he's Tea Party" (Hallerman 2016).

Given Trump's ideological and partisan inconsistency, Tea Party skepticism of his conservative credentials was not unwarranted. He had been a registered Democrat from 2001 through 2009 and had only registered as Republican in 2012, around the same time that he moved from being pro-choice to being pro-life (Politifacts 2015).

How successful would Trump be in attracting and holding Tea Party support in the primaries, and, after becoming the Republican nominee, in the general election? The latter was a significant concern, given the rancorous nature of the Republican nomination process, Cruz's failure to offer the expected Trump endorsement at the Republican convention, and Trump's divergence from traditional Tea Party positions on the deficit, free trade, and other key issues. After all, Tea Party supporters failed to warm up to Romney in 2012 even after he became the Republican nominee, and they failed to adopt his policies, even though they supported him over Obama (Rapoport 2013).

Although the role of the Tea Party and Tea Party activists in the Republican Party over the last ten years has been widely acknowledged, there have been few large-scale studies of Tea Party activists. Using a two-year panel study (2015–2017) of almost nine hundred FreedomWorks supporters (the largest Tea Party organization), we focus on the transformational role Trump has played in redirecting Tea Party supporters' attitudes and priorities. We find a major shift in priority from deficit to immigration, and a large increase in positive Trump evaluations, even among those with the most negative view of him during the 2016 nomination process. That such a process extended through the 2020 election should not be surprising.

Given their intense activity and ideological commitment, Tea Party activists in 2016 presented a significant challenge for persuasion by Trump. Their transition from one of the least pro-Trump constituencies to one of the most offers a unique lens through which to observe Trump's success in taking over the Republican Party. In early 2016, 61 percent of those with a positive view of the Tea Party (assessed in 2014–2015 before Trump's candidacy) rated Trump favorably on the 100-point feeling thermometer scale—a poor rating given the Tea Party's power and importance. Trump's selection of Tea Party candidates such as Mike Pence, Mike Pompeo, and Mark Meadows to fill key administration positions throughout his term acknowledged the centrality of Tea Party support to Trump's political base.

Tea Party support for Trump extended and increased after the 2016 election, even though Trump continued to pursue his own agenda, which often diverged significantly from traditional Tea Party and conservative positions. By 2018 positive evaluations had increased to 78 percent (Pew 2019), and by the time of the 2020 election to 84 percent (Pew 2020).[1] And that favorability far surpassed the Trump evaluations of other Republicans (by 20% in 2018 and 2020, up from 15% in 2016). Not surprisingly, this strong support translated into almost unanimous support for Trump in 2020 when 97 percent of this group voted for Trump, seven percent higher than among other Republicans (Pew 2020).

All of this suggests the transformation in Tea Party supporters' evaluations of Trump and issue priorities is a permanent departure from "traditional" Tea Party views in favor of "Trumpian" support.

TRUMP, THE TEA PARTY, AND FREEDOMWORKS

Although Trump commanded the lead among all Republicans in nomination preference from late July 2015 on, his support was far weaker among Tea Party supporters. In late January 2016, Trump led Cruz 2 to 1 (41% versus 19%) among all Republicans, but among Tea Party supporters it was far closer (37% versus 34%) (Agiesta 2016). We identified a similar difference in a survey of Republican identifiers, conducted between January 21 and February 8, 2016, in which Trump led Cruz among Tea Party backers 34 percent to 28 percent. Yet among the 34 percent of Tea Party supporters who identified as "strong" supporters, Cruz led Trump 41 percent to 25 percent. There was even less support for Trump among FreedomWorks activists than among strong Tea Party backers in the electorate: Cruz led Trump among this group by a better than 3 to 1 margin (55% to 15%). Though there was substantial Tea Party support for Trump, it was less than among Republicans at large, and it declined as the strength of Tea Party identification increased.

These "strong" Tea Party supporters and activists are an important subgroup, as the number of Tea Party activists in a district significantly impacts how members of Congress voted on issues salient to the Tea Party (Bailey et al. 2012). The number of Tea Party activists has a significant effect on congressional voting patterns even when district mean evaluations of the Tea Party do not, a finding that holds even with an extensive set of controls including the prior DWNOMINATE score for the member of Congress, presidential vote, Tea Party group endorsements, and selected demographics (Bailey et al. 2012).

METHODOLOGY

In this chapter, we use a panel survey of FreedomWorks email subscribers, carried out from 2015 to 2017. The initial survey of FreedomWorks activists was conducted in 2015–2016. At the time of the survey, FreedomWorks was the most dominant Tea Party group, as 45 percent of all 556,551 Tea Party group members belonged to FreedomWorks (Burghart and Zeskind 2015). From the Tea Party's inception, FreedomWorks had the largest support structure, even before its membership exploded (Burghart and Zeskind 2015).

FreedomWorks email subscribers was the universe from which we drew our respondents. This group constitutes a reasonable sample of Tea Party activists as 85 percent of respondents report either being actual members of a Tea Party group or actively participating in Tea Party activities between January 2014 and the date of the survey. We refer to our sample as FreedomWorks activists.

FreedomWorks is impressive not only in its size, but in its influence on election outcomes. An endorsement from FreedomWorks in 2010 was worth an increase in Republican vote of about 2.1 percent, while endorsements by Tea Party Express and other Tea Party groups had no significant effect (Karpowitz et al. 2011). (Bailey et al. 2012) finds an endorsement from FreedomWorks was associated with a 2.4 percent vote increase and was significantly related to support for Tea Party proposals among members of the 112th Congress.

The 2015 survey was disseminated to FreedomWorks email subscribers after Trump announced his candidacy but before the Iowa caucuses. The first email was sent in July 2015, with a reminder in January 2016. Surveys were sent to approximately 500,000 individuals, and 9,473 individuals completed surveys. On blast emails sent frequently by organizations such as Freedom-Works, the open rate tends to be small (around 10%). Therefore, about 50,000 individuals would be expected to open the survey invitation, of which approximately 20 percent completed the survey. These responses are referred to as the "2015 survey" since more than three-quarters of responses arrived prior to the January 2016 mailing.[2]

In March 2017, FreedomWorks sent another blast email to their subscribers. Of the 9,473 respondents who completed the 2015 survey, about 40 percent had unsubscribed from the FreedomWorks list or had entered incorrect ID numbers, so effectively only 6,687 individuals were eligible to take the 2017 survey. The 868 individuals who completed the 2017 survey comprise the panel on which this chapter is based.[3]

RESULTS AND DISCUSSION

Candidate Choice and Favorability

Among FreedomWorks subscribers, Cruz was the overwhelming favorite over Trump in the pre-Iowa survey. This fact simply shows the preference ordering, not the affect for Trump, as even those preferring Cruz or another candidate might have still viewed Trump favorably.

However, overall, FreedomWorks subscribers rated Trump relatively poorly pre-Iowa. Respondents rated candidates on a seven-point favorability scale ranging from poor to outstanding. The seven-point scale was condensed into a three-point scale with the three above-average categories ("outstanding," "well above average," and "slightly above average") combined and coded as 1, the three below average categories ("slightly below average," "well below-average," and "poor") combined and coded as −1, and "average" coded as 0. As figure 12.1 shows, taking the mean for each of the thirteen major candidates on the condensed three-point scale, Trump's mean rating places him ninth (and significantly below the top six rated candidates). Only Jeb Bush, Chris Christie, Lindsey Graham, and Mike Huckabee rated below him.[4]

Despite Trump's relatively low ratings among the full sample, there was still a distinguishable and significant constituency strongly attracted to him. As figure 12.2 shows, when respondents selected their top candidate for the nomination, although Cruz was the overwhelming favorite with 55 percent support, Trump's 15 percent support placed him second, ahead of other typical Tea Party favorites Ben Carson (11% support) and Rand Paul (9% support).[5]

But positive intensity toward Trump was accompanied by significant negative intensity, and his high level of each makes him unique among pre-nomination Republican candidates. In addition to indicating their top choice,

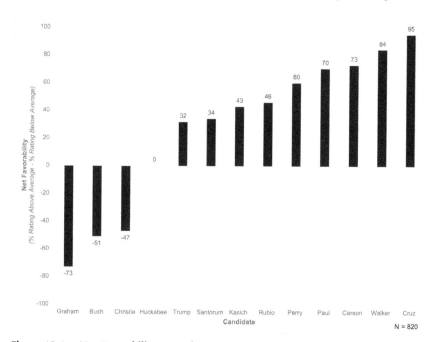

Figure 12.1. Net Favorability Toward 2016 Republican Nomination Candidates

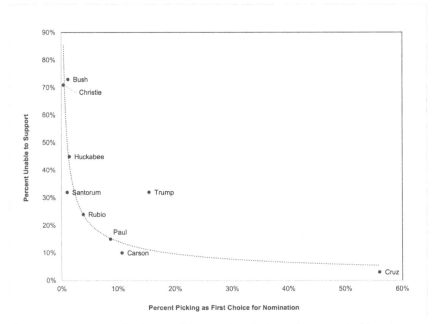

Figure 12.2.   Percent Selecting Candidate as First Choice and Percent Unable to Support

respondents selected candidates they could not support for the nomination. As expected, there was a strong inverse relationship between the percentage picking someone as the top choice and the percentage indicating they could not support them. For example, 55 percent selected Cruz as their first choice, but only about 3 percent said they could never support him. Conversely, candidates selected as a first choice by very few respondents have a larger number of respondents rejecting them outright. For example, Christie and Bush received only scant first choice support (1% each) but high levels of rejection (70% each).

Trump, on the other hand, was unique in receiving both significant first choice support (15%) and high levels of rejection (32%). Compared to other candidates with lower levels of support (such as Carson and Paul), two to three times as many respondents indicated they were unable to support Trump, whereas only 10 percent were unable to support Carson and 15 percent were unable to support Paul.

Change in Primary Candidate Favorability

Although net favorability ratings placed Trump near the bottom of the fourteen major Republican presidential candidates and many indicated they could not support him for the nomination, this survey came before he captured the Republican nomination and won the general election. What happened between 2015 and 2017? Did Tea Party activists overcome their doubts and embrace Trump once he become the nominee and once he won the election? Or did they turn on Trump as they had on Romney in 2012?

For each of the eight Republican politicians about whom we asked in both 2015 and 2017, we calculated net favorability for both the 2015 and 2017 waves by subtracting the proportion unfavorable from the proportion favorable. Trump not only shows the largest shift in the positive direction (from +32 to +82), but Trump's 2017 favorability ratings were nearly as high as those of Paul (+83) and Cruz (+88), and surpass Carson (+76), who rated far above him in 2015. Though 40 percent rated Trump average or below in 2015, only 12 percent did so in 2017, not much different from the ratings for Cruz, Carson, and Paul, and far below the 40 percent for Rubio in 2017. Conversely, establishment candidates Ryan, Kasich, and Bush showed significant declines in favorability over the same period with significantly more rating them negatively than positively.

As expected, Trump's 2017 evaluations among those already favorable toward him in 2015 remained extremely high. Even among the approximately 20 percent of respondents who both rated him below average and said they were unable to support him for the nomination in 2015, almost three-quarters (71%) rated him above average in 2017.

Individual-Level Change in Trump Evaluations

We examine three possible explanations for increased Trump favorability: a change in respondents' issue positions as the Trump campaign progressed to victory and his positions and agenda became more appealing; a change in priorities assigned to specific issues; and a change in which factors had the strongest impact on Trump evaluations.

Trump Support versus Cruz Support in 2015

Since Cruz was such a favorite of the Tea Party and our FreedomWorks sample, we used him as a proxy for a prototypical Tea Party candidate and compare bases of support for Trump to those for Cruz. Our predictors for 2015 evaluations include issues Trump emphasized during the primary campaign: immigration, law and order, and a populist domestic agenda promising to protect Social Security and Medicare. In addition, because immigration was a key issue for Trump (and the deficit—with his promise to protect Social Security and create a massive infrastructure program—much less so), we also measured the difference in priority assigned to immigration versus deficit reduction.[6] Along with a range of demographic variables, we also included attitudes more closely related to the Tea Party: ideology, evaluations of the Tea Party and evaluations of the Republican Party.

To the degree that Trump appealed to constituencies different from Cruz's, we should find the same variables having different effects on evaluations of each. For example, since immigration was more central to Trump's campaign than Cruz's we should expect a stronger effect on Trump's evaluations than on Cruz's. Conversely, because Cruz so strongly identified as conservative, we should find ideology more strongly related to Cruz's evaluations than to Trump's.

Examining results for Cruz evaluations in table 12.1, we find a clear effect of core Tea Party issues. Evaluations of the Tea Party and conservative ideology, but also willingness to cut Social Security and Medicare to reduce the deficit are the only significant predictors of Cruz evaluations (all $p < 0.001$). Surprisingly, immigration does not have a significant effect, nor do demographics or foreign policy attitudes. Cruz's embeddedness in the Tea Party, combined with ideology, overwhelms these other factors.

Looking at the same set of predictors for Trump evaluations, the lack of overlap was evident. Immigration—both the position on number of immigrants allowed and the priority of immigration compared with deficit reduction—as well as foreign policy all had significant effects on Trump evaluations ($p < 0.05$). Yet neither Tea Party evaluation nor conservative ideology—factors that strongly related to Cruz evaluations—had significant effects on Trump evaluations. Surprisingly, given Cruz's support for shutting down the government over repealing Obamacare, unwillingness to compromise had a significant effect on Trump evaluations but not on Cruz evaluations.

Attitudes about cutting the deficit even if it means cuts to social programs like Social Security and Medicare significantly affected both Cruz and Trump evaluations, but the effects go in opposite directions. While those more willing to cut social programs to balance the budget were more supportive of Cruz, those favoring protecting social programs over reducing the deficit were significantly more likely to support Trump, showing Trump's populist appeal even within our sample. For example, a respondent who strongly supported cutting these programs to reduce the deficit rates Trump more than 0.6 units lower (on the seven-point scale) than someone strongly opposed to cutting these programs, but rated Cruz 0.4 units higher.

Trump's campaign issues were uniquely important to Trump's evaluations in the FreedomWorks sample, but even with these included in the model, there remains significant unexplained variance in Trump evaluations. With all thirteen predictors the model explains only about 10 percent of the variance

Table 12.1. Regressions of Cruz and Trump Evaluations on Selected Variables

	Cruz Evaluations (2015)		Trump Evaluations (2015)		Trump Evaluations (2017)	
	Coefficient	Std. Error	Coefficient	Std. Error	Coefficient	Std. Error
Cut Social Security/ Medicare to Balance Budget	0.075*	0.021	−0.123***	0.05	−0.08***	0.032
Favor Compromise	−0.043	0.03	−0.173***	0.073	−0.051	0.047
Decrease Immigration	0.016	0.032	0.246**	0.078	0.172**	0.05
Immigration More Important Than Deficit Reduction	0.017	0.011	0.074**	0.027	0.04***	0.018
Terrorism More Important than Protecting Privacy	−0.053	0.03	0.114	0.073	0.146**	0.047
Evaluation of Tea Party	0.332*	0.035	0.122	0.084	0.155**	0.054
Evaluation of Republican Party	0.036	0.025	0.161[b]	0.06	0.167*	0.038
Male Gender	0.111	0.07	−0.196	0.169	−0.116	0.109
Education Level	−0.013	0.022	0.013	0.052	−0.033	0.034
Age	0.057***	0.026	0.151***	0.062	0.168*	0.04
Ideology (Liberal to Conservative)	0.237*	0.049	0.014	0.119	0.204**	0.077
Intervene to Protect US Interests	0.057	0.077	0.279	0.185	0.226	0.12
Intervene in Support of International Law	−0.011	0.066	−0.351***	0.159	−0.200	0.103
(Constant)	2.057*	0.424	4.365*	1.022	3.712*	0.66
N	558		558		558	
Adjusted R-Square	0.279		0.107		0.201	

Note: *p < 0.001; **p < 0.01; ***p < 0.05

(Adjusted R-sq = 0.107), while the same set of variables explain almost three times the variance in Cruz evaluations (Adjusted R-sq = 0.279).

Trump Support in 2017

At the beginning of his campaign, Trump was clearly not a typical Tea Party candidate in his bases of support and opposition. To assess whether his evaluations became more closely tied to typical Republican and Tea Party issues and groups as the campaign continued into the general election, we used the same independent variables from the 2015 model to predict Trump's 2017 evaluations. We evaluated whether the 2015 predictors structure evaluations of Trump two years later better than they did in 2015.

Since the independent and dependent variables were measured almost two years apart, it would be surprising if 2015 variables are equally predictive of 2017 Trump evaluations as they were of 2015 evaluations. As Trump became first the nominee and then president, issue attitudes that typically structure views toward Republicans and Tea Party candidates like Cruz might become more strongly related to Trump evaluations. Additionally, the selection of Mike Pence, a Tea Party caucus member, as vice president, as well as other Tea Party stalwarts like Ben Carson as secretary of HHS, Rick Perry as secretary of energy, and Mike Pompeo as CIA director emphasized Trump's links to the Tea Party at the beginning of his term. This relationship intensified as the 2020 election grew closer and as more prominent Tea Party supporters became part of his inner circle.

Table 12.1 (columns two and three) shows that most of the 2015 variables that significantly affected 2015 Trump evaluations—attitudes on immigration, deficit reduction versus social program protection, and foreign policy—continued to do so in 2017.[7] Unsurprisingly, the coefficients associated with each of these attitudes diminished in magnitude, but all remained statistically significant.

However, after showing virtually no effect on 2015 Trump evaluations, 2015 ideology becomes highly significant. Additionally, Tea Party evaluations had a greater effect on 2017 Trump evaluations compared to their effect on 2015 evaluations and evaluations of the Republican Party remain highly significant without decreasing in magnitude. The adjusted R-square of the 2017 model was almost double that of 2015 (0.107 versus 0.201). Even though they were measured two years before measures of the dependent variable, 2015 evaluations of the Republican Party and the Tea Party, as well as ideology, were more entwined with attitudes toward Trump in 2017 than they were in 2015.

Having established what factors explain attitudes toward Trump in both 2015 and 2017, we next explore changes in the sample beyond the increased positive affect for Trump and evaluate how the sample changed in other attitudes. Specifically, we investigated whether Tea Party activists have become part of the "Trump" Party between 2015 and 2017 by shifting away from traditional Tea Party orthodoxy in favor of Trump's issues and priorities, and, secondly, whether these changes were restricted to those who supported Trump initially or if it also affected those with negative evaluations of him in 2015.

Shifting Issue Priorities

If the Tea Party was becoming more Trump-like, we should find this change reflected not only in evaluations of Trump, but also in increased support for Trump policy positions. This shift should be evident among those who both favored and opposed Trump in 2015, since many became more favorable toward him. We examine shifts in the overall sample as well as among those who selected Trump as their top choice for the nomination in 2015, whom we label "Trump Supporters" and those who indicated they could not support Trump for the nomination, whom we label "Trump Rejectors." We first look at shifts in issue priorities and then examine changes in attitudes from 2015 to 2017, focusing on shifts in issue areas associated with Trump.

Respondents were generally stable in their top issue priority choice. As figure 12.3 shows, in both waves, "Shrinking Government" and "Repealing ACA" were at the top, and only three of the fourteen issues surveyed show changes greater than 2.7 percent.[8] However, two of those three were particularly interesting since they are so closely related to Trump's priorities: immigration and the budget deficit. As expected, these changes made our sample more reflective of Trump's priorities. Most strikingly, between 2015

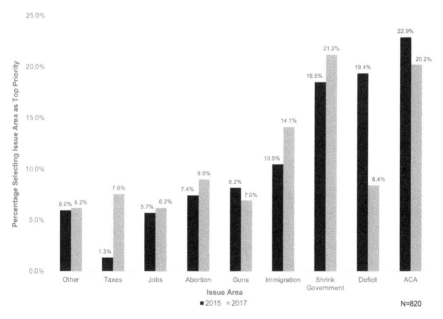

Figure 12.3. Percentage Selecting Each Issue Area as Top Priority

and 2017 the budget deficit became far less important to Tea Party activists, while immigration became much more important. While the deficit was a long-standing focus of the movement, immigration is not.

The *Contract from America*, a Tea Party manifesto emphasizing repeal of the Affordable Care Act (ACA), shrinking the size of government, and balancing the budget by reducing spending, does not even mention immigration (Davis 2010). Tea Party activists' prioritization of deficit reduction extends back at least to 2011, as surveys of FreedomWorks activists disseminated in 2011, 2014, and 2015 show that 20 percent or more of respondents in each survey rated the budget deficit as their top priority (Rapoport and Lienesch 2014).

However, between 2015 and 2017 the issue Tea Party activists selected as their highest priority shifted significantly. Although traditional Tea Party issues such as shrinking the size of government and repealing the ACA remained top priorities, the budget deficit, which had been the second highest priority in 2015, dropped to fifth, behind immigration, abortion, repealing the ACA, and shrinking the size of government. Fewer than half as many selected the deficit as their top priority issue in 2017 as had only two years earlier (8% in 2017 versus 19% in 2015).[9]

A significantly higher percentage of respondents selected taxes and immigration as top priorities in 2017 than in 2015. Given Trump's emphasis on immigration, this shift in priority was particularly important, especially since the relative priority assigned to immigration versus the deficit was a significant predictor of Trump evaluations in 2015 (see table 12.1).[10] Though different from immigration in important respects, the shift in priority for taxes demonstrates how quickly Trump positions were adopted by FreedomWorks activists. The survey was sent less than three weeks after Trump released his tax cut proposal on April 26.[11] Taxes, which had been the top priority of only 1.3 percent of respondents, more than tripled to seven percent.

The shift toward Trump positions from 2015 to 2017, even evident among Trump Rejectors who were initially less inclined toward Trump positions, reveals Trump's influence on Tea Party attitudes. Among both Trump Supporters and Rejectors the percentage of respondents ranking immigration as their top priority increased and the percentage ranking the budget deficit at the top decreased. Those least supportive of Trump prior to his nomination account for nearly all the increase in selecting immigration as a top priority, while the decline in the deficit ranking occurs among both Trump Supporters and Rejectors. The two groups were similar in their prioritization of the deficit in both the 2015 and 2017 waves of the survey.

Whereas in 2015 Trump Supporters were about as likely to prioritize immigration over the deficit (19%) as to prioritize the deficit over immigration

(15%), by 2017 twice as many Trump Supporters gave immigration a higher priority than the deficit (17% versus 8%). Trump Rejectors showed the same dynamic: in 2015, six times as many prioritized the deficit over immigration as the reverse (24% versus 6%); by 2017, more prioritized immigration over the deficit as the reverse (11% versus 7%).

Trump's disinterest in reducing the budget deficit was evident in his administration's first proposed budget for fiscal year 2018 and the 2018 Republican tax-reform bill, which were estimated to increase the federal deficit by approximately $1 trillion by 2020 (Jones 2018). Trump's position on the deficit was presaged by an interview in May 2016 when he stated, "[D]ebt was always sort of interesting to me. Now we're in a different situation with a country, but I would borrow knowing that if the economy crashed you could make a deal. And if the economy was good it was good so therefore you can't lose" (Kurtzleben 2016).

The decreased concern about the budget deficit is reflected in changes in support for spending on social programs. We asked respondents about their willingness to reduce the budget deficit even if it meant a cut in programs like Social Security and Medicare. Deficit hawks, whom we might expect to find among FreedomWorks activists, should show a willingness to make these cuts. Evidence from the 2015 survey supported this expectation, as almost twice as many respondents favored cutting the deficit even if it means cuts to social welfare programs as opposed it.[12] In 2017, these respondents still demonstrated more support than opposition for cutting the deficit, but the percentage supporting cuts to social programs diminished significantly.[13]

Figure 12.4 shows Trump Rejectors shift more than Trump Supporters on the deficit-social programs issue. In 2015, Trump Rejectors who favored cutting the deficit at the expense of social programs outnumbered opponents by 37 percentage points, but in 2017 this gap decreased by 15 points to 22 percentage points. Among Trump Supporters, opposition to cutting the deficit already outstripped support by about 11 percentage points in 2015, and this gap widened to about 20 percentage points in 2017. Although there is clear movement for both groups in opposition to cutting the deficit at the expense of social program spending, the increase is greater among Trump Rejectors. As a result, the difference between the groups declines even though Supporters and Rejectors remain on opposite sides of the issue.

Immigration issues played a central role in the Trump campaign and were closely linked to law and order, with claims that Mexicans were rapists and calls for banning Muslims, deporting illegal immigrants, and building a border wall becoming constant refrains at Trump's rallies. From 2015 to 2017 the percent of Tea Party activists indicating immigration as their top priority increased, reflecting a shift in support of Trump's policy priorities as

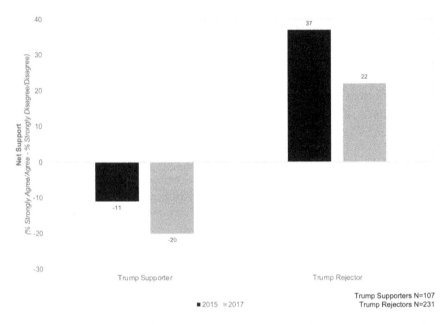

Figure 12.4. Net Support for Reducing the Deficit Even if it Means Cut to Social Security/Medicare

evaluations of him surged over the same two-year period. Since we did not ask identical questions on immigration across the two waves of the survey, examining change in issue positions was not possible. Nonetheless, the 2017 Tea Party sample was clearly aligned with Trump's immigration positions, though the intensity of support varies between Trump Supporters and Rejectors. Among Trump Supporters, 94 percent, 89 percent, and 79 percent, respectively, favor "building the wall," "deporting illegal immigrants," and "banning Muslims from entering the U.S." Among Trump Rejectors, the percentages are 72, 70, and 52. Just as the full sample had shifted to prioritize immigration issues more highly, FreedomWorks activists' show high support for Trump-specific policies regardless of initial support of Trump.

Evaluations of the Tea Party

Finally, we address whether positive affect for Trump has contributed to lowered evaluations of the Tea Party. Our argument that there has been a shift from Tea Party to Trump Party might suggest that Trump favorability supplanted Tea Party loyalty. If so, we should find that those most favorable toward Trump in 2015 became less favorable toward the Tea Party in 2017

Table 12.2. Effect of 2015 Candidate Evaluations on 2017 Tea Party Evaluation (Controlling for 2015 Tea Party Evaluation)

	Coefficient	Std. Error	Coefficient	Std. Error
Tea Party Evaluation (2015)	0.456***	0.033	0.412***	0.037
Trump Evaluation (2015)	0.073***	0.016	0.073***	0.017
Cruz Evaluation (2015)			0.037	0.04
Carson Evaluation (2015)			−0.026	0.026
Political Ideology			0.177***	0.051
Republican Party Evaluation (2015)			0.005	0.024
(Constant)	0.874***	0.089	2.117***	0.383
N	646		646	
Adjusted R-Square	0.252		0.264	

Note: *p < 0.001; **p < 0.01; ***p < 0.05

as the Tea Party was replaced by a Trump Party. Conversely, if the Tea Party and Trump have become more closely entwined and mutually supportive, we would expect to find 2015 Trump evaluations produce more positive attitudes toward the Tea Party in 2017.

Table 12.2 shows the results of two models used to test these possibilities. First, we simply regress 2017 Tea Party evaluations on 2015 evaluations and 2015 Trump evaluations. The results reveal Trump evaluations produce significantly higher Tea Party evaluations two years later. The coefficient for Trump evaluation is 0.073 ($p < 0.001$) and the difference between someone rating Trump as poor to someone rating him as excellent was an almost half point increase in Tea Party evaluation in 2017.

Since other candidates like Cruz and Carson were more closely tied to the Tea Party, the second model includes evaluations of Cruz and Carson, as well as political ideology and evaluations of the Republican Party. Compared to the first model, the coefficient for Trump does not change (b = 0.073; $p < 0.001$), but, surprisingly, none of the coefficients for evaluations of any other candidate is significant (in all cases $p > 0.20$) and the coefficient for Carson is negative. Similarly, the coefficient for Republican Party evaluations is effectively zero (b = 0.005). Other than Trump evaluations and the lagged Tea Party evaluation, only ideology has a significant impact on 2017 Tea Party evaluations, and its effect was less than that for Trump evaluations.

Though the change in attitudes between 2015 and 2017 aligns with Trump's agenda, it appears that affection for Trump contributed to more positive Tea Party evaluations, rather than detracted from them. Combined with the result that 2015 Tea Party evaluations positively impacted 2017 Trump evaluations, it appears that the Tea Party-Trump relationship was one of mutual reinforcement rather than a substitution effect.[14]

CONCLUSION

Among FreedomWorks activists, Donald Trump moved from being an unpopular candidate for the Republican nomination to becoming an extraordinarily popular president over a two-year period. Despite a small core of support early in the nomination process, Trump was unpopular among FreedomWorks activists overall, and only four of the thirteen Republican presidential candidates were rated less favorably. In 2015, nearly one-third of the sample indicated they were unwilling to support Trump for the nomination.

By 2017, Trump was almost as popular as Tea Party stalwart Ted Cruz, and even those who had rated him in the two lowest categories and were unwilling to support him for the nomination in 2015 had come around to high levels of support. At the beginning of the campaign, Trump support among Tea Party activists was more strongly related to support for issues not traditionally associated with the Tea Party: protecting social security; lack of concern about the deficit; and high priority for immigration issues. By 2017, Trump's support base included more typical predictors such as Tea Party and Republican Party affect.

Remarkably, those assigning highest priority to reducing the deficit dropped from 20 percent—a level it had held among FreedomWorks activists since 2011—to only 8 percent, while those selecting immigration increased. In addition, the large shift in support for protecting Social Security and Medicare over deficit reduction aligns with Trump campaign positions and directly contradicts policy preferences traditionally held by Tea Party members in 2015.

The Tea Party appears to have become a Trump Party. At the same time, positive affect for Trump did not detract from Tea Party evaluations but rather increased them. Additionally, Trump nomination activity, but not activity for other candidates, was significantly related to increased activity for the Tea Party between 2015 and 2017. Rather than concluding that the Tea Party has become the Trump Party, more accurately, a new form of Tea Party—a Trumpian Tea Party—emerged over the 2016 campaign.

Over the course of his term, the Trump administration became increasingly dominated by Tea Party figures, as Mike Pompeo took over as Secretary of State, Mick Mulvaney became head of OMB, and Mark Meadows became chief of staff. But Tea Party priorities like the budget deficit were no longer significant policy positions. For instance, Mulvaney, formerly a deficit hawk willing to shut down the government during the Obama Administration, oversaw a large increase in the deficit under Trump. During the early days of the coronavirus pandemic, the administration championed the Paycheck Protection Program, a massive spending bill that included direct aid for individuals and businesses—the kind of measure that would likely have been anathema to the pre-Trump Tea Party, but by 2020 raised virtually no criticism from its activists. In the aftermath of the 2020 election, Pompeo and Meadows further tied their political fates to Trump's, playing particularly crucial roles in denying the legitimacy of the Biden win. As the 2020 presidential campaign demonstrated, the shift in Tea Party activists' favorability toward Trump and his positions appears to now be a permanent transformation in Tea Party supporters' attitudes and issue positions. The continued relevance of Tea Party supporters and leaders during—and even after—the 2020 presidential election reinforces the shift from Tea Party to Trump Party.[15]

NOTES

1. We owe a special debt of gratitude to Scott Keeter for supplying us with the Tea Party variable from earlier baseline studies allowing us to merge it with wave 78 of the American Trends Panel.

2. The authors' agreement with FreedomWorks was to provide respondents a unique identification number to match respondents from different waves of the survey, rather than house the email list ourselves.

3. To assess whether 2015 characteristics influenced the decision to drop out of the survey we use an asymmetric ordinal statistic (Somer's d). Since the sample size is so large, even small substantive effects will be statistically significant. We evaluate ordinal statistics (Somer's d) for evaluations of Republican contestants for the nomination and for important groups, as well as for previous levels of activity for both the Tea Party and the Republican Party (Romney-Ryan in 2012 and Republican House candidates in both 2012 and 2014), and demographics.

In no case does the correlation exceed 0.050, with an average of 0.013. Only 10 of the 35 correlations is even significant at the 0.05 level. More importantly, it is not those who are most favorable to Trump who are likely to remain in the sample, but those who are slightly more negative (d = −0.025) while those more favorable to Cruz are slightly more likely to remain in the sample (d = 0.044). No activity level (Republican presidential or congressional) reaches even 0.01.

4. Using the full seven-point scale produces almost identical results.

5. When the July 2015 survey was initially disseminated, Walker and Perry were serious candidates. When the January 2016 follow-up was disseminated, they had already dropped out of the race. As a result, for respondents picking either of the two candidates as their first choice, their second choice was promoted to first choice. For the handful of respondents rating the two of them 1–2, their third choice was considered their first choice. This permits comparability between the two emailing's for the first wave of the survey.

6. Respondents were asked to select and rank the top five issue areas from a larger set of issue areas. If an area was not one of the top five, it was assigned six. The score for the immigration area was then subtracted from that for the deficit

area. If immigration was rated 1 and the deficit 4, this would give a score of 3. If the ranking were reversed, the score would be –3.

7. Using 2015 attitudes as predictors of 2017 Trump evaluations guards against reverse causation in which 2017 Trump evaluations might cause attitude shifts between 2015 and 2017 in line with Trump's positions and inflate the actual effect of respondent attitudes on 2017 Trump evaluations.

8. The areas were ACA, shrink government, deficit, immigration, guns, abortion, jobs, taxes, education, involvement in Middle East, gay marriage, reforming justice system, inequality of income, and environmental regulation.

9. A difference of means on the deficit as top issue priority comparing the first and second waves yields a highly significant difference for the sample as a whole and for both Rejectors and Supporters ($p < 0.01$). Immigration as the top issue shows a significant upward movement ($p < 0.01$) for the sample as a whole and for Trump Rejectors, but not for Trump Supporters ($p > 0.20$) who are already at a high level.

10. It is also the case that higher priority for immigration in 2017 was a significant predictor of Trump evaluations.

11. https://trumpwhitehouse.archives.gov/articles/president-trump-proposed-massive-tax-cut-heres-need-know/

12. The agree and strongly agree responses are combined into one category, the slightly agree and slightly oppose responses into a second category, and the disagree and strongly disagree responses into a third. Using the full range does not affect the results. Favor includes agree and strongly agree responses. 46.0 percent of respondents favored making these cuts compared to 25.3 percent of respondents who opposed it.

13. Support declined from 46.0 percent in 2015 to 39.4 percent in 2017. This result is significant, $p < 0.05$.

14. We also ran analysis to determine whether activity for Trump detracted/substituted for Tea Party activity. The results there reinforced our findings on Tea Party evaluations. Activity for Trump was associated with increased activity for Tea Party groups. So, rather than diminishing Tea Party activity, Trump activity actually increased Tea Party activity.

15. We would like to acknowledge the contributions of Rachel Lienesch, Andrew Langer, and Scott Keeter, as well as to FreedomWorks for their significant contributions to this article.

Part IV

WOMEN AND PARTY POLITICS

Chapter Thirteen

The Partisan Gap among Women in Elective Office

2020 and Beyond

Laurel Elder

The 2020 elections resulted in much to celebrate for those who believe American democracy is more legitimate, more representative, and produces better policy outcomes when our elected officials more accurately reflect the population in terms of gender. Most of the gains for women in 2020 were made by Republican women, leading CBS News to label 2020 as "The Year of The Republican Woman" (Ewall-Wice and Navarro 2020). The gains of Republican women helped women overall to reach historically high levels of representation. As of 2021, women form a record-breaking 31 percent of state legislators and 27 percent of Congress. These gains occurred among side the historic election of the first woman vice president, Kamala Harris.

Indeed, the election of Vice President Harris, Democrat, fits the large gap between women in the two parties, with Democratic women far outnumbering their Republican colleagues, despite the latter's gains in 2020. Of the 143 women in Congress, 73 percent are Democrats. Democrats are also two-thirds of the women in state legislatures. The partisan gap is also highly visible when we look at women as a percent of their party's caucuses. Women form 46 percent of Democrats in state legislatures, and 39 percent of Democrats in Congress. In contrast, women form only 19 percent of Republican state legislators and 15 percent of Republicans in Congress (see figures 13.1 and 13.2). While women in general are somewhat more likely to affiliate as Democrats than Republicans, the partisan gap among women in Congress and state legislatures significantly exceeds the partisan gap among women in the electorate.

This chapter seeks to answer two related questions: What explains the partisan gap among women in elective office? Will the partisan gap among women in office begin to close or widen further in future elections? This study applies the theoretical framework established in my book *The Partisan Gap* (2021) to the 2020 election and beyond. I argue that long-term, structural changes in American electoral politics including the ideological, regional, and racial realignments of the parties, as well as their distinctive cultures, have created an electoral and political environment conducive to the advancement of Democratic women office seekers and a much more challenging landscape for Republican women seeking office. Even with the strong performance of Republican women candidates in 2020, the structural factors behind the advantage of Democratic women over Republican women in state legislatures and Congress remained active in 2020 and the partisan gap is likely to remain a defining feature of American electoral politics for the near future.

This research is important for both theoretical and normative reasons. Plentiful research has examined how American partisan politics have undergone ideological, regional, and racial realignments over the past half century, but insufficient attention has been paid to the consequences of these realignments for women's representation. By centering analyses of these party realignments on gender, this study provides a critical and long overdue broadening of these theories. Second, much of the research seeking to understand why women's continued underrepresentation in the United States focuses on women as a cohesive group–seeking to understand why women still only compose 27 percent of Congress and 31 percent of state legislators. Yet when we break down women's representation by party, we see that vastly different dynamics are at play. By looking separately at women in elective office by party, this study provides a more precise understanding of the reasons for women's continued underrepresentation and what needs to be done in order to help women achieve parity in office. Finally, although many associate women's issues with a progressive policy agenda, the reality is that close to half of American women lean in a more conservative direction and these women are dramatically underrepresented in government. To have a truly representative government it is important to have moderate and strongly conservative women in elected positions, just as it is important to have descriptive representation for progressive women.

THE IDEOLOGICAL REALIGNMENT AND THE PARTISAN GAP AMONG WOMEN IN ELECTIVE OFFICE

Over the past several decades the Democratic and Republican Parties have polarized ideologically (see chapter 5 in this volume), with the Democratic Party becoming more liberal and the Republican Party moving significantly to the right. Political scientists Matt Grossman and Anthony Hopkins demonstrate empirically that the Republican Party has become, at its core, a party organized around the central motivating principle of conservatism (2015,

2016). This pattern is important as conservatism has long been associated with lower levels of women's representation (Darcy, Welch, and Clark 1994).

The ideological polarization of the parties extends to most issues, including issues of gender equality in the private and public spheres. Although at one point in the twentieth century, the Republican Party was arguably more progressive on issues of gender equality than the Democratic Party—for example, it embraced the Equal Rights Amendment in its platform before the Democrats—the parties have undergone a significant ideological realignment on these issues (Wolbrecht 2000). An ideology more supportive of traditional gender roles and hostile toward feminism has taken root in the Republican Party (Elder and Greene 2012, 2015; Elder, Greene, and Lizotte 2021). In its most recent platform, the Republican Party emphasizes traditional family values and makes no mention of the importance of women's political leadership (Och 2018). Only a minority of Republicans in the electorate, 37 percent, agree that the United States would be better off if there were more women serving in public office (Cooper et al. 2016). In contrast, the Democratic Party has become more vocal and active in supporting gender equality and making gender parity in elective office a goal. Today, 77 percent of Democrats feel the United States would be better off if there were more women serving in public office (Cooper et al. 2016).

The ideological polarization of the parties tracks closely with the emergence of the partisan gap among women in elective office. Across the 1970s and 1980s, there were not many women in Congress or in state legislatures (see figures 13.1 and 13.2), but those that did serve were equally likely to be Republicans and Democrats. Starting in the early 1990s, the partisan gap among women in elective office began to emerge. The Democratic Party's commitment to equality for women in the public sphere, and its support for policies designed to help women balance career and family, appears to have created a welcoming environment for women thinking about a political career (Elder 2012, 2015, 2018). Over the last several decades, the number of Democratic women has been on a strong upward trajectory in state legislatures and Congress. Democratic women are on track to reach, if not surpass, parity within their caucus at both the state and national level.

In contrast, for much of the past three decades progress for Republican women has stalled. As of 2021, only 19 percent of Republican state legislators are women, which is the same level of representation that Republican women had three decades ago (see figure 13.1). There are actually 15 states where women form a *smaller* portion of Republican state legislators today than they did three decades ago. The lack of meaningful progress for Republican women is also surprising given that the last three decades were a period of considerable educational and professional advancement for women, and

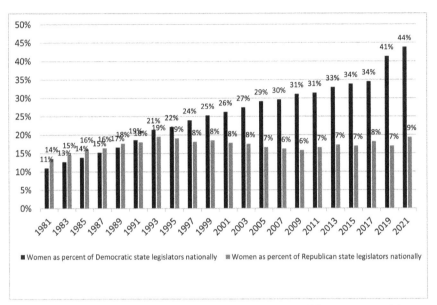

Figure 13.1. Women as a Percent of Democratic and Republican State Legislators, 1981–2021

Statistics calculated by author using data from the Center for American Women and Politics and The National Conference of State Legislatures.

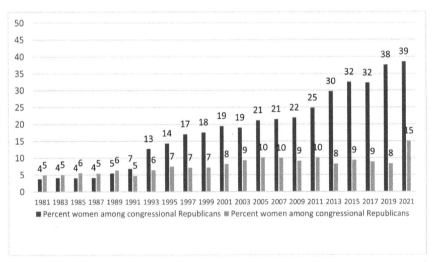

Figure 13.2. Women as Percent of Democrats and Republicans in Congress (Senate and House Combined), 1981–2021

Statistics calculated by author using data from the Center for American Women and Politics and Congressional Research Service 2021.

an overall electoral environment conducive for Republican candidates. The timing of Republican women's stalled progress suggests that the conservative shift of the Republican Party has made it comparatively more difficult for Republican women to consider running or to be recruited by their party. Given the Republican Party's greater emphasis on traditional values and hostility toward feminism, Republican women who work, especially mothers who work, may feel less encouraged to run for office within their party. Republican women may feel that their candidacies are not needed and perhaps not even wanted by their fellow partisans.

Figures 13.1 and 13.2 show that even though 2020 was a bad year for Democratic and a good year for Republican women, the overarching dynamics of the partisan gap among women in elective office did not change. While Democrats overall lost seats in state legislatures and Congress, women actually increased their representation among their Democratic colleagues in both Congress and state legislatures. In fact, the partisan gap between the representation of women among Democratic and Republican state legislators actually widened in the wake of the 2020 election. Moreover, correlation and multivariate regression analyses reveal that there is a significant negative relationship between the levels of representation of Republican women in state legislatures with the level of conservatism in a state (Elder 2021, 2018). In other words, not only are Republican women underrepresented, but their levels of representation are lowest in conservative states, where their party holds the majority, and they would have the most opportunities to influence policy. In contrast, the ideology of states no longer has any correlation with representation for Democratic women: Democratic women are achieving meaningful levels of representation in both liberal and conservative states (Elder 2021, 2018).

REGIONAL REALIGNMENT AND ITS IMPACT ON THE PARTISAN GAP

Another structural change to the American party system has been the regional realignment of the parties. Across the twentieth century and into the twenty-first century, the regional bases of the two parties in Congress have undergone significant shifts, which is critical because geographical regions have long had a profound impact on women's representation (Norrander and Wilcox 2005).

The most pronounced and consequential regional party shifts have been in the South, where Republicans made tremendous gains over the last half-century, while losing seats in the Northeast and West (Klinkner and Schaller

2006). The South is now the power base of the Republican Party and the region of greatest opportunities for Republican candidates. However, the South has long been the region of the country most hostile to women's candidacies due to its more traditional and conservative culture (Norrander and Wilcox 2015). The southern cultural climate used to act as a barrier for women in both parties, but as a result of conservatism becoming concentrated almost exclusively on the Republican side of the partisan aisle, the southern electoral landscape only acts to constrain Republican women.

Indeed, as of 2021, the South remains the region where Republican women have the fewest seats. Women form only 15 percent of Republican state legislators in the South compared to 19 percent nationally (see figure 13.3). There is only one southern state legislature, Florida, where women form more than 20 percent of Republicans. Similar patterns characterize women's representation in the House and in Congress. The number of Republicans holding seats in Congress from southern states more than doubled from 1989 to 2021, but these gains have not yielded many more Republican women. In the 117th Congress, women form only 9 percent of Southern Republicans, which is lower than all other regions (see figure 13.4). This pattern means that Republican women have their lowest levels of representation in the region of the country that is the power base of their party and that offers the most opportunities for Republican advancement and leadership.

In contrast, Democratic women have made big inroads among their party's representatives in all regions of the country. Women now form 50 percent or more of Democratic state legislators in the Midwest and the West (see figure 13.3). Women form over half of Democratic state legislators in twenty-two states including the southern states of Florida, Georgia, and Kentucky. Democratic women also perform well in all regions of the country in Congress. Women form 54 percent of congressional Democrats from the Midwest, 43 percent of congressional Democrats from the West, and 41 percent of congressional Democrats from the South (see figure 13.4).

In summary, the regional realignment of the parties has played a modest role contributing to the partisan gap among women in elective office. The concentration of Republican power in the South, combined with the ideological polarization of the parties, has created a challenging electoral environment for Republican women in where their party is the strongest. While Republican women posted modest gains in all regions of the country in the 2020 elections, the underlying regional dynamics of the partisan gap appear unchanged. The South remains the most challenging environment for Republican women despite new opportunities. Meanwhile, as legislative seats have turned over and opened up, Democratic women have been strategic and successful at seizing these opportunities, in all regions of the country.

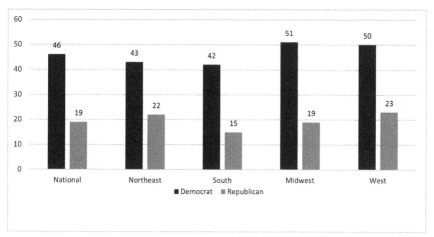

Figure 13.3. Women as a Percent of Democratic and Republican State Legislators by Region in 2021

Statistics calculated by author using data from National Conference of State Legislatures and Center for American Women and Politics.

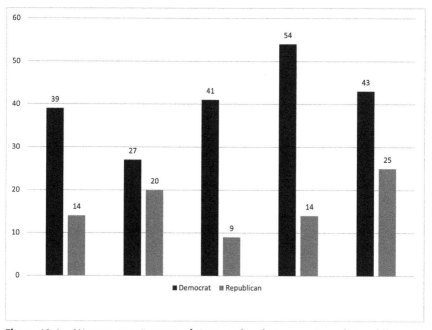

Figure 13.4. Women as a Percent of Congressional Democrats and Republicans in Congress as of 2021

Statistics calculated by author using date from Congress.gov and Center for American Women and Politics.

THE PARTISAN GAP AND WOMEN OF COLOR

A third structural change in American electoral politics has been the racial realignment of the parties. Americans of color were blocked from meaningful participation in electoral politics, including office holding, for much of American history. The passage of the Voting Rights Act (VRA) in 1965, opened the doors to increased political inclusion by Black Americans and other Americans of color. The VRA led to a dramatic influx of voters of color into the electorate and made it illegal for states to draw congressional district lines in a way to dilute the voting power of African Americans and other protected minority groups. In response to Supreme Court decisions, state governments created more majority-minority districts, and these districts have been the best opportunity for individuals of color, whether men or women, to enter elective office. These important legal and structural changes to American electoral politics led to a significant increase in representation by Black Americans and Hispanics in elective office.

Reflecting their formal and informal exclusion from national electoral politics, women of color entered Congress later than white women as well as later than men of color. Despite these barriers, since the 1980s, women of color have increased their numbers in elective office at a faster rate than non-Hispanic white women (see figure 13.5). As a result, women of color now form 43 percent of members of Congress of color, while white women form only 22 percent of white members of Congress.

The comparatively stronger performance of women of color compared to white women holds true for all non-white racial and ethnic groups. In 1987, women composed 5 percent of Black members of Congress and now women form 40 percent of the Black members of Congress. The first Hispanic woman did not enter Congress until 1989 with the election of Ileana Ros-Lehtinen. In the 117th Congress women form 29 percent of the Hispanic members of Congress. Women now form a stunning 58 percent of the Asian American/Pacific Islander members of Congress. In comparison, white women only form 22 percent of white members of Congress.

The success of women of color in winning election to the House and Senate is particularly striking given the double bind of racism and sexism that they face. While political ambition among women of color remains an area in need of greater attention, Brown and Dowe (2020) present compelling evidence that Black women have run and won seats, not as a result of party recruitment and support, but rather despite a lack of such support. Dowe (2020) uses the term "radical imagination" to capture the decision-making process among Black women to run for elective office. Bejarano (2013) as well as Garcia Bedolla, Tate, and Wong (2014) argue that women of color

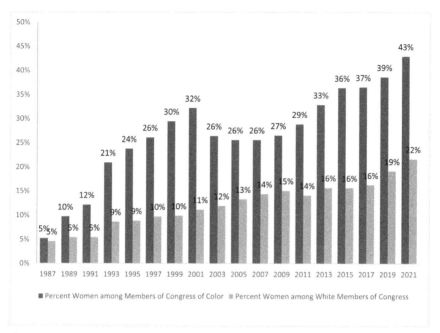

Figure 13.5. Women as Percent of White Members of Congress versus Members of Congress of Color, 1987–2021
Statistics calculated by author using data from Congressional Research Service.

are better positioned than white women to tap into preexisting political and organizational networks, and benefit more from both racial and gender based group solidarity.

The strong performance of women of color relative to white women has contributed to the partisan gap because of the strong Democratic partisanship of the women of color. Due to the ongoing partisan realignment over race—characterized by the Democratic Party coming to embrace a civil rights and racial justice issues while the Republican Party has taken on increasingly conservative positions on race and immigration, a trend further exacerbated by Donald Trump's explicit appeals to racial and ethnic resentment as a candidate and president—women of color in elective office are overwhelmingly Democratic. The 117th Senate convened with four women of color, and they are all Democrats (Catherine Cortez-Masto, Tammy Duckworth, Mazie Hirono, and Kamala Harris who vacated her seat on January 20 and assumed the vice presidency); 90 percent of the women of color in the 117th House are Democrats. A similar dynamic exists in state legislatures, with women of color, especially Black women, driving the success of Democratic women. A full 61 percent of the Democratic women in southern state legislatures are women of color including 100 percent of the Democratic women in Alabama's state legislature, 92 percent in Mississippi, and 87 percent in Alabama (CAWP 2021).

Taken together, the comparative success of women of color in obtaining seats in elective office compared to white women, combined with their heavily Democratic partisanship, has played a modest but driving role behind the partisan gap. If women of color were represented in Congress at the same, lower rate as white women—in other words, if women of color only represented only 22 percent of those of color in Congress rather than 40 percent—there would be roughly twenty fewer women in Congress and most likely twenty fewer Democratic women. Thus, without the strong performance by women of color in winning elections, the partisan gap among women would still exist, but would be considerably smaller.

PARTY CULTURE AND RECRUITMENT

A final factor behind the partisan gap of women in elective office concerns party culture and its implications for recruitment. In the 1980s, political scientist Joe Freeman (1986) argued that the two major parties had distinctive cultures. In a more recent analysis of party culture, Grossman and Hopkins explicitly build on Freeman's analysis and argue that the Democratic party is best understood "as a coalition of social groups seeking concrete government action" as opposed to the Republican Party, which is structured around conservative (Grossman and Hopkins 2015, 119). Drawing on extensive interview data reviewed in my book, I argue that the distinct cultures of the two parties have resulted in increasingly more robust recruitment efforts for Democratic women compared to Republican women (Elder 2021). Explicit encouragement and recruitment is particularly important when it comes to women candidates because women are more likely than men to need encouragement from others in order to conceive of themselves as candidates (Lawless and Fox 2018).

Freeman (1986) characterized the Democratic Party as having an open and decentralized culture, where power flows upwards, and where group identities and group-based activism are viewed as legitimate and valuable. As a result, the Democratic Party views activists making group-based demands and groups vying to shape party policy as the norm, rather than as an act of disloyalty toward the party or the party's liberal ideology. Cooperman and Crowder-Meyer further reaffirm this characterization of the Democratic Party culture arguing, "The Democratic Party is essentially organized to hear and respond to group-based demands" (2018, 111). The Democratic Party's distinctive culture has promoted the recruitment of women in several reinforcing ways. It has allowed feminists and those seeking to increase the representation of women in elective office to enter the party structure, to make group-based demands, and to have their demands viewed as legitimate. Secondly, as more individuals and groups committed to gender equality in public office have become integrated into the Democratic Party, especially in leadership roles, they are able to reinforce and deepen the Democratic Party's commitment to recruiting women. Finally, the Democratic Party's open culture where groups vie to shape policy as the normal course of action, rather than as an act of disloyalty, has allowed it to partner productively with an extended network of groups, most notably EMILY's List, that are committed to increasing women's representation. Rather than seeing such groups as competitors or disloyal segments of the party, the Democratic Party has, to a significant degree, integrated them into the party structure.

In contrast, several aspects of the Republican Party culture create a more challenging environment for Republican women interested in political careers. The Republican Party has a hierarchical, top-down culture, which embraces individualism, rejects group-based claims, and holds a strong commitment to gender-neutral recruiting (Och 2018). Explicit efforts to recruit women are only supported by a small faction within the party, which must fight against a dominant party culture viewing such efforts as problematic forays into the identity politics of the left. Indeed, the modest success of Republican women in achieving elective office in 2020 is in part due to women in the Republican partyespecially Representative Elise Stefanik—challenging Republican party culture (and receiving considerable pushback) to call out the lack of women in the party as a problem and specifically recruit and fund women candidates, starting early in the 2020 election cycle (Abramson 2019). Additionally, the hierarchical nature of Republican Party culture, with its emphasis on party and ideological loyalty, has undermined the party's ability to partner effectively with an extended network of groups focused on increasing Republican women's representation in elective office (Elder 2021).

CONCLUSION

Democratic and Republican women started making inroads into elective office at about the same time, but today Democratic women far outnumber their Republican women colleagues in state legislatures and Congress. The progress of women in elected office over the past several decades has quite simply been a tale of two parties, with Democratic women making consistent impressive gains, while representation for Republican women remains low.

Although Republican women made modest gains in 2020, the overall size and structure of the partisan gap remains very much in place. This study argues that several overlapping and reinforcing dynamics in American politics including the regional, racial, and ideological realignments of the political parties have contributed to the emergence and continuation of the partisan gap among women in office and are likely to continue reinforcing the partisan gap in future elections.

The progress of Democratic women in elective office has been fairly remarkable. Women are now close to 40 percent of Democrats in Congress and 46 percent of Democrats in state legislatures. Women form the majority of Democrats in twenty-two state legislatures. Democratic women have strong levels of representation in all regions of the country, and in both liberal and conservative states. Their success is driven in part by the "radical imagination" and remarkable success of women of color, who are disproportionately Democratic (Dowe 2020). The continued progress of Black, Hispanic, Asian Pacific Islander, and Indigenous women in achieving elective offices, which seems likely, will serve to reinforce and expand the partisan gap. There is also now a self-reinforcing dynamic at work. Women in elective office tend to be more committed than men to the idea that recruiting more women is a priority, and also tend to have more women in their social networks where much recruitment takes place (Sanbonmatsu 2006). This holds true for women in both parties (Dittmar, Sanbonmatsu and Carroll 2018; Elder 2021). But there are now many more Democratic women in elective office and leadership positions to carry out this recruitment work. The robust recruitment infrastructure on the Democratic side, led by EMILY'S List, is likely to ensure there are strong women candidates in place when opportunities arise to Democrats to gain a seat.

Republican women are likely to further increase their numbers in the 2022 election. Given President Biden's low approval ratings, combined with the reality that the president's party almost always loses seats during midterm elections, it is likely that 2022 will be a good year for Republicans. Also, there are signs that the Republican Party may field a historically large number of women candidates (Rubin 2021). Further success for Republican women in achieving elective office would be a positive development to all those who value women's representation, as there is no path for women to achieve proportional representation and hence gender equality in elective office without women's representation increasing in both the Democratic and the Republican Parties.

That said, gains by Republican women in 2022 and future elections are unlikely to change the underlying dynamics of the partisan gap, much as we saw in 2020. Even though a lot of Republican women have thrown their hat in the ring for 2022, even more Democratic women have done so (CAWP 2021). Given the much greater incumbency advantage among Democratic women, it will be hard for Republican women to meaningfully close the partisan gap. Further, the Republican Party remains a challenging place for women for seeking or holding elective office in several important respects. In 2021, the Republican Party pushed one of its women members, Liz Cheney, out of a leadership position and much of the party infrastructure is working against her reelection (Martin 2021). Moreover, as long as the most plentiful opportunities for Republican office-holding and advancement remain in the South, this will contribute to a comparatively less favorable electoral environment for Republican women. The challenging environment of the South for women can be seen in the Republican competition to replace Senator Richard C. Shelby (R, AL). Republican Katie Britt, who served as Chief of Staff to Richard Selby as well as having other relevant experience, is running for the open seat, yet former President Donald Trump and a Republican House member Mo Brooks, who is also running for the seat, dismissed her as an "assistant" and "unqualified." The Republican Party did not condone or respond to these sexist comments (Gonzalez 2021). Given the continued ideological and racial polarization of the parties, along with the much more robust recruitment efforts on the Democratic side of the partisan aisle, the partisan gap is likely to remain a prominent feature of American politics for elections to come.

The stakes surrounding the partisan gap are huge. As women have become better represented among Democratic Party officials, we have seen the Democratic Party work toward policies such as paid family leave, universal pre-K, expanded health care, and increased minimum wage which are critical in achieving gender equality. On the Republican side, the continued low levels of representation of women holds potentially negative consequences for the viability of the party. Even high profile members of the Republican Party themselves have indicated that the overwhelmingly white, male composition of their party-in-government threatens the future viability of their party (Abramson 2019). Moreover, conservative and Republican women have policy priorities and perspectives on issues that are distinctive from Republican and conservative men (Barnes and Cassese 2017; Deckman 2016). Without women gaining meaningful representation among Republicans in elective office, their distinctive views are not able to shape Republican Party priorities, internal discussions, and policy outcomes.

Chapter Fourteen

Fired Up or Falling Flat

Recruitment of Women Candidates during the Trump Administration

Shannon McQueen

In 2016, the election of Donald Trump had a psychological impact on women across the United States. Women spoke about sexual assaults on Twitter (Maas et al. 2018), protested in mass groups (Berry and Chenoweth 2018), and ran for office in record numbers (Dittmar 2020). Trump affected women's individual psychology and much of the scholarly attention focuses on this psychological impact (Shames et al. 2020, Lawless and Fox 2018; Mukhopadhyay and Harding 2017). But what about women's organizations?

Women's groups play an important role in increasing women's representation in US politics (Rozell 2000; Kreitzer and Osborn 2019; Piscopo 2019). These groups like EMILY's List, National Organization of Women, or General Federation of Republic Women, demonstrate women's leadership and ownership within the organization and provide support to candidates. But the importance of the existing infrastructure has been overlooked when exploring Trump's effect on mobilization women candidates. What changes in the candidate pool did these women's organizations witness after Trump's election in 2016?

Despite their growing importance, little is known about women's organization's perspective on recruitment changes during the Trump administration. Recruitment is key in developing the female-candidate pipeline, and scholars have noted the relevance of recruitment in combating the ambition gap (Sanbonmatsu and Carroll 2017; Frederick and Burrell 2007). Women's organizations have historically served as infrastructure to support women's entrance into the political realm, particularly during the second wave of feminism (Strachan et al. 2019). Furthermore, many Democratic and nonpartisan women's groups were the first political actors to draw attention to the increase of female candidates in 2018 (Shugerman n.d.) and Republican women's increase in 2020 (Conroy 2020b). Thus, it is essential to understand not only how women voters and potential candidates respond to the Trump years, but if and how the pool of candidates changed for women's groups. However, as women's organizations have grown in number and prominence, it is critical to examine the role of these outside actors in developing the women candidate pipeline.

To investigate these matters in the wake of Trump's 2016 election, I collected original data on the perspective of these groups with an original survey of state women's groups across the United States. I asked Democratic, nonpartisan, and Republican women's organizations. For added perspective, I conducted in-depth interviews with national women's organization leaders to assess their perception of change in recruitment.

The results indicate that the impact of Trump's election on women's groups drastically differed based on party identification. Republican groups tend to avoid acknowledging any "Trump effect." If an effect was noted, it tended to be negative and implied a greater problem for the group. Conversely, Democratic and nonpartisan groups readily acknowledge improvements in recruitment patterns and often reported growth within their organizations. Thus, partisan group identity impacts recruitment patterns, highlighting an infrastructure disparity negatively impacting Republican women candidates. Compared to Democratic women, Republican women have consistently lagged in gaining elected office. Scholars have explained this partisan gender gap through supply (Crowder-Meyer and Lauderdale 2014; Thomsen 2015), demand (Arceneaux 2001; Karpowitz, Monson, and Preece 2017; Elder 2021), and structural rationales (Schneider and Bos 2016). Adding to the understanding of the partisan gender gap, this chapter suggests scholars should consider the role of women's organizations in this long-standing pattern, as Republican women's groups may be at a disadvantage at responding to changes in the candidate pool. Understanding the differences in organizational capacity to respond to candidate pool changes clarifies partisan patterns in women's mobilizations.

EXPECTATIONS FOR RECRUITMENT AND THE CANDIDATE POOL

Inviting women to run for office is particularly important to combat self-perceived inadequacies and the gap in ambition (Sanbonmatsu and Carroll 2017; Frederick and Burrell 2007). Much of this scholarship highlights the role political parties play in recruitment (Kenny and Verge 2016; Dittmar 2015; Crowder-Meyer 2013; Niven 2006; Sanbonmatsu 2006). Republican women tend to find less recruitment opportunities from party elites that Democratic women, and this difference is a key rationale for the partisan gender gap (Och and Shames 2018; Crowder-Meyer and Lauderdale 2014; Elder 2012).

Women's organizations work alongside parties, mitigating the severity of the overall gender gap in recruitment (Lawless and Fox 2010) and ambition (Foos and Gilardi 2020; Preece et al. 2016). Although the literature on the party's recruitment is extensive (Crowder-Meyer 2013; Sanbonmatsu 2006), specific research on women's organizations and recruitment is quite sparse and what exists generally focuses on a small number of groups (Dittmar 2015). Preliminary evidence on recruitment during the Trump administration suggests that women's organizations that focus on candidate support saw a tremendous increase in women wanting to run for office. One pro-choice Democratic organization, EMILY's List, indicates that while 920 women contacted them about seeking office during the 2016 election cycle, 34,000 women contacted EMILY's List in the year after the 2016 election (EMILY's List 2018). However, often this more subjective data revolves around the perspective of large national Democratic groups, or candidates themselves, which do not reflect the larger norms and perspective of women's groups. Did all women's groups experience this rise of candidates, or only some groups?

There is strong reason to expect that women's groups experience different recruitment outcomes based on their partisan identity. Two key features of partisan-group identity, the preexisting candidate pools and long-standing partisan culture, likely minimized the change in recruitment for Republican women's groups and increased the change for Democratic and nonpartisan organizations. Considering candidate pools, more women identify as Democrats than Republicans (Box-Steffensmeier et al. 2004), Democratic women's groups have access to a greater pool of female potential candidates. Additionally, differences in women's organization's recruitment are likely connected to differences in party culture. Republican women's organizations that exist in a more complicated political culture compared to their Democratic counterparts. The Democratic Party's culture is generally associated with supporting women, as it is seen as pluralistic and more apt to respond to women's demands (Freeman 1986; Grossmann and Hopkins 2015; Crowder-Meyer and Cooperman 2018). The party is known for being pluralistic, and identity conscious, working on behalf of varied demographic groups. Conversely, the Republican Party advocates for a high degree of party loyalty, "doctrinal purity," and gender-blindness (Freeman 1986; Grossmann and Hopkins 2015). The Republican Party culture of hierarchy and avoidance of "identity politics" (Freeman 1986; Grossmann and Hopkins 2015) is unlikely to support changing candidate pools that highlight an increase in women candidates.

Although less recognized, nonpartisan groups compose most women's groups and their perspective on recruitment during the Trump administration should be considered. Due to the historical connection between the Democratic and nonpartisan groups, as well as the preexisting candidate pool compositions, I expect nonpartisan women's groups to support similar candidates as their Democratic counterparts, reporting changes in their candidate pool after Trump's election in 2016. The close alliance between nonpartisan women's organizations and the Democratic Party can be seen in the history of women's organization's connections to major political parties. The first women's groups, who took a bipartisan approach to support women's political involvement, pushing both major parties to support the ERA and abortion rights (Burrell 1996). As political parties clarified women's rights and responded to women's demands in the 1970s, the Democratic Party forged stronger alliances with feminist women's organizations (Ray 1995). This long-standing association may explain the similarity between the nonpartisan and Democratic women's groups' understanding of the environment. Additionally, like partisan groups, nonpartisan organizations will be impacted by preexisting candidate pools. If fewer Republican women are available to run for office (Crowder-Meyer and Lauderdale 2014; Sapiro 1982; Thomsen 2015), nonpartisan groups will likely support more Democratic women.

METHODS

There is no central repository of these organizations, nor a universal definition. To address this challenge, I first define women's groups. Scholars have defined women's groups based on feminist ideology (Ferguson 1984; Freeman 1979; Mansbridge 1994), the group's beneficiaries (Bordt 1997), or the group's members (Bordt 1994; Hatch and Cunliffe 1997). For this project, I build on a characteristic-based definition (Kusterer 1990), defining women's groups as entities with a structure and members, who use the collective action of individuals to solve problems, and demonstrate woman's ownership as women are incorporated into the leadership or organizational structure. This criterion means that women are incorporated into the leadership structure and are members and that the group identifies as a "women's organization." However, this definition does not specify membership, beneficiaries, or ideology. Thus, members can be composed of some men, men can be beneficiaries, and the group does not need to utilize the feminist label to be considered a women's organization in the frame.

Utilizing this definition, I am able to account for groups like the EMILY's List and Emerge, which are run by women and support women, along with the General Federation of Women's Clubs and Elevate PAC, which is run by women, but does not exclusively support women and will support male candidates. I limit the scope to only studying woman's organizations that provide support to candidates or potential candidates. Under this definition, women's organizations can be composed of mixed or female-only membership, have mixed or female-only clients, and are not limited by stringent definitions of "women's interest" or feminism.[1]

To develop the frame of women's groups, I supplemented an original frame of women's groups from Rutgers' Center for American Women and Politics with Internet searches for active women's organizations that provide some form of candidate support. This original frame included both national and state groups. I then cross-referenced this frame of organizations with fellow scholars who specialize in women's organizations and groups. As previous work on women's groups often relies on small-n analysis, developing a complete frame of women's organizations is a step forward for the field.

To determine how Trump's election as president affected the recruitment experiences of Republican, Democratic, and nonpartisan women's organizations, I utilize two different methodologies.[2] First, I surveyed the identifiable universe of state-based women's groups. The survey had twenty total questions and took about ten minutes to complete. I distributed it using email and Facebook Messenger to the 321 state-level organizations I identified, producing a response pool where 14.9 percent of respondents support Republican candidates, 32.18 percent support Democratic candidates, and 52 percent reported that they had no policy of supporting members from one party.[3] The response rate by party affiliation is generally reflective of the larger frame's partisan compositions. The survey was open for completion from June to August 2019.

I asked women's organizations the following prompt: "Since the election of President Donald Trump in 2016, has your organization found it easier or harder to recruit the following types of candidates?" The survey then presented different candidate identities. For example, organizations had to decide if recruiting candidates under thirty was easier, harder, or neither easier nor harder after Trump's election in 2016. These identities ranged in ideology, age, party, gender, and race. The order of these identities was randomized. I also provide a free-response question to gauge other, broader issues, stating, "What about your work, if anything, has changed after the election of President Trump?" Using content-based text analysis, I identified and analyzed the occurrence of repeated phrases utilizing an in vivo coding methodology. This coding methods looks for common trends, noting the specific change that occurred, and if that change was framed as positive or negative.

To complement my survey of state-based women's organizations in the United States, I conducted in-depth interviews with leaders of national women's organizations.[4] These interviews provide opportunities to add further depth and nuance to my analyses of changing recruitment from women's organizations. I invited all national partisan and nonpartisan national women's organizations to participate in these interviews via an email invitation or telephone call to the organization. I requested to speak with someone in a leadership position, meeting with executive directors, vice presidents, or board members. The interviews lasted around thirty to forty-five minutes and were semi-structured, meaning the interviewee had significant sway in determining the conversation's direction.

During these interviews, I asked national organizations a similar open response question, inquiring if anything about their organization has changed since the election of Donald Trump. I then transcribed the audio recordings of interviews, and then analysed the transcripts. Like the surveys, I used a content-based text analysis to personally identify and analyse the occurrence of phrases within these interview transcripts, utilizing In Vivo coding methods. In Vivo coding involves isolating and identifying repetitive phrases within the interview transcripts and grouping these phrases under categories. Table 14.1 depicts a table of coding examples for quotes that count as positive changes, negative changes, and no changes.

Table 14.1. Coding Examples

Code	Quote
No Change	"We haven't seen a huge shift in who we train."
	"I have not seen or heard anything different."
Negative Change	"There's not as much value on public service right now. . . . That's been a challenge."
	"With the election of president Trump, I feel as though some women are choosing to kind of take a back seat. They may, they may not want to be having the media scrutiny with, with the simple question of can you be a Republican woman and still support or do you still support the president?"
	"And it seems like as time goes on, there's less and less respect and less stability, and I think, you know, and we think that that is discouraging. So many women who might otherwise be interested in running for office."
	"These women are grieving alone. They're talking on Facebook. Some of them can't send their kids to school. They're crying every day. They're really upset."
Positive Change	"There are, there are more, more people now running for Congress and stepping up, but that's good."
	"We saw a surge in 2017 and 2018 with more women candidates. There's definitely been a surge of women who are more willing to run for office."
	"In 2017, the desire to fund state and local races went up. Our budget essentially doubled, because we could fundraise in a double capacity. Women got on the ballot on the ballot."
	"There's so many women who are running because of that, that have come to us."
	"After Trump you know, there was a surge of young women running for office at the federal and state and local level. And I think we made more endorsements than ever last cycle. And we're really proud of that helped elect bunch of young, new young women to Congress and to at the state and local level."

RESULTS

State Survey Results

When asked about recruiting women candidates, all nonpartisan and Democratic groups noted how it was easier to recruit women candidates' post-2016. In contrast, Republican groups were more divided. Depicted in figure 14.1, only 29 percent of Republican groups noted it was easier to elect women. Interestingly, 14 percent of Republican groups responded that it was harder to elect women, suggesting a negative impact of Trump's election.[5] For comparison, when asked about men candidates, depicted in figure 14.2, the majority of all groups responded that recruitment was the same post the 2016 election.

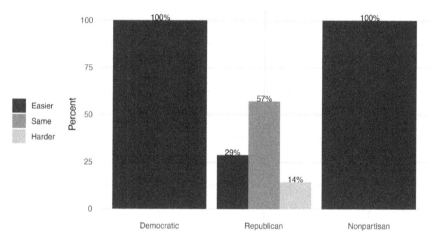

Figure 14.1.   How did recruitment of women change after 2016?

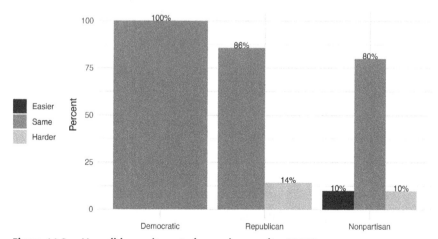

Figure 14.2.   How did recruitment of men change after 2016?

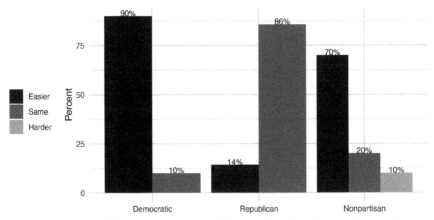

Figure 14.3. How did recruitment of candidates under thirty change after 2016?

Beyond women candidates, Republican women's groups consistently reported no changes to their recruitment of underrepresented and diverse candidates, while nonpartisan and Democratic women's groups reported great ease in electing a diverse set of candidates, such as those who were LGBTQ, Black, young, and progressive. For example, figure 14.3 depicts changes in the recruitment of candidates under thirty, as 90 percent of Democratic groups and 70 percent of nonpartisan groups report easier recruitment for candidates under thirty. Conversely, Republican groups note no difference in the recruitment of young candidates.

Likewise, when asked about candidates of non-white races, nonpartisan and Democratic groups report ease in recruitment. Evidenced in figure 14.4, 90 percent of Democratic and nonpartisan groups reported that it was easier to recruit Black candidates post-2016. Yet, the majority of Republican groups (71%) did not report a change. Similarly, 70 percent of Democratic groups

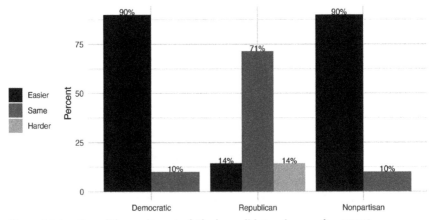

Figure 14.4. How did recruitment of Black candidates change after 2016?

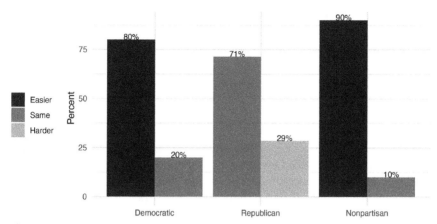

Figure 14.5. How did recruitment of liberals change after 2016?

and 60 percent of nonpartisan groups report an ease in recruiting Hispanic candidates. Although the pattern is muted for Asian candidates, there is similar results, suggesting an increased ease in recruiting minority candidates.

A similar pattern was found when asked about the recruitment of different ideologies. Figure 14.5 depicts changes in the recruitment of liberal candidates after 2016. Across all party affiliations, most groups report no change in recruitment for both moderate and conservative candidates. However, when asked about liberal candidates, the majority of Democratic and nonpartisan groups (about 75% of groups) report that the recruitment of liberal candidates is easier post-2016.

Finally, groups were asked about the different recruitment of alternative candidates, such as class-based differences, LGBTQ candidates, and veteran candidates. The recruitment of LGBTQ groups reflects the pattern previously found in young, liberal, women, and minority candidates. Depicted in figure 14.6, Democratic and nonpartisan groups report easier recruitment for LG-

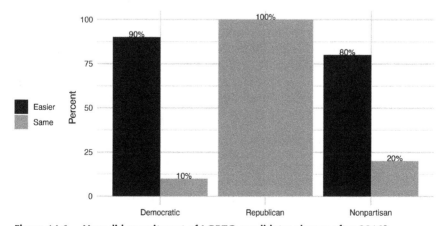

Figure 14.6. How did recruitment of LGBTQ candidates change after 2016?

Table 14.2. Survey Open Responses to Changes Post-2016

	Republican	Nonpartisan	Democratic
Increased Engagement	0	17	3
Increased Women Running	0	16	2
Emotional Shifts / Increased Partisanship	3	8	3
Organizational Changes	0	6	1
Nothing Changed	3	0	0

BTQ and working-class candidates, while most Republican groups report no change. Ninety percent of Democratic groups and 80 percent of nonpartisan groups report ease in recruiting LGBTQ candidates. Conversely, all Republican women's groups report the same recruitment for LGBTQ candidates as before 2016.

The qualitative open response question gauges how the organization's support of candidates has changed since the election of Donald Trump. Consistent with earlier trends, table 14.2 indicates that many Democratic and nonpartisan groups reiterated Trump's large effect on recruitment of women, women's mobilization, and overall increased engagement. One respondent noted, "We have seen an increase in applications, interest, and support of our work." Groups attributed this increased recruitment of women to a shift in emotions for their organizational members or clients. Many respondents used words like "hatred," "angrier," "MAD," and "traumatic" when describing how Trump has changed their organization's work. One respondent emphatically wrote, "I often hear that women feel they HAVE to fight. There is a sense of being on the right side of history and being able to tell our children and grandchildren what we did to fight this man." This respondent suggests that some groups believe women are in an active confrontation against Trump and articulates concern about a legacy associated with combating Trump.

Although there were few comments on this topic overall, a substantial group of Republican women's groups responded that Trump had not changed anything about their work or candidate recruitment (27% of all Republican comments). Comments reporting "nothing changed" about the organization after 2016 are unique to Republican groups. One respondent wrote, "Nothing. We stay true to our purposes and our goals." Another respondent noted, "Nothing, our focus is in our own backyard. If Trump does come up, we talk about it. But honestly, it hasn't been an issue in our program."

National Interview Results

When interviewing national women's groups, like survey findings, nonpartisan and Democratic organizational leaders described a change in the pool of eligible candidates to be recruited in the wake of Trump's election. Conversely, Republican women's groups did not note any changes in the candidate pools in the wake of Trump's election.

During interviews, many nonpartisan and Democratic women's groups described a "surge." This surge is more than an increase in women candidates (although many groups mentioned the increase in women candidates). Groups also mentioned an increase in funding, donors, volunteers, new women's groups, and urgency. The nonpartisan group Ignite describes the surge by saying, "When the Women's March happened, everything exploded. . . . We've been dealing with demand that is anywhere from 300 percent to 500 percent of what it was prior to 2016, and it kept up. . . . Like 70 people are showing up for a meeting that's supposed to be for 30 people."[6] Another group called this moment a "massive re-engagement of women."[7] Many groups, including the Electing Women PAC noted that women who are 'stepping up' are often new to politics. The Electing Women PAC eloquently commented that Trump's election meant "women realized that it mattered that they stayed on the sideline and that they really could have an impact by getting involved, and that we provided an opportunity, a place for women to engage who had not engaged in politics before."[8]

Many groups responded to this change in the recruitment pool by designing new institutional structures or organizations. For example, the Women's Campaign School at Yale had to respond to this increase of political novices with an entirely new program. Patti Russo, the executive director at the Campaign School, recalled that,

> After the 2016 presidential election, women just started calling us. It was really after the first global Women's March in 2017 in January that we were slammed with calls from women that marched, saying they wanted to run for office. As I started returning those calls, I discovered that a third of women weren't registered to vote. And I said I'm going to give you a local political homework assignment. The first thing to do is register to vote this week. Then the second third were registered but did not vote in the 2016 election because the candidates were so similar, they couldn't make up their minds, so two-thirds of the women who reached out to us were not ready to run! We needed to raise money to create a whole new level of training for women who have newly discovered a passion for politics but don't have the foundational skill set to launch themselves effectively. So, we created a one day intensive on the basics.[9]

Russo articulates a change in the candidate pool and how organizations often need to respond to these changes to be most effective. To accommodate the type of candidate reaching out for support, the Women's Campaign School at Yale had to create a new program, as their existing infrastructure was insufficient under this new context. Overwhelmingly, these excited political novices were Democratic women who were motivated to run for office by Trump's presence. In addition to Democratic women, candidates of color mobilized. Higher Heights, a group dedicated to supporting women of color, noted the increase in minority women candidates running for office in 2018.[10]

Even larger than programs, entire women's groups arose in response to changing candidate pools. Founder of WAVE (Women for American Values and Ethics) started the women's organizations in response to "seeing a lot of my friends on social media saying how upset they were with the election. . . . These women are grieving alone. . . . They're crying every day. And I just felt like we needed to bring women together and see what we can do."[11] After sharing feelings of grief about the election over some wine, the group progressed to political action and advocacy, attended the Women's March, advocated for immigrant and undocumented families, ran voter registration drives, and eventually created a PAC and organizational structure.

Conservative and Republican organizations stood out by not discussing an emergence of energy, urgency, new programs, or change in the candidate pools. Instead, groups with close partisan ties, such as Maggie's List, noted, "I have not seen or heard anything different, No I have not, truly."[12] If Republican groups did mention a change in the pools of candidates, the change was primarily negative. One Republican group noted that Trump makes it difficult to be Republican women if one does not fully support the President. Yet another noted an increase in the lack of respect for Republican women running for office.

DISCUSSION AND CONCLUSION

This study examines recruitment changes in the wake of Trump's 2016 election from the perspective of women's organizations. Given the importance of organizations in supporting women candidates—from the recruitment stage through campaign training and funding—it is critical to understand not only whether individual women sought to become more politically active in the wake of Trump's election but also whether there is infrastructure in place ready to assist them.

Results from the state survey and national interviews confirm that Democratic groups report easier recruitment post-2016 for women and traditionally underrepresented candidates, such as those who are working-class, Black and Hispanic, liberal, LGBTQ, and under thirty years old. This ease of recruitment paralleled the demographic shifts of who ran in 2018, as women and minorities flooded the candidate pool and made record-breaking shifts into elected positions (Schneider 2018). Like Democratic groups, nonpartisan groups acknowledge similar changes in recruitment post-2016. Nonpartisan groups noted that it was easier to recruit LGBTQ, working-class, liberal, Hispanic, female, and Black candidates after Trump's election. Entire groups or programs were created to respond to this increase in engagement. Compared to other women's groups, state and national Republican groups are an anomaly, reporting no change in recruitment post-2016.

Why did Republican women's groups differ so drastically in their response and fail to report any changes in their recruitment patterns? The lack of perceived change in the recruitment pools is likely due to two factors. First, the preexisting pool of women candidates for Republican groups is different than the pool for Democratic and nonpartisan groups. Although the Republican Party still has a large portion of support from white women, the majority of women tend to affiliate with the Democratic Party. Furthermore, Trump's 2016 election sparked an emotive response from the larger pool of candidates who are women, young, liberal, and from racial minorities. Ambition was seemingly ignited in these particular individuals due to a combination of affective polarization and the perception that Trump posed a threat to their particular identities. For example, one women's group representative noted, she feels "our bodies are at risk and our rights are at risk."[13] Many more groups noted the impact of seeing Hillary Clinton lose to Donald Trump. The director of the Electing Women PAC reported, "There was so much enthusiasm, and that quickly turned to anger, particularly with the history in Donald Trump's life."[14] This pool of politically ignited candidates tend to seek support from Democratic and nonpartisan women's groups, rather than Republican women's groups.

A second factor impacting the change in recruitment is the long-standing partisan culture. Democratic Party culture is more pluralistic and group based, compared to Republican Party cultures, which tend to avoid addressing "identity." Partisan women's organizations reflect these responses to group-based claims, resulting in Republican Women's groups that are less likely to directly advocate for women's unique identity. Due to these cultural differences, Republican groups are less likely to recognize changing candidate pools that highlight an increase in women and minority candidates. Conversely, Democratic groups are primed to be identity conscious and receptive to changing candidate pools.

Overall, this research advances our understanding of women's organizations' role in politics by drawing attention to both the cultural and logistical constraints women's groups face. Other scholars have argued that theories of movement mobilization are better equipped to explain the recent increase of electoral interest, rather than psychological approaches (Gordon 2020). Furthering that research aim, this chapter suggests that recruitment and support of candidates will be more successful when groups are identity-conscious and optimize exogenous shocks (such as Trump's election gain, or Clinton's electoral loss). Groups that recognize candidate pools with more women and minorities can thus take advantage or supporting these new candidates.

The results have two main implications. First, this project's findings hold implications for Republican women's groups. It does not appear as if Trump's presence positively impacted Republican women's organizations' growth of candidate pools in the wake of the election. This lack of change in recruitment of women has implications for the partisan gender gap, or disparity in representation between Democratic and Republican women. (Crowder-Meyer and Cooperman 2018; Lauderdale and Crowder-Meyer 2014.; Elder 2008; Thomsen 2015; Thomsen and Swers 2017). Scholars have identified a pattern of women's PACs benefiting Democratic women candidates (Burrell 1996; Uhlaner and Schlozman 1986; Sanbonmatsu 2006). These findings add theoretical context to the scholarship on the out-sized effect female donor networks have for Democratic women (Crespin and Deitz 2010; Francia 2001).

Additionally, although the rise of women candidate recruitment in 2018 is stressed, this research draws attention to the many other types of candidates whose recruitment changed after 2016. Changes in the pools of candidates being recruited by women's organizations has a large impact on representation. Women and minorities are still underrepresented in American politics. However, identities of candidates often historically denied from elected office had a moment in the wake of 2016, as Trump ignited political ambition within these individuals. This change in recruitment pools produced one of the most diverse Congresses thus far. The increased diversity of governing bodies has symbolic and substantive impacts, as diverse representation means women and minorities tend to be represented in a legislative agenda (Mansbridge 1999; Minta and Brown 2014; Juenke and Preuhs 2012). The connection between developing and supporting diverse candidate pools, and having diverse representation underscores the importance of studying changes to pool of eligible candidates that can be recruited, as well as the capacity of organizations to support changes in the candidate pools.

The "Trump phenomenon," in the recruitment of women candidates is not unique. There have been other historical rises of women candidates, such as in the first "Year of the Woman" in 1992. For instance, in 2020, the share of Republican female candidates increased by nearly 14 percent (Conroy 2020a). It's possible that while Democratic women and minorities were inspired to run due to Trump's election, Republican women were inspired to run because of the success Democratic women and minorities found in 2018. In similar echoes to 2018, women's groups claim increased interest from Republican women, such as the relatively new LBJ Women's Campaign School or the Women's Campaign School at Yale (Rodriguez 2020). Scholars have yet to understand what prompted this change in the candidate pools, nor to fully assess the extent of this change in recruitment pools. As indicated in this analysis, explorations of 2020 should consider how partisan group identity impacts women's organizations' recruitment patterns. Future research can suggest how effectively these partisan organizations responded to a rise of Republican women candidates of 2020.

NOTES

1. Groups that are not women-centered in their structure or leadership are not considered women's organizations. For example, groups that provide candidate training with no gendered specificity, or who have no gendered leadership component, are excluded, such as the LGBTQ Victory Institute.

2. For both the survey and interview methodologies, respondents first complete a voluntary informed consent form. The online survey presents the informed consent page and requires an online signature before respondents can begin the survey. For the interview process, phone respondents were emailed the informed consent and read the informed consent before beginning the interview. If the interview occurred in person, a paper version of the informed consent form was presented to the respondents.

3. The state survey was distributed to 290 organizations with clearly identified emails. Out of this group, 20 emails failed or were no longer active. Out of the 270 successfully sent emails, there were 83 responses, and 80 of these respondents answered every question. Thus, the email-distributed survey has a response rate of 40 percent and a completion rate of 80 percent. For the 31 groups that did not have email, I also distributed the survey via an anonymous link through Facebook messages and contact pages to 14 Facebook groups and 17 website contact forms and received 24 responses from these links. Seventy-four percent of all respondents completed every survey question, and 82.25 percent of respondents answered 60 percent of questions. In the frame of national and state women's organizations, 57.4 percent are nonpartisan, 23 percent are Democratic, and 19.5 percent are Republican.

4. My response rate to interview requests was 41 percent. If permission was granted from the interviewee, I recorded and later transcribed the interviews. The majority of interviews were administered via the phone. The entire interview data collection process lasted from June 2019 to August 2019. I then coded the interviews using in vivo coding and value coding. On the national level, I interviewed over twenty-five national women's organizations, including three Democratic groups, three Republican groups, and the rest as nonpartisan groups. This partisan/nonpartisan ratio is fairly consistent with the overall ratios of partisan and nonpartisan national woman's groups. The interview questions are located in the Appendix section A5, along with a full list of national organizations that spoke for attribution, Appendix section A4.

5. Nearly 60 percent of Republican groups did not answer this question, which may suggest an avoidance in addressing the impact Trump's election had on Republican women candidates.

6. Anne Moses, interviewed by author, phone, September 2019.
7. Rielly Karsh and Danielle Davies, interview by author, phone, August 2019.
8. Heather Lurie, interviewed by author, phone, August 2019.
9. Patti Russo, interviewed by author, phone, August 2019.
10. Glynda Carr, interviewed by author, phone, September 2019.
11. Joanna Weiss, interviewed by author, phone, September 2019.
12. Judith Albertelli, interviewed by author, phone, September 2019.
13. First Ask Representative, interviewed by author, phone, September 2019.
14. Heather Lurie, interviewed by author, phone, August 2019.

Chapter Fifteen

The Super Women and the Super Men behind Super PACs

A New Source of Inequality

Paul S. Herrnson and Jennifer Heerwig

Women have made tremendous strides in American politics and society in recent decades. They constitute almost 27 percent of all House members in the 117th Congress (2021–2022), a 9-percentage-point increase from the 112th Congress (2011–2012). Their numbers in the Senate grew from seventeen to twenty-four during this period. Women provided more than 36 percent of the contributions of $200 or more that individuals donated to congressional candidates in 2018 (OpenSecrets 2018). Women's voter turnout has equaled or exceeded that of men since the early 1980s (Center for American Women and Politics 2019). Although still underrepresented in the halls of power, women have claimed major electoral and policy victories at the federal, state, and local levels.[1]

The rise of Super PACs (also known as independent expenditure-only committees) has the potential to affect women's progress in politics. Super PACs differ from the traditional political action committees (PACs), party committees, and candidate campaign committees that participate in federal elections. Only Super PACs can legally raise unlimited contributions from virtually any source. Super PACs, like other outside spending groups, also can make unlimited independent expenditures to influence elections as long as they do not coordinate with a candidate's campaign. Super PACs made almost $5 billion in independent expenditures during the 2010 through 2020 election cycles. Congressional Super PACs, which spent money to influence at least one congressional race, accounted for 70 percent of these expenditures.[2] Super PACs' entry into the political arena has the potential to amplify or diminish women's voices in politics, particularly when these groups make independent expenditures to support or oppose women candidates.

We examine the gender gap in Super PAC financing using a new dataset that records the contributions congressional Super PACs raised from individuals between 2010 and 2016. We address three overarching questions: Do Super PACs exacerbate gender-based inequalities in campaign financing? Do the contributions of women Super PAC donors differ from those of men donors? In particular, do women provide more support to Super PACs committed to the election of women candidates? The first section of the analysis provides some descriptive analysis of gender gaps among congressional Super PACs and their donors. It identifies gendered differences in the donor pool, in the amounts donors contribute, and in the types of groups donors support. The second section investigates the impact of gender and Super PAC organizational characteristics on the likelihood a donor will contribute to a Super PAC. The next section assesses the influence of these factors on the amount of the contribution. The final section explores the degree to which women donors direct their funds to groups that provide the most wide-ranging support for women politicians. The findings reveal a steep gender gap among Super PAC donors. They have broad implications for elections, representation, the women's movement, and women's political progress.

SUPER PACS

The Supreme Court ruling in *Citizens United v. FEC* and other federal court rulings and agency decisions weakened the regulations governing campaign finance. They created new opportunities for raising and spending money in federal elections, and they led to the emergence of Super PACs. Numbering 83 in 2010 and 1,275 in 2012, Super PACs grew to just under 2,400 in 2014 and then plateaued. The financiers of Super PACs include individuals, corporations, labor unions, social welfare groups registered as 501(c)(4) organizations under the Internal Revenue Code, trade associations registered as 501(c)(6) organizations, limited liability corporations (LLCs), and other entities previously prohibited from participating in federal elections. Some contribute amounts thousands of times larger than the maximum allowable contribution to a candidate's campaign organization or other conventional political committee. Super PACs have amplified the voices of wealthy and well-organized interests (Herrnson, Heerwig, and Spencer 2018).

Super PACs vary along many of the same dimensions that distinguish traditional PACs from one another. A few raise millions of dollars, while some raise insufficient funds to influence an election—6 percent raise less than $1,000 and 63 percent raise no money. Most air TV advertisements that focus on candidates, but 44 percent focus on research, voter mobilization drives, contributing to other groups, or organizational maintenance (e.g., Dwyre and Braz 2015; Magleby, Goodliffe, and Olsen 2018). About 57 percent of active congressional Super PACs are multicandidate Super (MCSPs); they seek to advance the election of more than one candidate. Labor Super PACs account for 4 percent of the total, similar to their representation among traditional PACs. Business interests sponsor many traditional PACs, but only 3 percent of Super PACs. Many corporations and trade associations, and their leaders contribute to Republican-leaning conservative Super PACs. Super PACs associated with party committees, such as the Democrats' House Majority PAC and Senate Majority PAC and the Republicans' Congressional Leadership Fund and the Senate Leadership Fund, account for 3 percent. Ideological Super PACs, which have no parent organization, make up 45 percent. Single-candidate Super PACs (SCSPs) that exist to advance (or derail) the prospects of one candidate account for 43 percent of Super PACs.

Central to this study are women's Super PACs. Among the largest and most enduring is the pro-choice, Democratic-leaning *Women Vote!* This EMILY's List–affiliated MCSP raised $28.7 million between 2010 and 2016. Among the smallest and most short-lived is *Cowboy PAC*, a SCSP that raised $38,500 to support Republican Liz Cheney's (R-WY) unsuccessful bid for the Senate in 2014 and then disbanded.[3] Groups that support women constitute 11 percent of congressional Super PACs (see figure 15.1). Somewhat smaller than the percentage of women who run for Congress and larger than percentage of women candidates in competitive races, the percentage of women's congressional Super PACs is comparable to the percentage of traditional PACs devoted to electing women to Congress. The remaining Super PACs, referred to as mixed-gender groups, seek to advance the election of women and men, only men, or one man in the case of a SCSP.

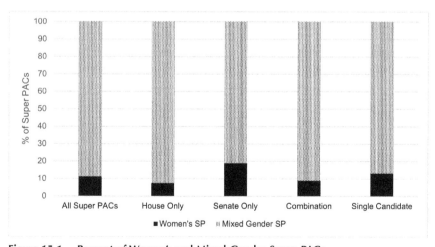

Figure 15.1.   Percent of Women's and Mixed-Gender Super PACs
Center for Responsive Politics, Federal Election Commission, data collected by authors.

Women's congressional Super PACs constitute 19 percent of the MCSPs that participate solely in Senate races, 8 percent of those that participate exclusively in House elections, 9 percent that participate in a combination of races, and 14 percent of all SCSPs. Although most women congressional candidates run as Democrats, the number of Democratic and Republican leaning women's Super PACs is roughly equal. However, 63 percent of all Republican women's congressional Super PACs are SCSPs, compared to only 39 percent of the Democratic groups (the remaining 37 percent of Republican and 61 percent of Democratic groups are MCSPs). Moreover, SCSPs account for 89 percent of all Republican and a paltry 12 percent of all Democratic women's Super PAC dollars. These differences probably result from dissimilarities in the parties' campaign finance networks and donor motives (Thomsen and Michele 2017; Crowder-Meyer and Cooperman 2018).

CAMPAIGN FINANCE AND THE GENDER GAP

Despite significant progress over the course of the twentieth and twenty-first centuries, gender inequality continues to structure the experiences of Americans across political, economic, and social institutions (Delli Carpini and Fuchs 1993; Gerson 2010; Fox and Lawless 2014; Damaske and Frech 2016; Thomsen and King 2020). Feminist theories predict women's motivations and strategies for participating in politics differ from those of men (Flammang 1997; Staeheli 2004). The gender affinity hypothesis states women seek to increase the number of women officeholders. However, it has received mixed empirical support (Lawless 2004; Paxton, Kunovich, and Hughes 2007; Dolan 2008, 2010; Grumbach, Sahn and Staszak 2020).

Gender gaps in partisan identification, vote choice, and policy preferences are well-documented (Shapiro and Mahajan 1986; Conover and Sapiro 1993; Howell and Day 2000; Kaufmann and Petrocik 1999; Box-Steffensmeier, De Boef, and Lin 2004; Pew 2016; Dolan and Lynch 2016; Barnes and Cassese 2017). Women vote at a higher rate than men (e.g., Center for American Women and Politics 2019). Fewer women make contributions, and those who do typically contribute smaller sums. Women donors also possess somewhat different motivations than men (Brown, et al. 1995; Burns, Schlozman and Verba 2001; Francia et al. 2003; Crowder-Meyer and Cooperman 2018). Women target their contributions to presidential and Senate candidates and ideological PACs, and men favor House candidates and industry-linked PACs (Heerwig and Gordon 2018).

Donor mobilization strategies likely contribute to the gender gaps in campaign finance. The efforts of EMILY's List and other women's groups to bundle or otherwise channel campaign contributions to candidates spurred an increase in Democratic women donors, led to the formation of a women's donor network. This has been particularly helpful to pro-choice Democratic female candidates (Crespin and Deitz 2010; Crowder-Meyer and Cooperman 2018), who raise as much if not more than male Democrats, including in primaries. Republican women enjoy no such advantages (Pearson and McGhee 2013; Burrell 2014; Kitchens and Swers 2016).

EXPECTATIONS

Whether the gender gap among donors to conventional political committees extends to Super PACs is an important question, in part, because while there is no limit to the size of a contribution that a Super PAC can accept, conventional groups are limited to relatively modest contributions. We base our expectations on studies of the financing of traditional political committees and semi-structured interviews with the leaders of a diverse group of Super PACs.[4]

Our first set of hypotheses focuses on the impact of donor gender on contributions. We expect women to demonstrate less support for Super PACs than men, both in terms of the numbers who make a contribution and the amounts they contribute. The interplay between donor gender and Super PAC characteristics informs our next set of hypotheses. We anticipate women provide more support for women's Super PACs than men. Women's preference for ideological causes and high-profile candidates implies they favor liberal Super PACs and Super PACs that participate in Senate elections or a combination of races. By contrast, men's material motives and interest in political access implies they focus on business Super PACs, House contests, and SCSPs.

Nonetheless, there are reasons not to set expectations too high. The literature on regulated contributions establishes donors tend to be wealthy, educated, older, and drawn from the business community, and wealthy individuals usually make the largest donations (e.g., McElwee, Schaffner, and Rhodes 2016). On the one hand, the link between education and the adoption of feminist attitudes (Bolzendahl and Myers 2004; Davis and Greenstein 2009; Crowder-Meyer and Lauderdale 2014) and the propensity of women donors to support women candidates could lay the foundation for an expansive gender gap among Super PAC contributors. On the other, economic interests may outweigh support for feminism, resulting in most women donors backing conservative Super PACs rather than women's or liberal groups, which implies that any gender gap among Super PAC donors is likely to be narrow. Moreover, because most contributors focus on the few competitive elections that occur in a given election cycle, there is likely to be considerable overlap in the Super PACs men and women support. Adding to the complexity of researching a potential gender gap among Super PAC donors as such a gap could manifest itself in the likelihood a donor will contribute to a specific group, the size of the contribution, or the amount a set of donors contributes to a class of Super PAC. We investigate all three possibilities.

DATA AND METHODS

We conduct our analysis using data from the Federal Election Commission (FEC), the Center for Responsive Politics (CRP), and other public sources. The data contain a wealth of information about Super PACs and Super PAC contributors, including itemization of their financial activities in federal elections. The first step in our research was to extensively clean the data, recode some variables, and create new ones (see the Appendix for details). Second, we aggregated the itemized contributions to create a dataset that has as its unit of analysis the sum of the contributions each individual made to each Super PAC in each election cycle between 2010 and 2016. The resulting dataset contains information for each active Super PAC (one that raised or distributed at least $1,000 and made at least one independent expenditure in at least one congressional race in a given election cycle) and information for each active individual donor (who contributed at least $200 to at least one of these groups in the same cycle).[5] This dataset only includes Super PACs that raised at least a portion of their funding from individuals. The variables for Super PAC characteristics record each group's support for women candidates and other aspects of its mission; its sponsorship (or affiliation); the offices it focuses on; and its finances. The contributor variables include the donor's gender and major economic or political association (based primarily on employer or profession), and the amount contributed to each Super PAC.

Next, we created a dataset for a multivariate analysis of congressional Super PACs that is an expansion of the first. This dataset includes a record for each *actual* contribution (from the first dataset) and a record for each *potential* contribution each donor could have made to a congressional Super PAC in a given election cycle, but did not (coded 0).[6] The inclusion of all actual and potential contributions results in a dataset that includes almost 13.9 million Super PAC–contributor dyads.

The first section of the analysis presents an overview of Super PAC donors and provides preliminary evidence of a gender gap. The second section uses the extended dataset and logit models to assess the impact of organizational and donor characteristics on the likelihood an individual will contribute to a congressional Super PAC. We first examine the effects of gender affinity across the entire sample of congressional Super PACs. Then, we assess the impact of gender on contributions to Super PACs that follow different spending strategies. To aid in the interpretation of the models, we present predicted probabilities for the effects of gender affinity on women and men. The third section of the analysis estimates the amounts women and men give to Super PACs, conditional on having given a donation. The unit of analysis for these models is the observed contributions an individual makes to a group. Because the amounts contributed to Super PACs are positively skewed, we use the natural log of the amount as the dependent variable. We use OLS to regress the logged contribution amount on Super PAC and donor characteristics. In the final section, we ascertain whether women or men allocate a greater portion of their contributions to Super PACs most committed to electing women candidates.

Each donor is coded as a woman or man. CRP codes for gender in its original data. We verified these codes using the Social Security Administration's gender distribution of first names and an imputation package supported in R. The few cases that could not be definitively verified were researched using public sources posted to the Internet.

Given the anticipated and observed differences between women's and men's Super PAC contributions, we estimate each of our multivariate models separately by gender.[7] The primary independent variable captures contributions to Super PACs that support women. *Women's Group*=1 for Super PACs that make all of their independent expenditures to promote the election of one or more women candidates or to oppose the candidacy of a man candidate running against a woman in the general election; mixed-gender Super PACs are the excluded comparison group. We chose this operationalization over others after some preliminary investigations of the data. We rejected classification by a group's name, in part, because few Super PACs have names that provide information about the gender of the candidates they support. Women's (and other) Super PACs convey this information when fundraising and through other means. We use a combination of candidate gender and group affiliation and spending to differentiate between women's and mixed-gender Super PACs. Women's SCSPs, which seek to elect one woman candidate (and have no organizational sponsor), constitute 56 percent of all women's Super PACs. Women's MCSPs, which seek to elect more than one woman candidate and no men, comprise the remaining 44 percent.[8]

Political perspective is based on a Super PAC's publicly stated goals or the objectives of its sponsoring organization: a Super PAC that seeks to elect liberal (mainly Democratic) candidates is coded *Liberal*=1 and Super PACs that back conservative (mostly Republican) candidates are the comparison group. The inclusion of this variable distinguishes the effects of the gender-based and the ideological components of a group's objectives on contributor behavior. The Super PAC strategy variables are based on the elections in which a Super PAC makes independent expenditures: *Senate Only*=1, *Combination* (of House, Senate, or presidential elections)=1, and Super PACs that participate only in House elections are the comparison group.

The analysis includes relevant organizational controls. Super PAC affiliation is coded as a series of dummy variables: *Single Candidate*=1 for a SCSP that makes positive independent expenditures in support of only one candidate, negative independent expenditures against that candidate's opponents, or some combination thereof. *Labor*=1 for a MCSP affiliated with one or more labor unions; *Business*=1 for a MCSP affiliated with one or more business entities; *Party connected*=1 for a MCSP associated with a party leader or party committee; and ideological Super PACs constitute the comparison group. A group that maintains a separate, segregated fund (i.e., a traditional PAC account) to contribute to federal candidates and other conventional political committees is coded *Hybrid=1* and pure Super PACs are the comparison group. *Ln(Receipts)* is the natural log of the total receipts a group raised in the election cycle. *Group Experience* is operationalized as the number of election cycles in which a group participated.

The analysis also includes donor control variables. We classify a donor's major primary economic or political sector using an approach similar to that used for Super PACs, where *Labor*=1; *Business*=1; *Party-connected (comprising* elected officials and party leaders)=1; *Other/miscellaneous*=1; and ideology is the excluded comparison group. One could argue this approach does not record a contributor's full range of interests. However, it is important to recognize that interests differ from associations; many interests lie dormant and have little impact on political activity, while associations result from the act of joining and have a greater impact. Most individuals' strongest association is rooted in their workplace or profession, and these have become increasingly important in motivating political participation (Hertel-Fernandez 2017). We control for a donor's propensity to participate in Super PAC financing: *Donor Experience*=the number of election cycles in which a donor contributed $200 or more to a Super PAC. The region in which the donor resides is coded *South*=1, *Midwest*=1, *West*=1, *Washington, DC* (the nexus for most campaign finance transactions)=1, and northeast is the excluded comparison group. The final controls are for the election cycle: *2010*=1, *2012*=1, *2014*=1, and 2016 is the comparison group.

RESULTS

How do the women who contribute to Super PACs differ from the men? To begin with, there are fewer of them (see figure 15.2, panel a). Women ac-

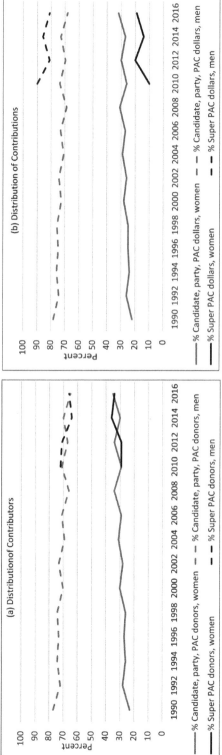

Figure 15.2. Women and Men Contributors to Super PACs and Candidates, Party Committees, and Traditional PACs

Compiled from data from the Center for Responsive Politics.

count for 35 percent of the individuals who contribute to a congressional Super PAC, similar to their participation among the larger set of individuals that contributes to candidates, party committees, or traditional PACs that participate in congressional elections.[9] Moreover, the increased participation of women contributors helped shrink by 9 percentage points the gender gaps for donors to both sets of committees. By 2016, men donors to each set of committees outnumbered women two to one. In contrast, women account for only 17 percent of the funds individuals contributed to Super PACs, compared to 45 percent of the funds contributed to conventional committees (see panel b). Although the gender gaps for the funds contributed to Super PACs and conventional committees fell at roughly the same rate, in 2016 men still contributed three times as much money to Super PACs as women, compared to only twice as much to conventional committees. In short, Super PACs do not appear to have widened the preexisting disparity in the number of women and men that make campaign contributions, but they have enabled men to become a more dominant force in campaign financing.

The gender gap in Super PAC contributions can be partially explained by the distributions of women's and men's contributions. Women make up roughly 40 percent of those who donate between $200 and $499 to congressional Super PACs, and their presence steadily declines among those who give substantially larger amounts (see figure 15.3). Women constitute only 23 percent of those who contribute $15,000 or more, compared to 67 percent for men.

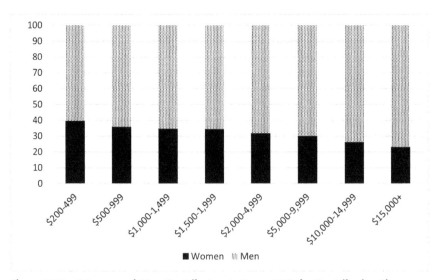

Figure 15.3.   Women and Men Contributors to Super PACs by Contribution Size
Center for Responsive Politics, Federal Election Commission, data collected by authors.

Table 15.1.   Overview of Women and Men Contributors to
Different Types of Super PACs

	Donors	
Super PAC Characteristics:	*Women*	*Men*
Gender of Candidates Supported		
Women's group	16.2%	5.2%
Mixed-gender group	83.8	94.8
Political Perspective		
Liberal	62.7%	36.2%
Conservative	37.3	63.2
Affiliation		
Single candidate	15.2%	14.7%
Party connected	7.3	7.2
Ideological	75.7	76.7
Labor	0.1	0.2
Business	1.7	1.2
Spending Strategy		
Senate only	10.5%	14.7%
House only	6.9	11.8
Combination	82.5	73.5

Sources: Center for Responsive Politics, Federal Election Commission, data
   collected by authors.

The initial results also suggest, as expected, there is a gender gap in the types of groups donors support. About 16 percent of the women support a women's Super PAC, compared to only 5 percent of the men (see table 15.1). Women donors favor liberal over conservative Super PACs by more than 26 percentage points, while men prefer conservative Super PACs by a similar margin. More women contribute to Super PACs that seek to elect candidates to a variety of offices, but more men contribute to Super PACs that seek to elect candidates solely to one chamber of Congress.

The Effects of Gender and Group Characteristics on Contributions to Super PACs

What effects do donor and recipient characteristics have on individuals' contributions to congressional Super PACs? Figure 15.4 presents the differences in the probability a woman or a man will contribute to a Super PAC based on logit models that control for donor attributes and Super PAC characteristics.[10] The first two bars demonstrate that a female donor has a 64 percent greater probability of contributing to a women's Super PAC than a mixed-gender Super PAC, while a male donor has a 38 percent lower probability

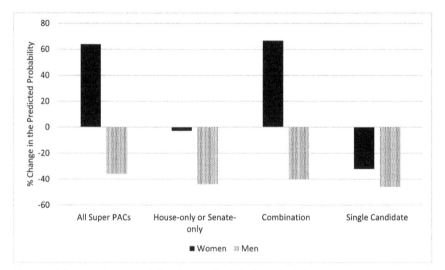

Figure 15.4. The Impact of Gender on the Likelihood of Contributing to a Women's Super PAC over a Mixed-Gender Super PAC

Note: Figure generated from models described in Appendix using average marginal effects (AMEs).

Center for Responsive Politics, Federal Election Commission, data collected by authors.

of doing so. The second set of bars, for groups that follow a single-chamber strategy, shows that neither set of donors shows a preference for contributing to a women's Super PAC over a mixed-gender Super PAC, but men are 40 percentage points less likely to do so.

The third set of bars demonstrates the widest gender gap is among donors who contribute to Super PACs that make independent expenditures in elections for different offices. Lacking a commitment to electing only one specific candidate and unencumbered by a strategy focused exclusively on one chamber of Congress, the women's Super PACs in this category provide the broadest support for women candidates. This makes them a prime target for ideological donors who support the Women's movement. A woman donor is 67 percent more likely to contribute to a women's combination Super PAC than to a mixed-gender combination Super PAC, while a man donor is 40 percent less likely to do so.

The last set of bars shows that the smallest gender gap exists among donors to women's SCSPs. The limited number of such groups undoubtedly contributes to women's (and men's) limited support for them. Some may reject a solicitation from a woman's SCSP in favor of a solicitation from a women's MCSP or a mixed gender MCSP that supports candidates more sympathetic to their views. The results also show that women have a propensity to support Democratic-leaning liberal Super PACs, particularly those that participate in Senate contests or a combination of races, while men prefer Republican-leaning conservative groups.

Figure 15.5 illustrates that men typically make the largest donation to Super PACs, irrespective of the recipient group's strategy or mission.[11] Women's contributions to women's and mixed gender Super PACs typically amount to about $1,600 and $1,200, respectively, and the former is 33 percent larger than the latter (see Figure 15.5, panel a). The corresponding donations for men, by contrast, are roughly $5,300 and $3,600—a difference of 47 percent. There are similar gender-based differences for donations to Super PACs that

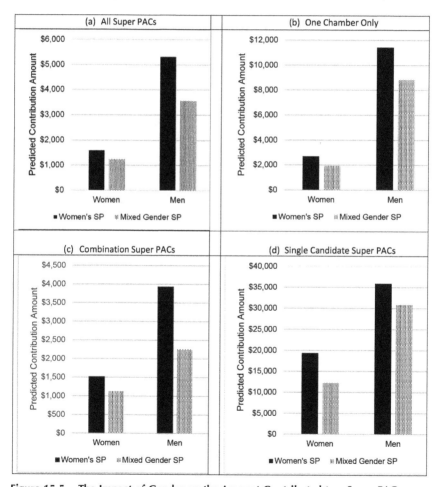

Figure 15.5.   The Impact of Gender on the Amount Contributed to a Super PAC

Note: Figure generated from models described in Appendix. One chamber only refers to groups that partici-pate in House or Senate elections, but not both.

Center for Responsive Politics, Federal Election Commission, data compiled by authors.

follow a single-chamber strategy and those active in elections for a combination of offices (see panels b and c). SCSPs constitute the only group of Super PACs where candidate gender has a greater impact on women's than men's donations: women's contributions to women's SCSPs are about 41 percent larger than their contributions to men's SCSPs, while the corresponding difference for men's contributions is only 17 percent (see panel d).

Women Donors and the Women's Movement

Having established the typical woman donor is more likely than the typical man donor to contribute to a women's Super PAC, but contributes fewer dollars to it (and to Super PACs in general), it is important to ask: Do women, as a group, commit a greater portion of their funds than men to Super PACs seeking to elect women? The answer to this question lends insights into the abilities of feminist organizations to mobilize women in support of Super PACs committed to women candidates. It also provides perspective on the political inclinations and allegiances of the small, elite group of women who contribute to Super PACs. As discussed earlier, it is possible these women share the priorities of similarly situated men, resulting in both sets of donors supporting Super PACs that pursue conservative goals. It is also possible that gender identity leads the women to prioritize feminist causes and liberal goals, resulting in a large gender gap in Super PAC support. Of course, it could be that women Super PAC donors' behavior is consistent with neither pattern. We use the percentages of the total Super PAC dollars contributed to women's Super PACs to assess women's ability to unite behind women's causes.

At first glance, the results provide moderate support for the expectation that the goal of electing female candidates heavily influences contributions of women Super PAC donors. Overall, women deliver 26 percent of their total Super PAC dollars to groups that only support women candidates, compared to 15 percent for men (see the first pair of bars in figure 15.6). Although a significant difference, the findings imply women Super PAC donors' allegiance to women's candidacies and causes is not overwhelming.

However, the divergent pattern across the various types of Super PACs paints a different picture. Notably, women's Super PACs collect 31 percent of the funds women contributed to groups participating in elections for a combination of offices. Unrestrained by ties to a single candidate or the pursuit of a narrow political strategy and constituting a mere 9 percent of all combination Super PACs, these groups provide the broadest support for women politicians and feminist causes. Women donors' robust backing of women's combination Super PACs (most of which support Democrats), contrasts sharply with

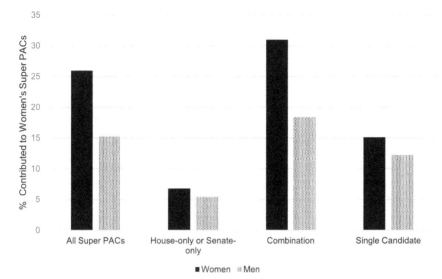

Figure 15.6. The Impact of Gender on the Allocation of Contributions to Women's Super PACs

Notes: The percentages are for the amounts women and men contributed to women's Super PACs; the remainder of the funds were contributed to mixed gender Super PACs, and when combined they sum to 100%.

Center for Responsive Politics, Federal Election Commission, data collected by authors.

their limited commitment to Super PACs that support women running for one chamber of Congress or Super PACs devoted to a single female candidate (most of which support Republicans). The results further support the argument that organizational characteristics and donor gender have a substantial impact on contributions to Super PACs.

CONCLUSION

Men have long dominated most aspects of American politics, but women have made substantial strides. The advent of Super PACs has the potential to affect the participation, election, and representation of women. Super PACs possess considerable fundraising advantages over conventional political committees. They vary in wealth, organizational affiliation, ideology, and campaign strategy. A relatively small number are dedicated solely to electing women.

Our analysis, based on a dataset comprising the contributions of individual donors to Super PACs, yields insights into the behavior of women and men Super PAC donors. The findings establish there is a gender gap among Super

PAC donors that dwarfs preexisting gender gaps in campaign finance and other realms of politics. The overview of Super PAC financing demonstrates fewer women than men donate to congressional Super PACs, women donors contribute smaller amounts, and women's contributions account for a fraction of Super PAC receipts. The multivariate analyses show that Super PAC characteristics combine with donor gender to structure the flow of Super PAC contributions. They confirm there is a gender gap in contribution strategies. One component of this gender gap is women donors' greater propensity to contribute to women's Super PACs, which is largely a product of their support for MCSPs that seek to elect women to a combination of offices. A second component is women donors' strong preference for Democratic-leaning liberal MCSPs. A third component is that women collectively deliver a larger portion of their funds to women's Super PACs.

The findings suggest that women Super PAC donors respond to the mobilization efforts of women's political organizations and liberal Democratic-leaning groups. They imply women Super PAC donors have a higher degree of solidarity with women who donate to conventional political committees than with men Super PAC donors who share their socioeconomic status. The findings also bolster speculation that absent gendered inequalities in disposable income, women's contributions to women's Super PACs would exceed those of men.

The findings have significant implications for American politics. Super PACs spend billions of dollars to influence elections. Their independent expenditures directly affect the information voters receive about candidates. Because they can lead to tactical adjustments by candidates and other political committees, Super PAC expenditures also indirectly influence the messages voters receive. Congressional Super PACs have their biggest impact on close elections, including where their spending outpaces that of one or both candidates. Super PACs' effects on policymaking are likely to be considerable given members of Congress respond to voting and financial constituencies. Partisan polarization and slim congressional majorities add to the potential for Super PACs to have an outsized impact on policy outcomes. The overall effects of the gender gap in Super PAC contributions are likely to benefit conservative candidates and causes. As such, the emergence of Super PACs may pose new obstacles to the advancement of workplace equality, gun control, and other policies that divide most women and men and most liberals and conservatives. The gendered disparities resulting from the rise of Super PACs will continue unless there is marked growth both in the number of women who donate to Super PACs and the amounts they contribute. Whether the gender gap among Super PAC contributors persists remains an open question.

APPENDIX

Data Coding and Cleaning

This research uses data collected by the FEC, then enhanced by CRP and other public sources. The earliest steps consisted of extensively cleaning the data, addressing inconsistencies in the coding of some variables, and recoding variables so they would better suit our research question. We also supplemented the dataset with new variables and data.

A major difference between CRP's coding and our coding concerns single-candidate Super PACs. CRP applied its single-candidate/multicandidate coding scheme to groups that made independent expenditures of $50,000 or more, leaving those that spent less $50,000 coded as MCSPs (their default category). Our preliminary investigation of the data showed that a substantial number of the Super PACs that spent less than $50,000 made independent expenditures solely to help elect (or oppose) only one candidate. Internet-based searches of these groups demonstrated that nearly all of them had no association with a parent organization, thereby confirming their single-candidate mission. We coded these groups as SCSPs (with the exception of the few associated with a parent organization). We also applied our coding scheme consistently, whereas CRP made some exceptions. Most notably, we coded Priorities USA as a MCSP in 2016 because it supported several federal candidates, while CRP coded it as an SCSP supporting Hillary Clinton. As a result, our data contain more SCSPs, and fewer MCSPs, than CRP's data.

Data Analysis

We tested several model specifications to ensure the robustness of the results. We include only theoretically relevant variables in the final models (results available upon request). Figure 15.4 panel is based on logistic regression models that estimate the likelihood an individual will contribute to a Super PAC. Figure 15.5 is based on models that estimate the amount an individual contributes to a Super PAC (in logged dollars). Analyses that included additional control variables or used other transformations produced substantively similar results.

NOTES

1. This project received support from the Democracy Fund. Data were provided by the Center for Responsive Politics and the Federal Election Commission. We thank Jay Goodliffe, Doug Spencer, Kyle Adams, Van Augur, and Christian Caron for assistance and Ray La Raja for helpful comments.

2. Compiled from data assembled by the Center for Responsive Politics, https://www.opensecrets.org/.

3. Following Cheney's election to the House, she created a traditional leadership PAC also called Cowboy PAC.

4. The interviewees include the founders, presidents, chief strategists, communications directors, treasurers, and legal councils of Super PACs that spent between $150,000 and almost $25 million in a single election. The groups vary in their support for women candidates, sponsorship, strategy, experience, ideology, and other organizational characteristics.

5. Contributions less than $200 are excluded because they are not itemized in disclosure reports.

6. The data expansion was done separately for each year because many Super PACs did not exist in every election, and it would be impossible to donate to a non-existent Super PAC.

7. The initial analysis with gender interaction terms confirmed substantial differences in women's and men's contributions.

8. Lowering the threshold to 90 percent results in the coding of few additional groups as women's Super PACs.

9. The figures for conventional political committees, from a different dataset, contains substantially more donors.

10. We present average marginal effects (AMEs) translated into percentage changes.

References

Abramowitz, Alan I. 1991. "Incumbency, Campaign Spending, and the Decline of Competition in U.S. House Elections." *Journal of Politics* 53: 34–56.

———. 2010. *The Disappearing Center*. New Haven, CT: Yale University Press.

———. 2012. "Grand Old Tea Party." In *Steep: The Precipitous Rise of the Tea Party*. Lawrence Rosenthal and Christine Trost, eds. Berkeley: University of California Press: 295–11.

———. 2018. *The Great Alignment: Race, Party Transformation and the Rise of Donald Trump*. New Haven, CT: Yale University Press.

———. 2021. "It's the Pandemic, Stupid! A Simplified Model for Forecasting the 2020 Presidential Election." *PS: Political Science and Politics*. 54: 52–54

Abramowitz, Alan I., and Kyle Saunders. 1998. "Ideological Realignment in the U.S. Electorate." *Journal of Politics*. 60: 634–52.

Abramowitz, Alan I., and Steven W. Webster. 2016. "The Rise of Negative Partisanship and the Nationalization of U.S. Elections in the 21st Century." *Electoral Studies* 41: 12–22.

Abramson, Alana. 2019. "Congresswoman Elise Stefanik has a Plan to get more Republican Congresswomen Elected." *Time*. May 9. www.time.com

Agiesta, Jennifer. 2016. "CNN/ORC Poll: Donald Trump dominates GOP field at 41%." *CNN Politics*. https://www.cnn.com/2016/01/26/politics/donald-trump-ted -cruz-polling/index.html.

Alba, Richard. 2020. *The Great Demographic Illusion*. Princeton, NJ: Princeton University Press.

Alba, Richard, Morris Levy, and Dowell Myers. 2021. "The Myth of a Majority-Minority America." https://www.theatlantic.com/ideas/archive/2021/06/myth-ma jority-minority-america/619190/.

Aldrich, John H., Brad Gomez, and John Griffin. 1999. "State Party Organizations Study, 1999; State Party Chair Questionnaire." Duke University.

Alemany, Jacqueline, Emma Brown, Tom Hamburger, and Jon Swaine. 2021. "Ahead of Jan. 6, Willard Hotel in Downtown D.C. Was a Trump Team 'Command

Center' for Effort to Deny Biden the Presidency." *Washington Post*. https://
www.washingtonpost.com/investigations/willard-trump-eastman-giuliani
-bannon/2021/10/23/c45bd2d4-3281-11ec-9241-aad8e48f01ff_story.html.

Anderson, Elijah. 2011. *The Cosmopolitan Canopy: Race and Civility in Everyday
Life*. New York: W.W. Wilson.

Ansolabehere, Stephen, John Mark Hansen, Shigeo Hirano, and James M. Snyder.
2007. "The Incumbency Advantage in U.S. Primary Elections." *Electoral Studies*
26: 660–68.

Ansolabehere, Stephen, Jonathan Rodde, and James N. Snyder, Jr. 2008. "The
Strength of Issues: Using Multiple Measures to Gauge Preference Stability,
Ideological Constraint and Issue Voting." *American Political Science Review* 102:
215–32.

Ansolabehere, Stephen, and Nathaniel Persily. 2007. "Vote Fraud in the Eye of the
Beholder: The Role of Public Opinion in the Challenge to Voter Identification Requirements Essay." *Harvard Law Review* 121: 1737–75.

Arceneaux, K., and David W. Nickerson. 2009. "Who Is Mobilized to Vote? A Re-
analysis of 11 Field Experiments." *American Journal of Political Science* 53: 1–16.

Arkansas Poll. 2020. University of Arkansas at Fayetteville. https://fulbright.uark
.edu/departments/political-science/partners/arkansas-poll.php.

Bacon, Perry, Jr. 2019. "The Six Wings of the Democratic Party." FiveThirtyEight
.com, March 11, https://fivethirtyeight.com/features/the-six-wings-of-the-demo
cratic-party/.

Bafumi, Joseph, and Michael C. Herron. 2010. "Leapfrog Representation and Extremism: A Study of American Voters and Their Members in Congress." *American
Political Science Review* 104: 519–42.

Bahrampour, Tara, and Ted Mellnik. 2021. "Census data shows widening diversity;
number of White people falls for first time." https://www.washingtonpost.com/dc
-md-va/2021/08/12/census-data-race-ethnicity-neighborhoods/.

Bail, Christopher, Lisa P. Argyle, Taylor W. Brown, John P. Bumpus, Haohan Chen,
M. B. Fallin Hunzaker, Jaemin Lee, Marcus Mann, Friedolin Merhout, and Alexander Volfovsky. 2018. "Exposure to Opposing Views on Social Media Can Increase
Political Polarization." *Proceedings of the National Academy of Sciences*. 115:
9216–21.

Bailey, Michael, Jon Mummolo, and Hans Noel. 2012. "Tea Party Influence: A Story
of Activists and Elites." *American Politics Research* 40: 769–804.

Ballhaus, Rebecca, Joe Palazzolo, and Andrew Restuccia. 2021. "Trump and His
Allies Set the Stage for Riot Well Before January 6." *Wall Street Journal*, https://
www.wsj.com/articles/trump-and-his-allies-set-the-stage-for-riot-well-before
-january-6-11610156283.

Balz, Dan, Scott Clement, and Emily Guskin. 2021. "Not Just Red and Blue: Large
Survey Explores Factions within Democratic and Republican Parties." *Washington
Post*, November 9. https://www.washingtonpost.com/politics/2021/11/09/demo
crat-republican-voters-survey/.

Banfield, Edward C., and James Q. Wilson. 1963. *City Politics.* New York: Vintage
Books.

Barber, Michael J., and Jeremy C. Pope. 2018. "Does Party Trump Ideology? Disentangling Party and Ideology in America." *American Political Science Review.* 113: 38–54.

———. 2019. "Conservatism in the Era of Trump." *Perspectives on Politics* 17: 719–36.

Barnes, Tiffany D., and Erin C. Cassese. 2017. "American Party Women: A Look at the Gender Gap within Parties." *Political Research Quarterly* 70: 127–41.

Barth, Jay. 2021. Interview with John C. Davis.

Barth, Jay, and Janine A. Parry. 2005. "Still Swingin': Arkansas and the 2004 Presidential Race," *American Review of Politics* 26: 133–54.

———. 2018. "Arkansas: Trump is a Natural for the Natural State." In *The Future Ain't What It Used to Be: The 2016 Presidential Election in the South.* Scott Buchanan and Branwell DuBose Kapeluck, eds. Fayetteville: University of Arkansas Press: 127–46.

Bateman, David A., Ira Katznelson, and John Lapinski. 2018. *Southern Nation: Congress and White Supremacy after Reconstruction.* Princeton, NJ: Princeton University Press.

Baylor, Christopher. 2017. *First to the Party: The Group Origins of Political Transformation.* Philadelphia: University of Pennsylvania Press.

Beck, Paul A., and Erik Heidemann. 2014a. "Changing Strategies in Grassroots Canvassing: 1956–2012." *Party Politics* 20: 261–74.

———. 2014b. "The Ground Game from the Voter's Perspective: 2012 and Before." In *The State of the Parties: The Changing Role of Contemporary American Parties*, 7th ed., John C. Green, Daniel J. Coffey, and David B. Cohen, eds. Lanham, MD: Rowman & Littlefield: 251–69.

Beck, Paul A., Richard Gunther, and Erik Nisbet. 2018. "What Happened to the Ground Game in 2016?" In *The State of the Parties 2018: The Changing Role of Contemporary American Parties*, John C. Green, Daniel J. Coffey, and David B. Cohen, eds. Lanham, MD: Rowman & Littlefield: 263–77.

Bejarano, Christina E. 2013. *The Latina Advantage: Gender, Race, and Political Success.* Austin: University of Texas Press.

Bell, Lauren Cohen, David Elliot Meyer, and Ronald Keith Gaddie. 2017. *Slingshot: The Defeat of Eric Cantor.* Thousand Oaks, CA: Congressional Quarterly Press.

Belluck, Pam. 2002. "A G.O.P. Primary Strains Party Ties and Bush Loyalties." *New York Times*, July 7.

Bendix, William, and Jon MacKay. 2017. "Partisan Infighting Among House Republicans: Leaders, Factions, and Networks of Interests." *Legislative Studies Quarterly* 42: 549–77.

Berkowitz, Edward D. 1991. *America's Welfare State: From Roosevelt to Reagan.* Baltimore: Johns Hopkins University Press.

Berry, Marie, and Erica Chenoweth. 2018. "Who Made the Women's March?" In *The Resistance: The Dawn of the Anti-Trump Opposition Movement.* David C. Meyer and Sidney Tarrow, eds. New York: Oxford University Press: 75–89.

Bishop, Bill. 2009. *The Big Sort: Why the Clustering of Like-Minded America is Tearing Us Apart.* Boston: Mariner Books.

Bishop, George F. 2004. *The Illusion of Public Opinion: Fact and Artifact in American Public Opinion Polls*. Lanham, MD: Rowman & Littlefield.

Black, Duncan. 1958. *The Theory of Committees and Elections*. London: Cambridge University Press.

Blair, Diane D. 1988. *Arkansas Politics: Do the People Rule?* Lincoln: University of Nebraska Press.

———. 1995. "The Big Three of Late-Twentieth-Century Arkansas Politics: Dale Bumpers, Bill Clinton, and David Pryor." *Arkansas Historical Quarterly* 54: 53–79.

Blair, Diane D., and Jay Barth. 2005. *Arkansas Politics and Government*, 3rd ed. Lincoln: University of Nebraska Press.

Blow, Charles M. 2018. "White Extinction Anxiety." https://www.nytimes.com/2018/06/24/opinion/america-white-extinction.html.

Blum, Rachel M. 2020. *How the Tea Party Captured the GOP: Insurgent Factions in American Politics*. Chicago: University of Chicago Press.

Boatright, Robert G. 2013. *Getting Primaried*. Ann Arbor: University of Michigan Press.

———. 2022. "What do the 2020 Congressional Primaries Tell Us About the Direction of the Democratic Party?" In *Polarization and Political Party Factions in 2020*, Christopher Galdieri, Jennifer Lucas, and Tauna Sisco, eds. Lanham, MD: Lexington Press: 38–100.

Boatright, Robert G., and Valerie Sperling. 2019. *Trumping Politics as Usual*. New York: Oxford University Press.

Boatright, Robert G., and Vincent J. Moscardelli. 2018. "Is There a Link Between Primary Election Competition and General Election Results?" In *Handbook of Primary Elections*, Robert G. Boatright, ed. New York: Routledge: 188–212.

Boatright, Robert G., and Zachary Albert. 2021. "Factional Conflict and Independent Expenditures in the 2018 Democratic House Primaries." *Congress and the Presidency* 48: 50–77.

Boatright, Robert G., Michael J. Malbin, and Brendan Glavin. 2016. "Independent Expenditures in Congressional Primaries after *Citizens United:* Implications for Interest Groups, Incumbents, and Political Parties." *Interest Groups and Advocacy* 5: 119–40.

Bolingbroke. 1997 [1738]. *Bolingbroke: Political Writings*, David Armitage, ed. New York: Cambridge University Press.

Bolzendahl, Catherine I., and Daniel J. Myers. 2004. "Feminist Attitudes and Support for Gender Equality: Opinion Change in Women and Men, 1974–1998." *Social Forces* 83: 759–89.

Book of the States. 1935. Chicago: Council of State Governments and American Legislators.

———. 2016. Lexington, KY: Council of State Governments, 2017.

Bordt, Rebecca Lea. 1992. "Form and content: An organizational analysis of women's non-profits." PhD diss., Yale University.

———. 1997. *The Structure of Women's Nonprofit Organizations*. Bloomington: Indiana University Press.

Box-Steffensmeier, Janet M., Suzanna De Boef, and Lin Tse-min. 2004. "The Dynamics of the Partisan Gender Gap." *American Political Science Review* 98: 515–28.

Brazile, Donna. 2017. *Hacks: The Inside Story of the Break-ins and Breakdowns That Put Donald Trump in the White House.* New York: Hachette Books.

Brennan Center for Justice and Bipartisan Policy Center, 2021. "Election Officials Under Attack." https://www.brennancenter.org/sites/default/files/2021-06/BCJ-130_Election%20Officials_fact%20sheet.pdf).

Brooks, David. 2019. "What Pelosi Versus the Squad Really Means." *New York Times*, July 15.

Brown, Heath, and Lindsey Cormack. 2021. "Angry about Fraud: How Congress Took up Trump's Claims of Fraud." *The Forum.* 19: 77–95.

Brown, Nadia E., and Pearl K. Dowe. 2020. "Late to the Party: Black Women's Inconsistent Support from Political Parties." In *Good Reasons to Run: Women and Political Candidacy*, Shauna L. Shames, Rachel I. Bernhard, Mirya R. Holman, and Dawn Langan Teele, eds. Philadelphia: Temple University Press: 153–66.

Brownstein, Ronald. 2018. "The prosperity paradox is dividing the country in two." CNN, https://www.cnn.com/2018/01/23/politics/economy-prosperity-paradox-divide-country-voters/index.html.

———. 2016. "Has the Balance of Power Shifted from the Rustbelt to the Sunbelt?" *The Atlantic.* http://www.theatlantic.com/politics/archive/2016/11/campaign-efforts-rustbelt-and-sunbelt/506873/.

Burghart, Devin, and Leonard Zeskind. 2015. *The Tea Party Movement in 2015.* Kansas City, MO: Institute for Research Education on Human Rights.

Burns, Nancy, Kay Lehman Schlozman, and Sidney Verba. 2001. *The Private Roots of Public Action: Gender, Equality, and Political Participation.* Cambridge, MA: Harvard University Press.

Burrell, Barbara C. 1996. *A Woman's Place is in the House: Campaigning for Congress in the Feminist Era.* Ann Arbor: University of Michigan Press.

———. 2014. *Gender in Campaigns for the U.S. House of Representatives.* Ann Arbor: University of Michigan Press.

Busch, Andrew E., and John J. Pitney, *Divided We Stand.* Lanham, MD: Rowman & Littlefield, 2021.

Cameron, Charles M., and Jonathan Kastellec. 2021. "Simulating the Future Ideological Composition of the Supreme Court." Working paper.

Campbell, Angus, Philip E. Converse, Warren E. Miller, and Donald E. Stokes. 1960. *The American Voter.* New York: John Wiley and Sons.

Canes-Wrone, Brandice, and Kenneth M. Miller. 2022. "Out-of-District Donors and Representation in the U.S. House." *Legislative Studies Quarterly* 47: 365–95.

Cantor, David M., and Paul S. Herrnson. 1997. "Party Campaign Activity and Party Unity in the U. S. House of Representatives." *Legislative Studies Quarterly* 22: 393–415.

Carew, Michele. 2021. "Partisan Attacks Drove Me Out of My Job as a Texas Elections Official." *Washington Post*, November 1.

Carmines, Edward G., and James Stimson. 1989. *Issue Evolution.* Princeton, NJ: Princeton University Press.

Carmines, Edward G., Michael J. Ensley, and Michael W. Wagner. 2014. "Why American Political Parties Can't Get Beyond the Left-Right Divide." In The *State of the Parties: The Changing Role of Contemporary American Parties*, 7th ed. John C. Green, Daniel J. Coffey, and David B. Cohen, eds. Lanham, MD: Rowman & Littlefield: 55–72.

———. 2016. "Ideological Heterogeneity and the Rise of Donald Trump." *The Forum* 14: 385–97.

Carmines, Edward G., and Nicholas J. D'Amico. 2015. "The New Look in Political Ideology Research." *Annual Reviews of Political Science* 18: 205–16.

Carter, Mark. 2019. "Bypassing Purple: Arkansas' Switch from Blue to Red Was Quick and Definitive." *Arkansas Money and Politics.* https://armoneyandpolitics.com/bypassing-purple-arkansas-switch-blue-red/.

Cassese, Erin C. 2021. "Partisan Dehumanization in American Politics." *Political Behavior* 43: 29–50.

Center for American Women and Politics. 2019. "Gender Differences in Voter Turnout." http://cawp.rutgers.edu/sites/default/files/resources/genderdiff.pdf.

———. 2020. "Women in Elective Office." www.cawp.rutgers.edu.

———. 2021. The Buzz 2022: Potential Women Candidates. https://cawp.rutgers.edu/election-2022-potential-women-candidates.

Claggett, William J. M., and Byron E. Shafer. 2010. *The American Public Mind: The Issue Structure of Mass Politics in the Postwar United States.* Cambridge: Cambridge University Press.

Claggett, William J. M., and Philip H. Pollock, III. 2006. "The Modes of Participation Revisited, 1980–2004," *Political Research Quarterly* 59: 593–60.

Clark, Peter B., and James Q. Wilson. 1961. "Incentive Systems: A Theory of Organizations." *Administrative Science Quarterly* 6: 129–66.

Clarke, Andrew J. 2020. "Party Sub-Brands and American Party Factions." *American Journal of Political Science* 64: 452–70.

Chen, Philip G., and Paul N. Goren. 2016. "Operational Ideology and Party Identification: A Dynamic Model of Individual Level Change in Partisan and Ideological Predispositions." *Political Research Quarterly* 69: 703–15.

Cohen, Marty, David Karol, Hans Noel, and John Zaller. 2008. *The Party Decides: Presidential Nominations Before and After Reform.* Chicago: University of Chicago Press.

Commager, Henry Steele. 1949. "American Political Parties." *Parliamentary Affairs.* III: 214–25.

Conger, Kimberly H., Rosalyn Cooperman, Gregory Shufeldt, Geoffrey C. Layman, Kerem Ozan Kalkan, John C. Green, and Richard Herrera. 2019. "Group Commitment Among U.S. Party Factions: A Perspective from Democratic and Republican National Convention Delegates." *American Politics Research* 47: 1376–1408.

Congressional Research Service. 2021. Profile of the 117th Congress. https://crsreports.congress.gov/product/pdf/R/R46705.

Conover, Pamela, and Virgina Sapiro 1993. "Gender, Feminist Consciousness, and War." *American Journal of Political Science* 37: 1079–99.

Conover, Pamela C., and Stanley Feldman. 1981. "The Origins and Meaning of Liberal/ Conservative Self-Identifications." *American Journal of Political Science* 25: 617–45.

Conroy, Meredith. 2020. "More Women Than Ever Are Running for Office. But Are They Winning Their Primaries?" FiveThirtyEight. September 2, 2020. https:// fivethirtyeight.com/features/more-women-than-ever-are-running-for-office-but -are-they-winning-their-primaries/.

———. 2020b. "How A Record Number of Republican Women Will and Won't Change Congress." FiveThirtyEight. November 16, 2020. https://fivethirtyeight .com/features/how-a-record-number-of-republican-women-will-and-wont-change -congress/.

Conroy, Meredith, Nathaniel Rakich, and Mai Nguyen. 2019. "We Looked at Hundreds of Endorsements. Here's Who Republican Voters are Listening to." FiveThirty-Eight, September 24. fivethirtyeight.com/features/we-looked-at-hundreds-of -endorsements-heres-who-republicans-are-listening-to/.

Converse, Philip E. 1964. "The Nature of Belief Systems in Mass Publics." In *Ideology and Discontent*, David Apter, ed. Glencoe, IL: The Free Press: 206–61.

Cooper, Betsy, Daniel Cox, Rachel Lienesch, and Robert P. Jones. 2016. "The Divide over America's Future: 1950 or 2050?" *PRRI*. www.prri.org.

Cowburn, Mike, and Oswald, Michael T. 2020. "Legislator Adoption of the Fake News Label: Ideological Differences in Republican Representative Use on Twitter." *The Forum* 18: 389–413.

Crespin, Michael, and Barry Edwards. 2016. "Redistricting and Individual Contributions to Congressional Candidates." *Political Research Quarterly* 69: 220–32.

Crespin, Michael H., and Janna L. Deitz. 2010. "If You Can't Join 'Em, Beat 'Em: The Gender Gap in Individual Donations to Congressional Candidates." *Political Research Quarterly* 63: 581–93.

Crowder-Meyer, Melody. 2013. "Gendered Recruitment without Trying: How Local Party Recruiters Affect Women's Representation." *Politics & Gender* 9: 390.

Crowder-Meyer, Melody A., and Benjamin E. Lauderdale. 2014. "A Partisan Gap in the Supply of Female Potential Candidates in the United States." *Research and Politics* 1: 1–7

Crowder-Meyer, Melody A., and Rosalyn Cooperman. 2018. "Can't Buy Them Love: How Party Culture among Donors Contributes to the Party Gap in Women's Representation." *The Journal of Politics* 80: 1211–1224.

Crowley, Michael. 2020. "Trump's False Election Fraud Claims Split Republicans." *New York Times*, November 6. https://www.nytimes.com/2020/11/06/us/politics /trump-election-republicans.html.

Cutright, Phillips. 1963. "Measuring the Impact of Local Party Activity on the General Election Vote." *Public Opinion Quarterly* 27: 372–86.

Cutright, Phillips, and Peter H. Rossi. 1958. "Grassroots Politicians and the Vote." *American Sociological Review* 23: 171–79.

Cybersecurity & Infrastructure Security Agency. 2020. "Joint Statement from Elections Infrastructure Government Coordinating Council & the Election Infrastructure Sector Coordinating Executive Committees | CISA." https://www.cisa.gov

/news/2020/11/12/joint-statement-elections-infrastructure-government-coordinat
ing-council-election.

Damaske, Sarah, and Adrianne Frech. 2016. "Women's Work Pathways Across the
Life Course." *Demography* 53: 365–91.

Damore, David F., Robert E. Lang, and Karen A. Danielsen. 2021a. *Blue Metros, Red
States: The Shifting Urban-Rural Divide in America's Swing States.* Washington,
DC: Brookings Institution Press.

———. 2021b. "In 2020, the largest metro areas made the difference for the Democrats." Brookings Metro, Brookings Institution, February 4, 2021b. www.brook
ings.edu/research/in-2020-the-largest-metro-areas-made-the-difference-for
democrats/.

Damore, David F., and Robert E. Lang. 2016. "The End of the Democratic Blue
Wall?" Brookings Mountain West. https://digitalscholarship.unlv.edu/brookings
_pubs/45/.

Damore, David F., and Thomas G. Hansford. 1999. "The Allocation of Party Controlled Campaign Resources in the House of Representatives, 1989–1996." *Political Research Quarterly* 52: 371–85.

Darr, Joshua. 2020. "In 2020, the Ground Game is All Trump." *Mischiefs of Faction*,
October 9.

Darr, Joshua, and Matthew Levendusky. 2014. "Relying on the Ground Game: The
Placement and Effects of Campaign Field Offices." *American Politics Research*
42: 529–48.

Davenport, Lauren. 2018. *Politics Beyond Black and White*. New York: Cambridge.

Davis, John C., Andrew J. Dowdle, and Joseph D. Giammo. 2017. "The 2016 Elec-
tions in Arkansas: Did Playing in Hillary's "Home Court" Make a Difference?"
In *The New Politics of the Old South*, 6th ed., Charles S. Bullock III and Mark J.
Rozell, eds. Lanham, MD: Rowman & Littlefield: 242–54.

———. 2021. "Arkansas: Should We Color the State Red with a Permanent Marker?"
In *The New Politics of the Old South*, 7th ed., Charles S. Bullock III and Mark J.
Rozell, eds. Lanham, MD: Rowman & Littlefield: 289–302.

Davis, John C. 2014 "The Natural State in a Time of Change: A Survey-Based Analysis of State Party Organizations in Arkansas, 1999–2013." *Midsouth Political Science Review* 15: 81–102.

Davis, John C., and Drew Kurlowski. 2017. "Campaign Inc.: Data from a Field Survey of State Party Organizations." *Midsouth Political Science Review* 18: 1–26.

Davis, Shannon N., and Theodore N. Greenstein. 2009. "Gender Ideology: Components, Predictors, and Consequences." *Annual Review of Sociology* 35: 87–105.

Davis, Teddy. 2010. "Tea Party Activists Unveil Contract from America." *ABC
News.* April 15. http://abcnews.go.com/Politics/tea-party-activists-unveilcontract
america/story?id=10376437.

Deckman, Melissa. 2016. *Tea Party Women: Mama Grizzlies, Grassroots Activists,
and the Changing Face of the American Right.* New York: NYU Press.

Delli Carpini, Michael X., and Ester R. Fuchs. 1993. "The Year of the Woman? Candidates, Voters, and the 1992 Elections." *Political Science Quarterly* 108: 29–36.

Denton, Nancy. 2013. "Interpreting U.S. Segregation Trends: Two Perspectives." *City & Community* 12: 156–59.

DeSante, Christopher D., and Candis Watts Smith. 2020. "Fear, Institutional Racism, and Empathy: The Underlying Dimensions of Whites' Racial Attitudes." *PS: Political Science & Politics* 53: 639–45.

Desilver, Drew. 2021. "Turnout Soared in 2020 as Nearly Two-Thirds of Eligible U.S. Voters Cast Ballots for President." Pew Research Center, January 28. https://www.pewresearch.org/fact-tank/2021/01/28/turnout-soared-in-2020-as-nearly-two-thirds-of-eligible-u-s-voters-cast-ballots-for-president/.

DiSalvo, Daniel. 2012. *Engines of Change: Party Factions in American Politics, 1868–2010*. New York: Oxford University Press.

Dittmar, Kelly. 2015. "Encouragement is not Enough: Addressing Social and Structural Barriers to Female Recruitment." *Politics & Gender* 11: 759.

———. 2020. "Urgency and Ambition: The Influence of Political Environment and Emotion in Spurring US Women's Candidacies in 2018." *European Journal of Politics and Gender* 3: 143–60.

Dittmar, Kelly, Kira Sanbonmatsu, and Susan J. Carroll. 2018. *A Seat at the Table: Congresswomen's Perspectives on Why Their Presence Matters*. New York: Oxford University Press.

Dolan, Kathleen. 2008. "Is There a 'Gender Affinity Effect' in American Politics? Information, Affect, and Candidate Sex in U.S. House Elections." *Political Research Quarterly* 6: 79–89.

———. 2010. "The Impact of Gender Stereotyped Evaluations on Support for Women Candidates." *Political Behavior* 32: 69–88.

Dolan, Kathleen, and Timothy Lynch. 2016. "The Impact of Gender Stereotypes on Voting for Women Candidates by Level and Type of Office." *Politics & Gender* 12: 573–95

Dowdle, Andrew, and Joseph Giammo. 2010. "Arkansas: Deep Blue and Bright Red at the Same Time?" in *The New Politics of the Old South*, 4th ed., Charles S. Bullock III and Mark J. Rozell, eds. Lanham, MD: Rowman & Littlefield: 207–18.

Dowdle, Andrew J., and Gary D. Wekkin. 2007. "Arkansas: The Post-2000 Elections in Arkansas: Continued GOP Growth or a Party That Has Peaked?" In *The New Politics of the Old South*, 3rd ed., Charles S. Bullock III and Mark J. Rozell, eds. Lanham, MD: Rowman & Littlefield: 213–36.

Dowe, Pearl K. Ford. 2020. "Resisting marginalization: Black women's political ambition and agency." *PS: Political Science & Politics* 53: 1–5.

Downs, Anthony. 1957. *An Economic Theory of Democracy*. New York: Wiley.

Dreier, Peter, and Christopher Martin. 2010. "How ACORN was Framed: Political Controversy and Media Agenda Setting." *Perspectives on Politics* 8: 761–92.

Drutman, Lee. 2020. *Breaking the Two Party Doom Loop*. New York: Oxford University Press.

———. 2017. "Political Divisions in 2016 and Beyond: Tensions Between and Within the Two Parties." The Democracy Fund Voter Study Group, https://www.voterstudygroup.org/publication/political-divisions-in-2016-and-beyond.

Dunn, Amina. 2021. "Two-Thirds of Republicans Want Trump to Retain

Major Political Role; 44% Want Him to Run Again in 2024." Pew Research Center. https://www.pewresearch.org/fact-tank/2021/10/06/two-thirds-of-republicans -want-trump-to-retain-major-political-role-44-want-him-to-run-again-in-2024/.

Dunn, Susan. 2012. *Roosevelt's Purge*. Cambridge, MA: Harvard University Press.

Duverger, Maurice. 2021. "Political Party." *Encyclopedia Britannica* https://www .britannica.com/topic/political-party.

Dwyre, Diana, and Evelyn Braz. 2015. "Super PAC Spending, Strategies, and Goals." *The Forum* 13: 245–67.

Edmondson, Catie, and Luke Broadwater. 2021. "Before Capitol Riot, Repub- lican Lawmakers Fanned the Flames." *New York Times.* https://www.nytimes .com/2021/01/11/us/politics/republicans-capitol-riot.html.

Eggers, Andrew, Garro Haritz, and Justin Grimmer. 2021. "No Evidence for System- atic Voter Fraud: A Guide to Statistical Claims About the 2020 Election." *Proceed- ings of the National Academy of Sciences* 118: e2103619118.

Ekins, Emily. 2017. "The Five Types of Trump Voters: Who They Are and What They Believe." The Democracy Fund Voter Study Group, https://www.voterstudygroup .org/publication/the-five-types-trump-voters.

Elazar, Daniel J. 1966. *American Federalism: A View from the States.* New York: Thomas Y. Crowell.

Elder, Laurel. 2008. "Whither Republican Women: The Growing Partisan Gap among Women in Congress." In *Forum* 6: 000102202154088841204.

———. 2012. "The Partisan Gap among Women State Legislators." *Women, Politics & Policy,* 33: 65–85.

———. 2014. "Contrasting Party Dynamics: A Three Decade Analysis of the Repre- sentation of Democratic versus Republican Women State Legislators." *The Social Science Journal* 51: 377–85.

———. 2018. "Why So Few Republican Women in State Legislatures?" In, *The Right Women: Republican Party Activists, Candidates, and Legislators*. Malliga Och, and Shauna L. Shames, eds. Praeger: Santa Barbara: 157–75.

———. 2021. *The Partisan Gap: Why Democratic Women Get Elected, but Republi- can Women Don't.* New York: NYU Press.

Elder, Laurel, and Steven Greene. 2012. *The Politics of Parenthood: Causes and Con- sequences of the Politicization and Polarization of the American Family*. Albany: SUNY Press.

———. 2016. "Red Parents, Blue Parents: The Politics of Modern Parenthood." *The Forum: A Journal of Applied Research in Contemporary Politics.* 14: 143–67.

Elder, Laurel, Steven Greene, and Mary-Kate Lizotte. 2021. "Feminist and Anti- Feminist Identification in 21st Century United States." *Journal of Women Politics & Politics.* 42: 243–59.

Ellis, Atiba R. 2014. "The Meme of Voter Fraud." *Catholic University Law Review* 63:879.

EMILY's List. 2018. "Over 34,000 Women Want to Run for Office." https://www. emilyslist.org/news/entry/over-34000-women-want-to-run-for-office.

English, Art. 2003. "Term Limits in Arkansas: Opportunities and Consequences." *Spectrum: Journal of State Government* 76: 30–33.

Epstein, Reid J., and Katie Glueck. 2021. "10 Republicans Voted to Impeach Trump. The Backlash has been Swift." *New York Times*, January 23.

Erikson, Robert S., and Christopher Wlezien. 2021. "Forecasting the 2020 Presidential Election: Leading Economic Indicators, Polls, and the Vote." *PS: Political Science and Politics*. 54: 55–58

Ewall-Wice, Sarah, and Aaron Navarro. 2020. "Year of the Republican Women: GOP Adds Record Number of Women to Congress." CBS News. November 20.

Federal Election Commission. 2021a. "Candidate Expenditure Reports." https://www.fec.gov/data/browse-data/?tab=candidates.

———. 2021b. "Independent Expenditure Reports." https://www.fec.gov/data/browse-data/?tab=spending.

Feinberg, Andrew. 2021. "Texas Lt. Governor Pays Out $25k Reward for Proof of Election Fraud-but Over a Republican Who Tried to Vote Twice." *The Independent.* https://www.independent.co.uk/news/world/americas/us-politics/texas-lt-governor-election-fraud-b1943709.html.

Feldman, Stanley, and Christopher Johnston. 2014. "Understanding the Determinants of Political Ideology: Implications of Structural Complexity." *Political Psychology* 35: 337–58.

Ferguson, Kathy E. 1984. *The Feminist Case Against Bureaucracy*. Philadelphia, PA: Temple University Press.

Finkel, Eli J., Christopher A. Bail, Mina Cikara Peter H. Ditto, Shanto Iyengar, Samara Klar, Lilliana Mason, Mary C. McGrath, Brendan Nyhan, David G. Rand, Linda J. Skitka, Joshua A. Tucker, Jay J. Van Bavel, Cynthia S. Wang, and James N. Druckman. 2020. "Political Sectarianism in America." *Science 370*: 533–36.

Fiorina, Morris. 2002. "Parties, Participation, and Representation in America: Old Theories Face New Realities." In *Political Science: State of the Discipline*. Ira Katznelson and Helen Milner, eds. New York: Norton.

———. 2013. "America's Missing Moderates: Hiding in Plain Sight." *The American Interest* 8: 58–67.

———. 2018. *Unstable Majorities: Polarization, Party Sorting & Political Stalemate*. Stanford, CA: Hoover Institution Press.

———. 2020. "Economic Anxiety or Cultural Backlash: Which Was Key to Trump's Election?" Unpublished paper.

———. 2021. "The Myth of a Majority Minority Nation." https://www.realclearpolitics.com/articles/2020/12/08/the_myth_of_a_majority-minority_nation_144799.html.

Fiorina, Morris, with Samuel Abrams. 2011. *Disconnect: The Breakdown of Representation in American Politics*. Norman: Oklahoma University Press.

Fiorina, Morris, Samuel J. Abrams, and Jeremy C. Pope. 2010. *Culture War? The Myth of a Polarized America*. Boston: Longman.

Fischer, Claude S. 1984. *The Urban Experience*, 2nd ed. New York: Harcourt Brace Jovanovich.

Flammang, Janet A. 1997. *Women's Political Voice: How Women Are Transforming the Practice and Study of Politics*. Philadelphia: Temple University Press.

Florida, Richard, Marie Patino, and Rachael Dottle. 2020. "How Suburbs Swung the 2020 Election." CityLab. www.bloomberg.com/graphics/2020-suburban-density -election/.

Foos, Florian, and Fabrizio Gilardi. 2020. "Does Exposure to Gender Role Models Increase Women's Political Ambition? A Field Experiment with Politicians." *Journal of Experimental Political Science* 7: 157–66.

Ford, Henry Jones. 1898. *The Rise and Growth of American Politics.* New York: Macmillan.

Forstall, Richard L., and James D. Fitzsimmons. 1993. "Metropolitan Growth and Expansion in the 1980s." Technical Working Paper Series. Washington, DC: Population Division, U.S. Bureau of the Census.

Fox, Richard L., and Jennifer L. Lawless. 2014. "Uncovering the Origins of the Gender Gap in Political Ambition." *American Political Science Review* 108: 499–519.

Francia, Peter L. 2001 "Early Fundraising by Nonincumbent Female Congressional Candidates: The Importance of Women's PACs." *Women & Politics* 23: 7–20.

Francia, Peter. 2018. "Free Media and Twitter in the 2016 Presidential Election: The Unconventional Campaign of Donald Trump." *Social Science Computer Review* 36: 440–55.

Francia, Peter L., John C. Green, Paul S. Herrnson, Lynda W. Powell, and Clyde Wilcox. 2003. *The Financiers of Congressional Elections.* New York: Columbia University Press.

Franz, Michael M. 2011. "What Motivates Interest Groups to Participate?" In *Guide to Interest Groups and Lobbying in the United States.* Burdett A. Loomis, Dara S. Strolovitch, and Peter L Francia, eds. Washington, DC: CQ Press.

Frederick, Brian, and Barbara Burrell. 2007. "Political Windows of Opportunity: Recruitment Pools, Gender Politics and Congressional Open Seats." Annual meeting of the Southern Political Science Association, New Orleans.

Freedlander, David. 2021. *The AOC Generation.* Boston, MA: Beacon Press.

Freeman, Jo. 1986. "The Political Culture of the Democratic and Republican Parties." *Political Science Quarterly.* 101: 327–56.

Freeman, Jo. 1979. "Resource Mobilization and Strategy: A Model for Analyzing Social Movement Organization Actions." Mayer N. Zald and John D. McCarthy, eds. In *The Dynamics of Social Movements*: 167–89.

Frey, William H. 2015. "The Browning of America: The Next 15 Years." https://frey -demographer.org/browning-america-next-15-years.

———. 2018. *Diversity Explosion: How New Racial Demographics are Remaking America.* Washington, DC: Brookings Institution Press.

Galston, William A. 2020. "Election 2020: A Once-in-a-Lifetime Massive Turnout?" Brookings Institution, August 14. https://www.brookings.edu/blog/fix gov/2020/08/14/election-2020-a-once-in-a-century-massive-turnout/.

Garcia Bedolla, Lisa, Katherine Tate, and Janelle Wong. 2014. "Indelible Effects: The Impact of Women of Color in the U.S. Congress." In *Women and Elective Office: Past, Present and Future*, 3rd ed. Sue Thomas and Clyde Wilcox, eds. New York: Oxford University Press: 235–52.

Gardner, Amy. 2021. "In Ramp Up to 2022 Midterms, Republican Candidates Center Pitches on Trump's False Election Claims." *Washington Post*, July 5. https://www .washingtonpost.com/politics/republican-trump-2022-midterms-election-falsehoods /2021/07/04/3a43438c-d36f-11eb-ae54-515e2f63d37d_story.html.

Gardner, Amy, and Paulina Firozi. 2021. "Here's the Full Transcript and Audio of the Call between Trump and Raffensperger." *Washington Post*, January 3.

Garrison, Joey. 2020. "Record-breaking Donations Pour in From the Left After Ruth Bader Ginsburg's Death." *USA Today*, September 20.

Geng, Lucia. 2020. "From South Carolina to Maine, out-of-state donors give big in Senate races." OpenSecrets.org, October 22.

Gerson, Kathleen. 2010. *The Unfinished Revolution: How a New Generation is Reshaping Family, Work, and Gender in America.* New York: Oxford University Press.

Gimpel, James G., Frances E. Lee, and Joshua Kaminski. 2006. "The Political Geography of Campaign Contributions." *The Journal of Politics* 68: 626–39.

Gimpel, James G., Frances E. Lee, and Shanna Pearson-Merkowitz. 2008. "The Check is in the Mail: Interdistrict Funding Flows in Congressional Elections." *American Journal of Political Science* 52: 373–94.

Gimpel, James G., and Iris Hui. 2017. "Inadvertent and Intentional Partisan Residential Sorting." *The Annals of Regional Science* 58: 441–68.

Gimpel, James G., Nathan Lovin, Bryant Moy, and Andrew Reeves. 2020. "The Urban–Rural Gulf in American Political Behavior." *Political Behavior* 42: 1343–68.

Gonzales, Nathan L. 2015. "What Happened to The Rothenberg Political Report?" *Roll Call* January 12.

———. 2021. "Sexist Comments Followed by Silence Mar Alabama Senate Race." *Rollcall* August 4.

Gosar, Paul. 2020. "Congressman Paul Gosar's open letter to Arizona: Are we witnessing a coup d'etat?" *Revolver.* https://www.revolver.news/2020/12/congress man-paul-gosars-open-letter-to-arizona-are-we-witnessing-a-coup-detat/.

Gosnell, Harold Foote. 1927. *Getting Out the Vote.* Chicago: University of Chicago Press.

Grantham, Dewey W. 1994. *The South in Modern America: A Region at Odds.* New York: HarperCollins.

Gratzinger, Ollie. 2020. "Four of the 10 Most Expensive House Races of all Time Happened in 2020." OpenSecrets.org, December 18.

Green, Donald, Bradley Palmquist, and Eric Schickler. 2002. *Partisan Hearts and Minds: Political Parties and the Social Identities of Voters.* New Haven, CT: Yale University Press.

Green, Donald P., and Alan S. Gerber. 2008. *Get Out the Vote: How to Increase Voter Turnout.* Washington, DC: The Brookings Institution.

Green, John C., and Daniel Coffey, eds. 2006. *The State of the Parties: The Changing Role of Contemporary American Parties.* 5th ed. Lanham, MD: Rowman & Littlefield.

———. 2010. *The State of the Parties: The Changing Role of Contemporary American Parties.* 6th ed. Lanham, MD: Rowman & Littlefield.

Green, John C., Daniel M. Coffey, and David B. Cohen, eds. 2014. *The State of the Parties: The Changing Role of Contemporary American Parties.* 7th ed. Lanham, MD: Rowman & Littlefield

Green, John C., Daniel M. Coffey, and David B. Cohen, eds. 2018. The State of the Parties: The Changing Role of Contemporary American Parties. 8th ed. Lanham, MD: Rowman & Littlefield.

Green, John C., and Rick Farmer, eds. 2003. *The State of the Parties: The Changing Role of Contemporary American Parties.* 4th ed. Lanham, MD: Rowman & Littlefield.

Green, John C., and Daniel M. Shea, eds. 1999. *The State of the Parties: The Changing Role of Contemporary American Parties.* 3rd ed. Lanham, MD: Rowman & Littlefield.

———. 1996. *The State of the Parties: The Changing Role of Contemporary American Parties.* 2nd ed. Lanham, MD: Rowman & Littlefield.

Groenendyk, Eric, Michael W. Sances, and Kirill Zhirkov. 2020. "*Intra*party Polarization in American Politics." *Journal of Politics* 82: 1616–20.

Gronke, Paul, William D. Hicks, Seth C. McKee, Charles Stewart III, and James Dunham. 2019. "Voter ID Laws: A View from the Public." *Social Science Quarterly* 100: 215–32.

Grossmann, Matt, and Hopkins, David A. 2015. "Ideological Republicans and Group Interest Democrats." *Perspectives on Politics* 13:119–39.

———. 2016. *Asymmetric Politics: Ideological Republicans and Group Interest Democrats.* New York: Oxford University Press.

Grumbach, Jacob M., Alexander Sahn, and Sarah Staszak. 2020. "Gender, Race, and Intersectionality in Campaign Finance." *Political Behavior.* https://link.springer.com/article/10.1007/s11109-020-09619-0.

Gunther, Richard, Paul A. Beck, Pedro C. Magalhães, and Alejandro Moreno, eds. 2016. *Voting in Old and New Democracies.* New York: Routledge.

Gura, David. 2010. "'I'm Not a Witch,' Republican Candidate Christine O'Donnell Tells Delaware Voters." https://www.npr.org/sections/thetwo-way/2010/10/05/130353168/-i-m-not-a-witch-republican-senate-candidate-christine-o-donnell-says-in-new-ad.

Haberman, Maggie. 2021. "A survey of Republicans shows 5 factions have emerged after Trump's presidency." *New York Times*, March 12. https://www.nytimes.com/2021/03/12/us/politics/republican-factions-.html.

Hacker, Jacob S., and Paul Pierson. 2006. *Off Center: The Republican Revolution and the Erosion of American Democracy.* New Haven, CT: Yale University Press.

Hatch, Mary Jo, and Ann L. Cunliffe. 1997. *Organization Theory: Modern, Symbolic, and Postmodern Perspectives.* New York: Oxford University Press.

Hainmueller, Jens, Daniel J. Hopkins, and Teppei Yamamoto. 2014. "Causal Inference in Conjoint Analysis: Understanding Multidimensional Choices via Stated Preference Experiments." *Political Analysis* 22: 1–30.

Hajnal, Zoltan L., and Taeku Lee. 2011. *Why Americans Don't Join the Party.* Princeton, NJ: Princeton University Press.

Hallerman, Tamar 2016. "Tea Partyer Jenny Beth Martin Takes on Trump at CPAC," *The Atlanta Journal-Constitution*. March 4. https://www.ajc.com/blog/politics /tea-partyer-jenny-beth-martin-takes-donald-trump-cpac/a5UDd9r6wao0pFzBfm 5TVK/.

Hammer, Josh. 2021. "The Republican Party's Multiethnic, Working Class Coalition is Taking Shape." https://amgreatness.com/2021/12/09/the-republican-partys -multiethnic-working-class-coalition-is-taking-shape/.

Hansen, John Mark, Shigeo Hirano, and James M. Snyder Jr. 2017. "Parties within Parties: Parties, Factions, and Coordinated Politics, 1900–1980." In *Governing in a Polarized Age: Elections, Parties, and Political Representation in America*, Alan S. Gerber and Eric Schickler, eds. New York: Cambridge University Press: 143–90.

Hansen, Ronald J. 2020, November 17. "Fact Check: Reps. Andy Biggs, Paul Gosar Still Touting Baseless Election-Fraud Claims." *Arizona Republic.* https://www .azcentral.com/story/news/politics/fact-check/2020/11/17/andy-biggs-paul-gosar -still-touting-baseless-election-fraud-claims/6334872002/.

Hassell, Hans J. G. 2017. *The Party's Primary: The Influence of the Party Hill Committees in Primary Elections for the House and Senate.* New York: Cambridge University Press.

Healy, Jack. 2021. "These are the 5 People Who Died in the Capitol Riot." *New York Times*, January 11. https://www.nytimes.com/2021/01/11/us/who-died-in-capitol -building-attack.html.

Hebda, Dwain. 2019. "From Worst to First: Arkansas GOP Rises in Prominence Nationally." *Arkansas Money and Politics*. https://armoneyandpolitics.com/arkansas -gop-rises-prominence-nationally/.

Heberlig, Eric S., and Bruce A. Larson. 2005. "Redistributing Campaign Funds by U.S. House Members: The Spiraling Costs of the Permanent Campaign." *Legislative Studies Quarterly* 30: 597–624.

Heersink, Boris. 2018. "Trump and the Party-in-Organization: Presidential Control of National Party Organizations." *Journal of Politics* 80: 1474–82.

Heerwig, Jennifer A., and Gordon, Katie M. 2018. "Gendered Contribution Careers among Affluent Political Donors to Federal Elections." *Sociological Forum* 33: 805–25.

Helderman, Rosalind. 2021. "The Stuff of Which Violent Insurrections are Made: Federal Judge Punishes Colorado Lawyers for 2020 Election Lawsuit." *Washington Post*, August 4. https://www.washingtonpost.com/politics/colorado-sanctions -trump-lawsuit/2021/08/04/704dec92-f53a-11eb-a49b-d96f2dac0942_story.html.

Herrnson, Paul S. 1988. *Party Campaigning in the 1980s.* Cambridge, MA: Harvard University Press.

Herrnson, Paul S., Jennifer A. Heerwig, and Douglas M. Spencer. 2018. "The Impact of Organizational Characteristics on Super PAC Financing" In *The State of the Parties*, 8th ed. Lanham, MD: Rowman & Littlefield: 248–62.

Hersh, Eitan. 2020. *Politics Is for Power: How to Move Beyond Political Hobbyism, Take Action, and Make Real Change.* New York: Scribner.

Hertel-Fernandez, Alexander. 2017. "American Employers as Political Machines." *Journal of Politics* 9: 105–17.

Hicks, William D., Seth McKee, Mitchell Sellers, and Daniel A. Smith. 2015. "A Principle or a Strategy? Voter Identification Laws and Partisan Competition in the American States." *Political Research Quarterly,* 68: 18–33.

Hightower, Mary. 2018. "Two-Thirds of Arkansas' Counties Lost Population: What Are The Consequences?" *University of Arkansas Division of Agriculture Research and Extension.* May 21. https://www.uaex.uada.edu/media-resources /news/2018/may2018/05-21-2018-Ark-Population-Changes.aspx (Accessed December 20, 2021).

Hirano, Shigeo, and James M. Snyder, Jr. 2019. *Primary Elections in the United States.* New York: Cambridge University Press.

Hook, Janet. 2015. "First Three GOP Presidential Candidates Share Tea Party Roots." *Wall Street Journal.* April 12. https://www.wsj.com/articles/first-three-gop -presidential-candidates-share-tea-party-roots-1428867635?mod=rss_US_News.

Howell, Susan E., and Christine L. Day. 2000. "Complexities of the Gender Gap." *Journal of Politics* 62: 858–74.

Huckabee, Mike. 2021. Interview with John C. Davis.

Huggins, Christopher M., and Jeffrey S. Debies-Carl. 2015. "Tolerance in the City: The Multilevel Effects of Urban Environments on Permissive Attitudes." *Journal of Urban Affairs* 37: 255–59.

Hutchinson, Asa. 2021. Interview with John C. Davis.

Ingram, D. D., and S. J. Franco. 2014. "NCHS Urban-Rural Classification Scheme for Counties." 166. Vital Health Stat. Vol. 2. National Center for Health Statistics.

Ipsos Poll. 2021. Ipsos/Reuters Poll: The Big Lie. Public Poll Findings and Methodology. https://www.ipsos.com/sites/default/files/ct/news/documents/2021-05 /Ipsos%20Reuters%20Topline%20Write%20up-%20The%20Big%20Lie%20 -%2017%20May%20thru%2019%20May%202021.pdf.

Ipsos Poll. 2022: Core Political Data. https://www.ipsos.com/en-us/news-polls/ipsos -core-political-presidential-approval-tracker-03232022.

Issacharoff, Samuel, and Jeremy Peterman. 2013. "Special Interests After *Citizens United*: Access, Replacement, and Interest Group Response to Legal Change." *Annual Review of Law and Social Science* 9: 185–205.

Issenberg, Sasha. 2012. *The Victory Lab.* New York: Crown.

Iyengar, Shanto, Gaurav Sood, and Yphtach Lelkes. 2012. "Affect, Not Ideology: A Social Identity Perspective on Polarization." *Public Opinion Quarterly* 76: 405–31.

Iyengar, Shanto, and Sean J. Westwood. 2015. "Fear and Loathing across Party Lines: New Evidence on Group Polarization." *American Journal of Political Science* 59: 690–707.

Iyengar, Shanto, Yphtach Lelkes, Matthew Levendusky, Neil Malhotra, and Sean J. Westwood. 2019. "The Origins and Consequences of Affective Polarization in the United States." *Annual Review of Political Science* 22: 129–46.

Jackson, David. 2016. "Trump: I'll Accept the Election Results—'If I Win.'" *USA Today*, October 20. https://www.usatoday.com/story/news/politics/elec tions/2016/10/20/donald-trump-election-results-debate-hillary-clinton/92450922/.

Jacobson, Gary C. 1985–86. "Party Organization and Distribution of Campaign Resources: Republicans and Democrats in 1982." *Political Science Quarterly* 100: 603–25.

———. 2013. "Partisan Polarization in American Politics: A Background Paper." *Presidential Studies Quarterly* 43: 688–708.

———. 2015. "It's Nothing Personal: The Decline of the Incumbency Advantage in U.S. House Elections." *Journal of Politics* 77: 861–73.

———. 2016. "Polarization, Gridlock and Presidential Campaign Politics in 2016." *Annals of the American Academy of Political and Social Science* 667: 226–46.

Jacobson, Gary C., and Jamie L. Carson. 2019. *The Politics of Congressional Elections.* 9th ed. Lanham, MD: Rowman & Littlefield.

Jardina, Ashley. 2019. *White Identity Politics.* New York: Cambridge.

Johnson, Jenna. 2016. "Trump Alleges Widespread Voter Fraud: 'This Voting System is Out of Control.'" *Washington Post.* https://www.washingtonpost.com/news/post-politics/wp/2016/01/05/trump-alleges-widespread-voter-fraud-this-voting-system-is-out-of-control/.

Johnson, Lauren R., Deon McCray, and Jordan M. Ragusa. 2018. "#NeverTrump: Why Republican Members of Congress Refused to Support Their Party's Nominee in the 2016 Presidential Election." *Research & Politics* 5: 2053168017749383.

Johnston, Ron, Kelvyn Jones, and David Manley. 2016. "The Growing Spatial Polarization of Presidential Voting in the United States, 1992–2012: Myth or Reality?" *PS: Political Science & Politics* 49: 766–70.

Jones, Chuck. 2018. "Trump's Federal Budget Deficit: $1 Trillion and Beyond." *Forbes.* February 9. https://www.forbes.com/sites/chuckjones/2018/02/09/trumpsfederal-budget-deficit-1-trillion-and-beyond/63236af1544f.

Jones, Jeffrey. 2021a. "Americans Revert to Favoring Reduced Government Role." https://news.gallup.com/poll/355838/americans-revert-favoring-reduced-government-role.aspx.

———. 2021b. "Last Trump Job Approval 34%; Average is Record-Low 41%." *USA Today*, January 18. https://news.gallup.com/poll/328637/last-trump-job-approval-average-record-low.aspx.

Jost, John T. 2006. "The End of the End of Ideology." *American Psychologist* 61: 651–70.

Judis, John B. 2021. "The Emerging Republican Advantage." https://www.nationaljournal.com/s/32748/emerging-republican-advantage.

Judis, John, and Ruy Teixeira. 2002. *The Emerging Democratic Majority.* New York. Scribner.

Juenke, Eric Gonzalez, and Robert R. Preuhs. 2012. "Irreplaceable Legislators? Rethinking Minority Representatives in the New Century." *American Journal of Political Science* 56: 705–15.

Jurkowitz, Mark, Amy Mitchell, Elisa Shearer, and Mason Walker. 2020. "U.S. Media Polarization and the 2020 Presidential Election: A Nation Divided." Pew Research Center, January 24: https://www.journalism.org/2020/01/24/u-s-media-polarization-and-the-2020-election-a-nation-divided/.

Kahn, Chris, Soyoung Kim, Jason Lange, James Oliphant, and Tim Reid. 2021. "Special Report: Stolen Election? Republican Lawmakers Paralyzed by Trump's False Fraud Claims." Reuters, February 4. https://www.reuters.com/article/us-usa-trump-lawmakers-special-report/special-report-stolen-election-republican-lawmakers-paralyzed-by-trumps-false-fraud-claims-idUSKBN2A41CP.

Kalmoe, Nathan P., and Lilliana Mason. 2022. *Radical American Partisanship*. Chicago: University of Chicago Press.

Kamarck, Elaine, and Alexander R. Podkul. 2018. "The 2018 Primaries Project: What are the internal divisions within each party?" The Brookings Institution, https://www.brookings.edu/research/the-2018-primaries-project-what-are-the-internal-divisions-within-each-party/.

Karpowitz, Christopher F., J. Quinn Monson, et al. 2011. "Tea Time in America? The Impact of the Tea Party Movement on the 2010 Midterm Elections." *PS: Political Science and Politics* 44: 303–309.

Katz, Daniel, and Samuel J. Eldersveld. 1961. "The Impact of Local Party Activity upon the Electorate." *Public Opinion Quarterly* 25: 1–24.

Kaufmann, Karen M., and John R. Petrocik. 1999. "The Changing Politics of American." *American Journal of Political Science* 43: 864–87.

Kennedy, Courtney, Jesse L. Lopez, Scott Keeter, Arnold Lau, Nick Hatley, and Nick Bertoni. 2021, "Confronting 2016 and 2020 Polling Limitations," Pew Research Center, April 8. https://www.pewresearch.org/methods/2021/04/08/confronting-2016-and-2020-polling-limitations/.

Kenny, Meryl, and Tania Verge. 2016. "Opening Up the Black Box: Gender and Candidate Selection in a New Era." *Government and Opposition* 51: 351–69.

Key, V. O, Jr. 1949. *Southern Politics in State and Nation*. New York: Alfred A. Knopf.

———. 1958. *Politics, Parties, and Pressure Groups*, 4th ed. York: Thomas Y. Crowell Company.

Khanna, Kabir, and DePinto Jennifer. 2021. "CBS News Analysis: What Drives Republican and Trump Voters' Belief in Widespread Voter Fraud?" *CBS News*, July 21. https://www.cbsnews.com/news/republicans-belief-voter-fraud-opinion-poll/.

Kimball, David C., Joseph Anthony, and Tyler Chance. 2018. "Political Identity and Party Polarization in the American Electorate." In *The State of the Parties*, 8th ed. eds. John C. Green, Daniel J. Coffey, and David B. Cohen. Boulder, CA: Rowman & Littlefield: 169–84.

Kinder, Donald R. 2006. "Belief Systems Today." *Critical Review: A Journal of Politics and Society* 18: 197–216.

Kinder, Donald R., and Nathan P. Kalmoe. 2017. *Neither Liberal nor Conservative: Ideological Innocence in the American Public*. Chicago: University of Chicago Press.

Kingzette, Jon, James N. Druckman, Samara Klar, Yanna Krupnikov, Matthew Levendusky, and John Barry Ryan. 2021. "How Affective Polarization Undermines Support for Democratic Norms." *Public Opinion Quarterly* 85: 663–77.

Kitchens, Karin E., and Michele L. Swers. 2016. "Why Aren't There More Republican Women in Congress? Gender, Partisanship, and Fundraising Support in the 2010 and 2012 Elections." *Politics & Gender* 12: 648–76.

Klar, Samara, and Alexandra McCoy. 2021. "Partisan-Motivated Evaluations of Sexual Misconduct and the Mitigating Role of the #MeToo Movement." *American Journal of Political Science* 65: 777–89.

Klinkner, Philip A., and Thomas F. Schaller. 2006. "A Regional Analysis of the 2006 Midterms." *The Forum* 4. <bepress.com/forum/vol4/iss3/ast9>

Koger, Gregory, Seth Masket, and Hans Noel. 2010. "Cooperative Party Factions in American Politics." *American Politics Research* 38: 33–53.

Kolodny, Robin, and Diana Dwyre. 1998. "Party-Orchestrated Activities for Legislative Party Goals: Campaigns for Majorities in the US House of Representatives in the 1990s." *Party Politics* 4: 275–95.

———. 2017. "Convergence or Divergence?" *American Politics Research* 6: 375–401.

Kovacs-Goodman, Jacob. 2021. Post-election litigation analysis and summaries, March 10. Stanford-MIT Health Elections Project.

Kreitzer, Rebecca J., and Tracy L. Osborn. 2019. "The Emergence and Activities of Women's Recruiting Groups in the US." *Politics, Groups, and Identities* 7: 842–52.

Kurtzleben, Danielle. 2016. "Donald Trump's Messy Ideas For Handling The National Debt, Explained." *NPR.* May 9. https://www.npr.org/2016/05/09/477350889/donaldtrumps-messy-ideas-for-handlingthe-national-debt-explained.

Kusterer, Ken. 1990. "The Imminent Demise of Patriarchy." In *Persistent Inequalities, Women and World Development*, Irene Tinker, ed. New York: Oxford University Press: 239–55.

La Raja, Raymond J., and Brian Schaffner. 2015. *Campaign Finance and Political Polarization.* Ann Arbor: University of Michigan Press.

Lang, Robert E., and Jennifer B. LuFurgy. 2007. *Boomburbs: The Rise of America's Accidental Cities.* Washington, DC: Brookings Institution Press.

Lang, Robert, Thomas Sanchez, and Alan Berube. 2008. "The New Suburban Politics: A County-Based Analysis of Metropolitan Voting Trends since 2000." In *Red, Blue, & Purple America,* Ruy Teixeira, ed. Washington, DC: Brookings Institution Press: 25–50.

Lawless, Jennifer L. 2004. "Politics of Presence: Women in the House and Symbolic Representation." *Political Research Quarterly* 53: 81–99.

Lawless, Jennifer L., and Richard L. Fox. 2010. *It Still Takes a Candidate: Why Women Don't Run for Office,* Cambridge: Cambridge University Press.

———. 2018. "A Trump Effect? Women and the 2018 Midterm Elections." *The Forum* 16: 665–86. De Gruyter, 2018.

Lee, Frances. 2016. *Insecure Majorities: Congress and the Perpetual Campaign.* Chicago: University of Chicago Press.

Lelkes, Ypthach, Gaurav Sood, and Shanto Iyengar. 2017. "The Hostile Audience: The Effect of Access to Broadband Internet on Partisan Affect." *American Journal of Political Science* 61: 5–20.

Levendusky, Matthew. 2013. *How Partisan Media Polarize America.* Chicago: University of Chicago Press.

Levin, Matt. 2020. "How California expats are helping turn Texas into a battleground state." Cal Matters. https://calmatters.org/politics/2020/10/california-expats-texas-battleground-state/.

Levine, Sam, and Spencer Mestel. 2020. "'Just Like Propaganda': The Three Men Enabling Trump's Voter Fraud Lies." https://www.theguardian.com/us-news/2020/oct/26/us-election-voter-fraud-mail-in-ballots.

Lewis-Beck, Michael S., and Charles Tien. 2021 "The Political Economy Model: A Blue Wave Forecast For 2020." *PS: Political Science and Politics.* 54 (1): 59–62

Lilla, Mark. 2016. "The End of Identity Liberalism." https://www.nytimes.com/2016/11/20/opinion/sunday/the-end-of-identity-liberalism.html.

Link, Arthur S., and Richard L. McCormick. 1983. *The Progressives.* Arlington Heights: Harlan Davidson.

Loeffler, Kelly. @KLoeffler. 2020. Joint statement from @Perduesenate and myself #gapol #gasen. [tweet]. Twitter. https://twitter.com/KLoeffler/status/1325892918700290048.

Lofland, Lynn. 1998. *The Public Realm: Exploring the City's Quintessential Social Territory.* New Brunswick, NJ: Transaction.

Logan, John R. 2013. "The Persistence of Segregation in the 21st Century Metropolis." *City & Community* 12: 160–68.

Maas, Megan K., Heather L. McCauley, Amy E. Bonomi, and S. Gisela Leija. 2018. "'I was grabbed by my pussy and its# NotOkay': A Twitter backlash against Donald Trump's degrading commentary." *Violence Against Women* 24: 1739–50.

Magleby, David B. 2014. "Classifying Super PACs." In *State of the Parties*, 7th ed., John C. Green, Daniel J. Coffey, and David B. Cohen, eds. Lanham, MD: Rowman & Littlefield: 231–50.

Magleby, David B., Jay Goodliffe, and Joseph A. Olsen. 2018. *Who Donates in Campaigns? The Importance of Message, Messenger, Medium, and Structure.* New York: Oxford University Press.

Maisel, Sandy L., and Mark D. Brewer. 2010. *Parties and Elections in America: The Electoral Process.* Lanham, MD: Rowman & Littlefield.

Mann, Thomas E., and Norman J. Ornstein. 2016. *It's Even Worse than it Looks: How the American Constitutional System Collided with the New Politics of Extremism.* New York: Basic Books.

Mansbridge, Jane. 1994. "Feminism and the Forms of Freedom." In *Critical Studies in Organization and Bureaucracy*, Frank Fisher and Carmen Sirianni, eds. Philadelphia, Temple University Press: 544–43.

———. 1999. "Should Blacks Represent Blacks and Women Represent Women? A Contingent 'yes.'" *The Journal of Politics* 61: 628–57.

Mar, Kristinn. 2020. "Partisan Affective Polarization: Sorting, Entrenchment, and Fortification." *Public Opinion Quarterly* 84: 915–35.

Marcus, George E., James Piereson, and John Sullivan. 1980. "Rural-Urban Differences in Tolerance: Confounding Problems of Conceptualization and Measurement." *Rural Sociology* 45: 731–37.

Martherus, James L., Andres G. Martinez, Paul K. Piff, and Alexander G. Theodoridis. 2021. "Party Animals? Extreme Partisan Polarization and Dehumanization." *Political Behavior* 43: 517–40.

Martin, Jonathan. 2021. "Liz Cheney's Consultants are Given an Ultimatum: Drop Her, or Be Dropped." *New York Times*, October 21.

Masket, Seth. 2020. *Learning from Loss: The Democrats, 2016–2020*. New York: Cambridge University Press.

Masket, Seth E. 2014. *No Middle Ground: How Informal Party Organizations Control Nominations and Polarize Legislatures*. Ann Arbor: University of Michigan Press.

Masket, Seth, John Sides, and Lynn Vavreck. 2016. "The Ground Game in the 2012 Presidential Election." *Political Communication* 33:169–87.

Mason, Lilliana. 2018. *Uncivil Agreement: How Politics Became Our Identity*. Chicago: University of Chicago Press.

———. 2014. "'I Disrespectfully Agree': The Differential Effects of Partisan Sorting on Social and Issue Polarization." *American Journal of Political Science* 59: 128–45.

Maxwell, Angie. 2021. Interview with John C. Davis.

Maxwell, Angie, and Todd Shields. 2019. *The Long Southern Strategy: How Chasing White Voters in the South Changed American Politics.* New York: Oxford University Press.

Mayhew, David. 2004. *Electoral Realignments*. New Haven, CT: Yale University Press.

McElwee, Sean, Brian Schaffner, and Jesse Rhodes. 2016. "Whose Voice, Whose Choice? The Distorting Influence of the Political Donor Class in Our Big-Money Elections." Demos Research Report. https://www.demos.org/research/whose-voice-whose-choice-distorting-influence-political-donor-class-our-big-money, accessed July 30, 2019.

McEvoy, Jemima. 2021. "Trump Votes by Mail (Again) Despite Months of Voter Fraud Claims." *Forbes* March 9: https://www.forbes.com/sites/jemimamcevoy/2021/03/09/trump-votes-by-mail-again-despite-months-of-voter-fraud-claims/?sh=285c034052da.

McGregor Burns, James. 1964. *The Deadlock of Democracy*. Englewood Cliffs, NJ: Prentice-Hall.

Medvic, Stephen K. 2007. "Old Democrats in New Clothing? An Ideological Analysis of a Democratic Party Faction." *Party Politics* 13: 587–609.

Mickey, Robert. 2015. *Paths Out of Dixie*. Princeton, NJ: Princeton University Press.

Miller, Eliana. 2020. "Nine of the 10 most Expensive Senate Races of all Time Happened in 2020." OpenSecrets.org, December 9.

Miller, Kenneth M. 2017. "Cooperative Media Spending in Senate Campaigns Post-Citizens United." *The Forum* 15: 269–89.

Miller, Patrick R., and Pamela Johnston Conover. 2015. "Red and Blue States of Mind: Partisan Hostility and Voting in the United States." *Political Research Quarterly* 68: 225–39.

Minnite, Lorraine C. 2010. *The Myth of Voter Fraud*. Ithaca, NY: University of Cornell Press.

Minta, Michael D., and Nadia E. Brown. 2014. "Intersecting interests: Gender, race, and congressional attention to women's issues." *Du Bois Review: Social Science Research on Race* 11: 253–72.

Montanaro, Domenico. 2021. "These Are the 10 Republicans Who Voted to Impeach Trump." *National Public Radio*. https://www.npr.org/2021/01/14/956621191 /these-are-the-10-republicans-who-voted-to-impeach-trump.

Moritz, John. 2019. "Records Lay Bare Debt Load of Party; State Democrats Lag in Fundraising." *Arkansas Democrat-Gazette*. https://www.arkansasonline.com /news/2019/aug/10/records-lay-bare-debt-load-of-party-201/.

Mukhopadhyay, Samhita, and Kate Harding. 2017. *Nasty Women: 2017. Feminism, Resistance, and Revolution in Trump's America*. New York: Picador.

Muro, Mark, and Jacob Whiten. 2018. "Geographic Gaps are Widening while U.S. Economic Growth Increases," Brookings Institution. www.brookings.edu/blog/the -venue/2018/01/22/uneven-growth/.

Myers, Dowell, and Morris Levy. 2018. "Racial Population Projections and Reactions to Alternative News Accounts of Growing Diversity." *Annals of the American Academy of Political and Social Science* 677: 215–28.

Myers, John. 2016. "Donald Trump Alleges Widespread Voter Fraud in California: There's no Evidence to Back it Up." *Los Angeles Times*, November 27. https://www.latimes.com/politics/la-pol-ca-trump-tweet-california-voter-fraud -20161127-story.html.

NCSL. 2021. "State Partisan Composition." National Conference of State Legislatures. www.ncsl.org.

———. 2021. "Women in State Legislatures for 2021." National Conference of State Legislators. www.ncsl.org.

Nilsen, Ella. 2018. "The 2018 Midterms Had the Highest Turnout Since Before World War I: How Trump Made Political Engagement Great Again." *Vox*, December 10: https://www.vox.com/policy-and-politics/2018/12/10/18130492/2018-voter -turnout-political-engagement-trump.

Niven, David. 2006. "Throwing Your Hat Out of the Ring: Negative Recruitment and the Gender Imbalance in State Legislative Candidacy." *Politics & Gender* 2: 473.

Noble, Alex. 2021. "Tucker Carlson Insists There Are 'Non-White People Cheering the Extinction of White People.'" https://www.yahoo.com/now/tucker-carlson -insists-non-white-181108285.html.

Noel, Hans. 2016. "Ideological Factions in the Republican and Democratic Parties." *Annals of the American Academy of Political and Social Science* 667: 166–88.

Nokken, Timothy P. 2003. "Ideological Congruence Versus Electoral Success: Distribution of Party Organization Contributions in Senate Elections, 1990–2000." *American Politics Research* 31: 3–26.

Norpoth, Helmut. 2021. "Primary Model Predicts Trump Reelection." *PS: Political Science and Politics*. 54: 63–66

Norrander, Barbara, and Clyde Wilcox. 2014. "Trends in the Geography of Women in the U.S. State Legislatures." In *Women and Elective Office: Past, Present and Future*. 3rd ed. Sue Thomas and Clyde Wilcox, eds. Oxford, UK: Oxford University Press: 273–67.

Norris, Pippa. 1995. "May's Law of Curvilinear Disparity Revisited: Leaders, Officers, Members and Voters in British Political Parties." *Party Politics* 1: 29–47.

Och, Malliga. 2018. "The Grand Old Party of 2016." In *The Right Women: Republican Party Activists, Candidates, and Legislat*ors." Malliga Och and Shauna L. Shames, eds. Denver: Praeger, 3–24.

Och, Malliga, and Shauna L. Shames, eds. 2018. *The Right Women: Republican Party Activists, Candidates, and Legislators.* Santa Barbara: ABC-CLIO.

Olsen, Henry. 2021. "The GOP has five factions now. They all see a different future for their party." *Washington Post*, July 26. https://www.washingtonpost .com/opinions/2021/07/26/gop-has-five-factions-now-they-all-see-different-future -their-party/,accessed October 20, 2021.

OpenSecrets. 2018. "Democratic Women Outraise Men among Female Donors." https://www.opensecrets.org/news/2018/10/democratic-women-outraise-men -among-female-donors-another-record-breaking-first/.

———. 2021. "Cost of Election." https://www.opensecrets.org/elections-overview /cost-of-election.

———. 2022a. "2020 Cost of Election." https://www.opensecrets.org/elections -overview/cost-of-election, accessed March 28, 2022.

———. 2022b. "2020 Democratic National Committee." https://www.opensecrets .org/parties/totals.php?cycle=2020&cmte=DNC, accessed March 28, 2022.

———. 2022c. "2020 Presidential Race." https://www.opensecrets.org/2020-presi dential-race, accessed March 13, 2022.

———. 2022d. "2020 Republican National Committee." https://www.opensecrets .org/parties/totals.php?cycle=2020&cmte=RNC, accessed March 28, 2022.

Osmundsen, Mathias, Alexander Bor, Peter Bjerregaard Vahlstrup, Anja Bechmann, and Michael Bang Petersen. 2021. "Partisan Polarization Is the Primary Psychological Motivation behind Political Fake News Sharing on Twitter." *American Political Science Review* 115: 999–1015.

PBS. 2014. "Obama and His Politics Prove Toxic for Arkansas Democrats." 2014. *PBS News Hour*, January 13. https://www.pbs.org/newshour/politics/obama-poli cies-prove-toxic-arkansas-democrats.

Palmer, Ewan. 2021. "MAGA Supporters Left Confused by Donald Trump's Call Not to Vote in Midterms, 2024." https://www.newsweek.com/maga-supporters -confused-donald-trump-vote-2024-election-qanon-midterms-1639286.

Panagopoulos, Costas. 2016. "All About the Base: Changing Campaign Strategies in U.S. Presidential Elections." *Party Politics* 22: 179–90.

Parker, Ashley, and Marianna Sotomayor. 2021. "For Republicans, Fealty to Trump's Election Falsehood Becomes a Defining Loyalty Test." *Washington Post*, May 2: https://www.washingtonpost.com/politics/republicans-trump-election-falsehood /2021/05/01/7bd380a0-a921-11eb-8c1a-56f0cb4ff3b5_story.html.

Parks, Mary Alice, and Kendall Karson. 2020. "A step-by-step look at Trump's false-hoods on mail-in voting: Analysis." ABC News, October 1. https://abcnews.go.com /Politics/step-step-trumps-falsehoods-mail-voting-analysis/story?id=73354979.

Pasley, Jeffrey L. 2013. *The First Presidential Contest: The Election of 1796 and the Founding of American Democracy*, Lawrence: University Press of Kansas.

Paxton, Pamela, Sheri Kunovich, and Melanie M. Hughes. 2007. "Gender in Politics." *Annual Review of Sociology* 33: 263–84.

Pearson, Kathryn. 2018. "Rising Partisan Polarization in the U.S. Congress." In *Parchment Barriers: Political Polarization and the Limits of Constitutional Order* Zachary Courser, Eric Helland and Kenneth P. Miller, eds. Lawrence: University Press of Kansas: 35–57.

Pearson, Kathryn, and Eric McGhee. 2013. "What It Takes to Win: Questioning 'Gender Neutral' Outcomes in U.S. House Elections." *Politics & Gender* 9: 439–62.

Peters, Gerhard, and John T. Woolley. 2020a. "Presidential Debate at Case Western Reserve University in Cleveland, Ohio." September 29, *The American Presidency Project*, https://www.presidency.ucsb.edu/documents/presidential-debate -case-western-reserve-university-cleveland-ohio.

———. 2020b. "Tweets of November 4, 2020." November 4, 2020, *The American Presidency Project*, https://www.presidency.ucsb.edu/documents/tweets-november -4-2020.

———. 2021a. "Donald J. Trump, Tweets of January 6, 2021." January 6. *The American Presidency Project*. https://www.presidency.ucsb.edu/documents/tweets -january-6-2021.

———. 2021b. "Donald J. Trump, Remarks to Supporters Prior to the Storming of the United States Capitol." January 6. *The American Presidency Project*, https:// www.presidency.ucsb.edu/documents/remarks-supporters-prior-the-storming-the -united-states-capitol.

Pew Research Center. 2016. "A closer look at the gender gap in presidential voting." https://www.pewresearch.org/fact-tank/2016/07/28/a-closer-look-at-the-gender -gap-in-presidential-voting/, accessed July 30, 2019.

———. 2019. "Trump's Staunch GOP Supporters Have Roots in the Tea Party." May 2019. https://www.pewresearch.org/politics/2019/05/16/trumps-staunch-gop -supporters-have-roots-in-the-tea-party/.

———. 2020. *American Trends Panel Wave 78*. Fielded November12–17, 2020.

———. 2020. "Election 2020: Voters Are Highly Engaged, But Nearly Half Expect to Have Difficulties Voting."

Piscopo, Jennifer M. 2019. "The Limits of Leaning In: Ambition, Recruitment, and Candidate Training in Comparative Perspective." *Politics, Groups, and Identities* 7: 817–28.

Polifacts. 2015. https://www.politifact.com/factchecks/2015/aug/24/jeb-bush/bush -says-trump-was-democrat-longer-republican-las/.

Poole, Keith T., and Rosenthal, Howard L. 2007. *Ideology and Congress*. Piscataway, NJ: Transaction Publishers.

Preece, Jessica Robinson, Olga Bogach Stoddard, and Rachel Fisher. 2016. "Run, Jane, Run! Gendered Responses to Political Party Recruitment." *Political Behavior* 38: 561–77.

ProPublica. 2020. "House Members Who Signed a Brief Asking the Supreme Court to Consider Overturning the Election." *ProPublica Google News Initiative.*

"Quick Facts." 2019. *United States Census*. https://www.census.gov/quickfacts/AR.

Ranchino, Jim. 1972. *Faubus to Bumpers: Arkansas Votes, 1960–1970.* Arkadelphia, AR: Action Research.

Ranney, Austin, and Willmoore Kendall. 1956. *Democracy and the American Party System.* New York: Harcourt, Brace and Company.

Rapoport, Ronald B. 2013. "Epilogue: What 2012 nomination contests tell us about the future of the Republican Party." *Electoral Studies* 40: 509–13.

Rapoport, Ronald B., Jack Reilly, and Walter J. Stone. 2020. "It's Trump's Party and I'll Cry if I Want To." *The Forum* 17: 693–709.

Rapoport, Ronald B., and Rachel Lienesch. 2014. *Freedom Works Supporters 2011–2014: Stability and Change in Opinions over Time.* Unpublished Report.

Rattner, Nate. 2021. "Trump's election lies were among his most popular tweets." CNBC January 13: https://www.cnbc.com/2021/01/13/trump-tweets-legacy-of-lies-misinformation-distrust.html.

Reiter, Howard L. 2004. "Factional Persistence Within Parties in the United States." *Party Politics* 10: 251–71.

Rev.com. 2020. "Donald Trump 2020 Election Night Speech Transcript." November 4. https://www.rev.com/blog/transcripts/donald-trump-2020-election-night-speech-transcript.

Riordan, William L., *Plunkitt of Tammany Hall* (1905; reprint, New York: E. P. Dutton, 1963): 3–6.

Rodden, Jonathan A. 2019. *Why Cities Lose: The Deep Roots of the Urban-Rural Population Divide.* New York: Basic Books.

Rodriguez, Barbara. 2020. "Can the LBJ Women's Campaign School Build a Pipeline for Women Candidates?" August 7. https://19thnews.org/2020/08/what-it-takes-to-build-a-nonpartisan-pipeline-for-women-candidates/.

Rose, Richard. 1974. *The Problem of Party Government.* New York: Penguin Books.

———. 1964. "Parties, Factions and Tendencies in Britain." *Political Studies* 12: 33–46.

Rosenstone, Steven J., and John Mark Hansen. 1993. *Mobilization, Participation, and Democracy in America.* New York: Macmillan.

Rozell, Mark J. 2000. "Helping Women Run and Win: Feminist Groups, Candidate Recruitment and Training." *Women & Politics* 21: 101–16.

Rubin, Gabriel T. 2021. "More Republican Women Plan Runs for House, Building on Party's 2020 Wins. The Wall Street Journal. July 2. https://www.wsj.com/articles/more-republican-women-plan-runs-for-house-building-on-partys-2020-wins-11625218202.

Saad, Lydia. 2009. "In U.S., Majority Now Say Obama's Policies 'Mostly liberal.'" https://news.gallup.com/poll/124094/majority-say-obama-policies-mostly-liberal.aspx.

Sabato, Larry. 1991. *Feeding Frenzy.* New York: Free Press.

Sabato, Larry J., Kyle Kondik, and J. Miles Coleman, eds. 2021. *A Return to Normalcy? The 2020 Election that (Almost) Broke America.* Lanham, MD: Rowman & Littlefield.

Saldin, Robert, and Steven Teles. 2020. *Never Trump: The Revolt of the Conservative Elites.* New York: Oxford University Press.

Sanbonmatsu, Kira. 2006. "The Legislative Party and Candidate Recruitment in the American States." *Party Politics* 12: 233–56.

———. 2006. *Where Women Run: Gender & Party Politics in the American States.* Ann Arbor: University of Michigan Press.

Sanbonmatsu, Kira, and Susan J. Carroll. 2017. "Women's decisions to run for office: A relationally embedded model." In *The Political Psychology of Women in U.S. Politics*, A. L. Bos and M. C. Schneider, eds. Philadelphia: Routledge/Taylor & Francis Group: 148–64.

Sances, Michael W., and Charles Stewart III. 2015. "Partisanship and Confidence in the Vote Count: Evidence from U.S. National Elections Since 2000." *Electoral Studies* 40:176–88.

Sartori, Giovanni. 1976. *Parties and Party Systems: A Framework for Analysis, Volume 1.* New York: Cambridge University Press.

Sawyer, Elizabeth M., Byron E. Shafer, and Regina L. Wagner. 2021. "Misreporting: Social Scientists, Political Commentators, and the Politics of Presidential Selection," *The Forum* 19, Issue 1.

Scherer, Michael, and Josh Dawsey. 2021. "Would-Be Speaker Kevin McCarthy Walks the Trump Tightrope, Pursuing a GOP House." *Washington Post.* https://www.washingtonpost.com/politics/2021/10/22/kevin-mccarthy-trump/.

Schmidt, Michael S., and Luke Broadwater, 2021. "Officers' Injuries, Including Concussions, Show Scope of Violence at Capitol Riot." *New York Times*, February 11. https://www.nytimes.com/2021/02/11/us/politics/capitol-riot-police-officer-injuries.html.

Schneider, Elena. 2018. "'Something has actually changed': Women, minorities, first-time candidates drive Democratic House hopes. White men are in the minority among Democratic House nominees." *Politico*, September 11 https://www.politico.com/story/2018/09/11/white-men-democratic-house-candidates-813717.

Schneider, Monica C., and Angela L. Bos. 2016. "The Interplay of Candidate Party and Gender in Evaluations of Political Can." *Journal of Women, Politics & Policy* 37: 274–94.

Shafer, Byron E. 1983. *Quiet Revolution: The Struggle for the Democratic Party and the Shaping of Post-Reform Politics.* New York: Russell Sage Foundation.

Shafer, Byron E., and Regina L. Wagner. 2019. *The Long War over Party Structure.* New York: Cambridge University Press.

Shafer, Byron, and Richard Johnston. 2006. *The End of Southern Exceptionalism.* Cambridge, MA: University of Harvard Press.

Shames, Shauna L., Rachel I. Bernhard, Mirya R. Holman, and Dawn Langan Teele, eds. 2020. *Good Reasons to Run: Women and Political Candidacy.* Philadelphia: Temple University Press.

Shapiro, Robert Y., and Harpreet Mahajan. 1986. "Gender Differences in Policy Preferences." *Public Opinion Quarterly* 50: 42–61.

Shaw, Adam. 2020. "'Trump Promises 'Wild' Protest in Washington DC on Jan. 6, Claims it's 'Impossible' He Lost." *Fox News*, December 19. https://www.foxnews.com/politics/trump-wild-protest-washington-dc-jan-6.

Shaw, Daron R. 2006. *The Race to 270: The Electoral College and Campaign Strategies of 2000 and 2004.* Chicago: University of Chicago Press.

Shea, Daniel M, and John C. Green, eds. 1994. *The State of the Parties: The Changing Role of Contemporary American Parties.* Lanham, MD: Rowman & Littlefield.

Shugerman, Emily. n.d. "'Incredible Explosion': 40,000 US Women Interested in Running for Office Since Trump's Election." https://www.emilyslist.org/news/entry /incredible-explosion-40000-us-women-interested-in-running-for-office-since-.

Siders, David, and Zach Montellaro. 2021. "It's Spreading: Phony Election Fraud Conspiracies Infect Midterms." *Politico*, September 20. https://www.politico.com /news/2021/09/20/election-fraud-conspiracies-infect-midterms-512783.

Sides, John. 2015. "Why does Trump remain atop the polls? You can still blame the media." *Washington Post.* August 28.

Sides, John, and Lynn Vavreck. 2013. *The Gamble: Choice and Chance in the 2012 Presidential Election.* Princeton, NJ: Princeton University Press.

Sides, John, Michael Tesler, and Lynn Vavreck. 2018. *Identity Crisis: The 2016 Presidential Campaign and the Battle for the Meaning of America.* Princeton, NJ: Princeton University Press.

Skelley, Geoffrey. 2021. "Biden Has Lost Support Among All Groups of Americans—But Especially Independents and Hispanics." https://fivethirtyeight.com /features/biden-has-lost-support-across-all-groups-of-americans-but-especially -independents-and-hispanics/.

Smith, Glen, and Kathleen Searles. 2014. "Who Let the (Attack) Dogs Out? New Evidence for Partisan Media Effects." *Public Opinion Quarterly* 78: 71–99.

Smith, Patricia. 2020. "An Election Like No Other." *New York Times Upfront*, November 2. https://upfront.scholastic.com/issues/2020-21/110220/an-election-like -no-other.html.

Snyder, James M. 1989. "Election Goals and the Allocation of Campaign Resources." *Econometrica* 57: 637–60.

Snyder, James M., and Steven Ansolabehere. 2002. "The Incumbency Advantage in U.S. Elections: An Analysis of State and Federal Offices, 1942–2000." *Election Law Journal* 1: 315–38.

Sorauf, Frank. 1992. *Inside Campaign Finance: Myth and Realities.* New Haven, CT: Yale University Press.

South, Scott J., and Kyle D. Crowder. 1997. "Escaping Distressed Neighborhoods: Individual, Community, and Metropolitan Influences." *American Journal of Sociology* 102: 1040–84.

Spring, Marianna. 2020. "'Stop the Steal': The Deep Roots of Trump's 'Voter Fraud' Strategy." *BBC News*, November 23. https://www.bbc.com/news/blogs -trending-55009950.

Sprunt, Barbara. 2021. "7 GOP Senators Voted to Convict Trump. Only 1 Faces Voters Next Year." *National Public Radio.* https://www.npr.org/sections/trump -impeachment-trial-live-updates/2021/02/15/967878039/7-gop-senators-voted-to -convict-trump-only-1-faces-voters-next-year.

———. 2021b, June 15. "Trump Pressed the Justice Department to Reverse The Election Results, Documents Show." *National Public Radio.* https://www.npr.org

/2021/06/15/1006570584/trump-pressed-the-justice-department-to-reverse-the-election-results-documents-s.

Staeheli, Lynn A. 2004. "Mobilizing Women, Mobilizing Gender: Is It Mobilizing Difference?" *Gender, Place and Culture: A Journal of Feminist Geography* 11(3): 347–72.

Stein, Sam. 2010. "Arkansas Senate Runoff Obama Disengages from Race as Blanche Lincoln Sinks in the Polls." *Huffington Post*, June 7.

Steward, Frank Mann. 1950. *A Half-Century of Municipal Reform: The History of the National Municipal League.* Berkeley: University of California Press.

Stewart, Charles III. 2020. "How We Voted in 2020: Version 0.1." MIT Election Data Science Lab.

Stoddard. A. B. 2021. "If Polls are Right, Democrats are Doomed. If They're Wrong, It's Worse." https://www.realclearpolitics.com/articles/2021/10/11/if_polls_are_right_dems_are_doomed_if_theyre_wrong_its_worse_146544.html.

Stoker. Laura, and M. Kent Jennings. 2008. "Of Time and the Development of Partisan Polarization." *American Journal of Political Science* 52: 619–35.

Stouffer, Samuel. 1955. *Communism, Conformity and Civil Liberties.* New York: Doubleday.

Strahan, Randall, and Daniel J. Palazzolo. 2004. "The Gingrich Effect." *Political Science Quarterly* 119: 89–114.

Tajfel, Henri, and John Turner. 1979. "An Integrative Theory of Intergroup Conflict." In *The Social Psychology of Intergroup Relations*, William Austin and Stephen Worchel, eds.,. Monterey, CA: Brooks/Cole: 33–37.

Tam, Wendy K., Tam Cho, James G. Gimpel, and Iris S. Hui. 2013. "Voter Migration and the Geographic Sorting of the American Electorate." *Annals of the Association of American Geographers* 103: 856–70.

Tavernese, Sabrina. 2018. "Why the Announcement of a Looming White Minority Makes Demographers Nervous." https://www.nytimes.com/2018/11/22/us/white-americans-minority-population.html.

Teixeira, Ruy. 2012. "The Emerging Democratic Majority Turns Ten." https://www.theatlantic.com/politics/archive/2012/11/the-emerging-democratic-majority-turns-10/265005/.

———. 2021. "The Dems' Hispanic Problem is Way Worse Than You Think." https://www.realclearpolitics.com/2021/12/10/the_dems_hispanic_problem_is_way_worse_than_you_think_558484.html.

Teixeira, Ruy, and Joel Rogers. 2001. *America's Forgotten Majority: Why the White Working Class Still Matters.* New York: Basic.

Tesler, Michael, and David O. Sears. 2010. *Obama's Race.* Chicago: University of Chicago Press.

Theriault, Sean M. 2008. *Party Polarization in Congress.* New York: Cambridge University Press.

Thompson, Wilbur R. 1965. *A Preface to Urban Economics.* Baltimore: Johns Hopkins University Press.

Thomsen, Danielle M. 2015. "Why So Few (Republican) Women? Explaining the Partisan Imbalance of Women in the US Congress." *Legislative Studies Quarterly* 40: 295–323.

———. 2017. "Joining Patterns Across Party Factions in the US Congress." *The Forum* 15: 741–51.

Thomsen, Danielle M., and Aaron S. King. 2020. "Women's Representation and the Gendered Pipeline to Power." American Political Science Review 114: 989–1000.

Thomsen, Danielle M., and Michele L. Swers. 2017. "Which Women Can Run? Gender, Partisanship and Candidate Donor Networks." *Political Research Quarterly* 70: 449–63.

Tiebout, Charles M. 1956. "A Pure Theory of Local Expenditures." *Journal of Political Economy* 54: 416–24.

Timberg, Craig, Elizabeth Dwoskin, and Reed Albergotti. 2021. "Inside Facebook, Jan. 6 Violence Filled Anger, Regret Over Missed Warning Signs. *Washington Post.* https://www.washingtonpost.com/technology/2021/10/22/jan-6-capitol-riot -facebook/.

Tomer, Adie Tomer, and Joseph Kane. 2014. "Mapping Freight: The Highly Concentrated Nature of Goods Trade in the United States," Washington, D.C.: Brookings Institution, Metropolitan Policy Program, Global Cities Initiative. Accessed December 7, 2021. www.brookings.edu/wpcontent/uploads/2016/06/Srvy_GCI FreightNetworks_Oct24.pdf.

Trounstine, Jessica. 2018. *Segregation by Design: Local Politics and Inequality in American Cities.* New York: Cambridge University Press.

Troyer, Madison. 2020. "Top Trump Tweets since Election Day 2020." *Stacker* (December 30: https://stacker.com/stories/6057/top-trump-tweets-election-day-2020).

Udani, Adriano, and David C. Kimball. 2018. "Immigrant Resentment and Voter Fraud Beliefs in the U.S. Electorate." *American Politics Research* 46: 402–33.

Uhlaner, Carole Jean, and Kay Lehman Schlozman. 1986. "Candidate Gender and Congressional Campaign Receipts." *Journal of Politics* 48: 30–50.

Urwin, Cathy Kunzinger. 1991. *Agenda and Reform: Winthrop Rockefeller as Governor of Arkansas 1967–1971.* Fayetteville: University of Arkansas Press.

U.S. Census Bureau. "2014. Projecting Majority-Minority." https://www.census.gov /content/dam/Census/newsroom/releases/2015/cb15-tps16_graphic.pdf.

Vickery, Bill. 2021. Interview with John C. Davis.

Viebeck, Elise. 2012. "Republican Says Evolution, Big Bang Theory 'Lies Straight from the Pit of Hell.'" http://thehill.com/blogs/blog-briefing-room/news/260641 -house-republican-says-evolution-big-bang-theory-lies-straight-from-the-pit-of-hell.

Vigdor, Jacob L. 2013. "Weighing and Measuring the Decline in Residential Segregation." *City & Community* 12: 169–77.

Vosoughi, Soroush, Deb Roy, and Sinan Aral. 2018. "The Spread of True and False News Online." *Science* 359(6380): 1146–51.

Walshe, Shushannah. 2013. "RNC Completes 'Autopsy' on 2012 Loss, Calls for Inclusion Not Policy Change." *ABC News*, March 18. https://abcnews.go .com/Politics/OTUS/rnc-completes-autopsy-2012-loss-calls-inclusion-policy /story?id=18755809.

Wang, Vivian. 2019. "House Democrats Prepare for Civil War as Challengers Plot Primary Battles." *New York Times*, July 19.

Ware, Alan. 2002. *The American Direct Primary: Party Institutionalization and Transformation in the North.* New York: Cambridge University Press.

Wattenberg, Martin P. 1991. *The Rise of Candidate-Centered Politics: Presidential Elections in the 1980's.* Cambridge, MA: Harvard University Press.

WBUR Newsroom. 2021. "'Go Home': Trump Tells Supporters Who Mobbed Capitol to Leave, Again Falsely Claiming Election Victory." *WBUR*, January 6. https://www.wbur.org/news/2021/01/06/go-home-trump-supporters-us-capitol-transcript.

Webster, Steven W. 2020. *American Rage: How Anger Shapes Our Politics.* New York: Cambridge University Press.

Wekkin, Gary D. 1998. "Arkansas: Electoral Competition in the 1990s." In *The New Politics of the Old South* 2nd ed., Charles S. Bullock III and Mark J. Rozell, eds. Lanham MD: Rowman & Littlefield: 195–222..

West, Emily A., and Shanto Iyengar. 2020. "Partisanship as a Social Identity: Implications for Polarization." *Political Behavior* 44: 807–38.

Wheelock, David C. 2020. "Comparing the COVID-19 Recession with the Great Depression." *Economic Synopses*.

Wilson, David C., and Paul R. Brewer. 2013. "The Foundations of Public Opinion on Voter ID Laws: Political Predispositions, Racial Resentment, and Information Effects." *Public Opinion Quarterly*. 77: 962–84.

Wolbrecht, Christina. 2000. *The Politics of Women's Rights: Parties, Positions, and Change.* Princeton, NJ: Princeton University Press.

Wooldridge, Jeffrey M. 2003. *Introductory Econometrics: A Modern Approach*, 2nd ed. Cincinnati, OH: South-Western College Publishing.

Yost, B.A. 2003. "Disappearing Democrats: Rethinking Partisanship Within Pennsylvania's Electorate." *Commonwealth* 12: 77–86.

Yourish, Karen, Larry Buchanan, and Denise Lu. 2021. "The 147 Republicans Who Voted to Overturn Election Results." *New York Times*, January 7: https://www.nytimes.com/interactive/2021/01/07/us/elections/electoral-college-biden-objectors.html.

Zaller, John R. 1992. *The Nature and Origins of Mass Opinion.* Cambridge: Cambridge University Press.

Zelizer, Julian E. 2020. *Burning Down the House: Newt Gingrich and the Rise of the New Republican Party.* New York: Penguin Books.

Zhang, Lingling, and Doug J. Chung. 2020. "The Air War Versus the Ground Game: An Analysis of Multi-Channel Marketing in U.S. Presidential Elections." *Marketing Science* 29: 872–92.

Index

295

About the Contributors

Alan I. Abramowitz is the Alben Barkley Professor Emeritus of Political Science at Emory University. He has written extensively on public opinion, partisanship, and polarization. He is the author of *The Great Alignment: Race, Party Transformation and the Rise of Donald Trump* (2018).

Paul A. Beck is Academy Professor of Political Science at The Ohio State University, and co-coordinator of the Comparative National Elections Project. He has published nine books and numerous articles in leading journals on voting behavior and political parties.

Robert G. Boatright is professor and chair of the Department of Political Science at Clark University and the director of research for the National Institute for Civil Discourse at the University of Arizona. He is the author of *Getting Primaried* (2013).

David B. Cohen is a professor of political science, director of the Applied Politics Program, and Fellow of the Ray C. Bliss Institute of Applied Politics at the University of Akron. He teaches courses and conducts research on the American presidency, Congress, and homeland security.

W. Henry Crossman graduated from the College of William & Mary in 2019 with a BA in international relations and is currently pursuing an MA in security studies at Georgetown University. He lives and works in the Washington, DC, area.

David F. Damore is professor and chair of the Department of Political Science and the interim executive director of The Lincy Institute and Brookings

Mountain West at the University of Nevada–Las Vegas. His research focuses on electoral politics and applied public policy.

Karen A. Danielsen is associate professor in the School of Public Policy and Leadership at the University of Nevada–Las Vegas. Her research interests include urban planning theory, political geography, housing policy, growth management, metropolitan structure, and urban design.

John C. Davis is an associate professor of political science at the University of Arkansas at Monticello. His research interests include political parties, state politics, and public policy. He is currently writing a book on the rise of the Republican Party in Arkansas.

Laurel Elder is a professor of political science at Hartwick College. She is the author of *The Partisan Gap: Why Democratic Women Get Elected, But Republican Women Don't* (2021).

Morris P. Fiorina is the Wendt Family Professor of Political Science at Stanford University and a senior fellow of the Hoover Institution. He has written or edited thirteen books, most recently, *Unstable Majorities: Party Sorting, Polarization and Political Stalemate* (2017).

John C. Green is the emeritus director of the Ray C. Bliss Institute of Applied Politics at the University of Akron. A respected analyst of Ohio and national politics, his work has been widely cited and quoted by scholars and journalists alike.

Jennifer A. Heerwig is an associate professor of sociology at SUNY Stony Brook. Her work in political sociology uses longitudinal methods to examine the role of individual donors in the American campaign finance system and the influence of money on American politics.

Paul S. Herrnson is a professor of political science at the University of Connecticut and a fellow at OpenSecrets. His recent publications include *Congressional Elections: Campaigning at Home and in Washington* (2020), *Under the Iron Dome: Congress from the Inside* (2021), and articles on campaign finance and election administration. He served as president of the Southern Political Science Association, chair of the Political Organizations and Parties section of the American Political Science Association, and as an APSA Congressional Fellow.

David C. Kimball is professor of political science at the University of Missouri–St. Louis. He has written extensively on voting behavior, election administration, public opinion, and interest group lobbying in the United States. He is coeditor of *Controversies in Voting Behavior*, 5th ed. (2011).

Robert E. Lang is professor emeritus in the School of Public Policy and Leadership at the University of Nevada–Las Vegas. He was the inaugural holder of the Lincy Endowed Chair in Urban Affairs and the founding executive director of The Lincy Institute and Brookings Mountain West at the University of Nevada–Las Vegas, and a Senior Resident Fellow in the Brookings Institution's Metropolitan Policy Program. Previously, Dr. Lang was director of the Metropolitan Institute and a professor and chair in Urban Planning at Virginia Tech and director of Urban and Metropolitan Research at the Fannie Mae Foundation. His research specialties include suburban studies, national and state politics, political geography, real estate, demographic and spatial analysis, economic development, and metropolitan policy.

Anita Manion is an assistant professor of political science at the University of Missouri–St. Louis. Her research focuses on the impact of policy on issues of equity, particularly in areas of elections and education.

Shannon McQueen is an assistant professor of political science at West Chester University. Her research interests include the mobilization of women's groups, and the institutional, cultural, and policy obstacles women face when running for office.

Stephen K. Medvic is The Honorable and Mrs. John C. Kunkel Professor of government and director of the Center for Politics and Public Affairs at Franklin and Marshall College. His research interests include campaigns and elections, political parties, public opinion, and ideology.

Kenneth M. Miller is an assistant professor of political science at the University of Nevada–Las Vegas. His research interests and publications include campaign finance, elections, and representation.

Ronald B. Rapoport is professor emeritus in government at the College of William & Mary. His research has focused on party activists. He is coauthor of *Three's a Crowd: The Dynamic of Third Parties, Ross Perot and Republican Resurgence* (2005). His current projects are on democratic factionalism and American emigrant participation.

Byron E. Shafer is the Hawkins chair of political science at the University of Wisconsin–Madison. He has written extensively on numerous aspects of the structure of American politics and is the coauthor of *The Long War Over Party Structure: Democratic Representation and Policy Responsiveness in American Politics* (2019).

Adriano Udani is an associate professor of political science and director of the Public Policy Administration Program at the University of Missouri, St. Louis. He specializes in the study of political attitudes toward immigrant groups and policy decisions that affect immigrant treatment in the United States.

Regina L. Wagner is assistant professor of political science at the University of Alabama. Her research interests include political parties, political representation, and gender and politics. She is the coauthor of *The Long War Over Party Structure: Democratic Representation and Policy Responsiveness in American Politics* (2019).

Berwood A. Yost is director of the Floyd Institute for Public Policy and the director of the Center for Opinion Research at Franklin & Marshall College. He is also the director of the Franklin & Marshall College Poll, which tracks public attitudes toward public policy issues and political campaigns in Pennsylvania. His scholarship is multidisciplinary and has appeared in journals in the fields of criminology, human rights, political science, psychology, and public health.

Printed in the USA
CPSIA information can be obtained
at www.ICGtesting.com
LVHW092343260823
756177LV00011B/994